Image Critique &
the Fall of the Berlin Wall

for
PDM and the quiet philosophizing you entrust...
YLM and those first trips to the library...

Image Critique & the Fall of the Berlin Wall

Sunil Manghani

intellect Bristol, UK / Chicago, USA

First Published in the UK in 2008 by
Intellect Books, The Mill, Parnall Road, Fishponds, Bristol, BS16 3JG, UK

First published in the USA in 2008 by
Intellect Books, The University of Chicago Press, 1427 E. 60th Street, Chicago,
IL 60637, USA

A catalogue record for this book is available from the British Library.

Cover Image: New Year celebrations at the Brandenburg Gate, 31st December 1989.
Courtesy of Zuma Press
Cover Design: Gabriel Solomons
Copy Editor: Holly Spradling
Typesetting: Mac Style, Nafferton, E. Yorkshire

ISBN 978-1-84150-190-1

Printed and bound by Gutenberg Press, Malta.

Contents

LIST OF ILLUSTRATIONS

The Fall of the Berlin Wall (...an Imaginary)

I have kept only the images which enthral me, without knowing why (such ignorance is the very nature of fascination, and what I shall say about each image will never be anything but...imaginary)

Roland Barthes,
Roland Barthes on Roland Barthes

I'm standing on top of the Berlin Wall, which for years has been the most potent symbol of the division of Europe. And there can be few better illustrations of the changes which are sweeping across this continent, than the party which is taking place here on top of it tonight.

Brian Hanrahan
BBC News, 10.11.89

Berlin is tonight alight with celebration. The world beyond is rife with speculation for no one has yet established the limits to which the changes in East Germany will now go. [...] we report from both sides of the Wall as families lift their loved ones across it. As East Germans literally hug the border guards who for so long have kept them from it, and as revellers savour the right to cross and re-cross it...

Jon Snow
Channel Four News, 10.11.89

Knowledge comes only in lightning flashes. The Text is the long roll of thunder that follows.
Walter Benjamin
The Arcades Project

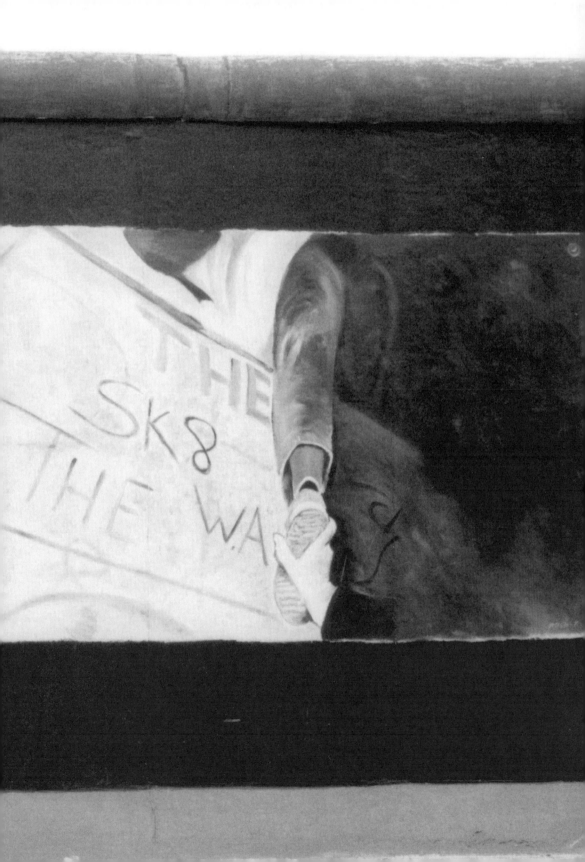

Before Words...

Over a period of some four years or so, in a manner not too dissimilar to Patrick Keiller's character Robinson in the film *London* (1993), who travels about the capital city undertaking what he purports to be research into a supposedly very real, though never really defined, 'problem' of London, I carried with me my own particular research problem. I generally referred to this as 'images of the fall of the Berlin Wall'. Its conundrum remained with me as I wandered in and out of the corridors of my university and as I sat in various libraries home and abroad, watched numerous films and TV broadcasts and, of course, read countless books and articles. There is no doubt the images can be found in all manner of places, and in all number of forms. The only trouble had been knowing *exactly* what I was looking for once I came upon them. The fact that the Berlin Wall came to its 'end' on the 9th of November 1989 seems simple enough. Witnessed live by millions around the world, the media images (now synonymous with the wider collapse of communism) were all too plain to see. As the saying goes, 'a picture is worth a thousand words.' So what more is there to say?

It is perhaps with the same familiarity of a nursery rhyme that this simple phrase 'the fall of the Berlin Wall' remains with us. It is a chapter heading, a footnote and, of course, a turning point in a conversation or flow of an argument, *after the fall...it all changes*. It denotes a time, a place and a sense of change. It marks a new beginning, as well as an 'end of history.' We live in a post-Wall era and that carries with it certain responsibilities, not least how we choose to respond and relate to the sorts of media news events that the fall of the Wall prefigures. However, whilst I certainly take issue with any simplistic readings of the images of the fall of the Berlin Wall, it is not my intention to look at what went on *behind* those images, as if somehow there is a truer, pure reality that is not pictured. I am not concerned so much with analysing images in order to elucidate some new critical interpretation (in hope of setting us all right in the matter). Instead, I aim to look the *other* way and ask what it is we think when we think about images in the first place, and how this process of pictured/picturing thought might itself be a useful critical practice.

*   *   *

The Berlin Wall will surely always remain a startling fact of history. It stands at the heart of one of the great dramas of the second half of the twentieth century. When I first went to school I vaguely knew about it, though could never quite get my head around the idea. Who could blame me, for since when had a wall dividing a nation been a reasonable thing to grasp? As a child there were only questions and more questions. How high was this Wall, and did it *really* encircle a whole country? Naturally, when I came across a map of Germany I soon realized that it *only* cut a city clean in half; but, of course, that was no small feat and no easier to grasp. And what was still further inconceivable was just why half a city stood like an island in the middle of another country. How crazy was that? Since East Germany was smaller than West, why not just let Berlin be fully integrated with the East? I realize now that I was hardly alone in my naivety. The way in which we think about our socio-political landscapes seem so often to be anchored in simplified metaphors and narratives. I have frequently found the same incredulousness when speaking to a variety of people with no immediate experience of the Wall. And all too often the same overall fascination: what did it look like, was the graffiti on both sides, and did it run along the entire East/West Border? It is perhaps no real surprise that when the Wall 'fell' it really came down with a bang (...and everyone went to the after-show party)!

Today, wandering about the city it is increasingly difficult to imagine what the Wall would have looked like, and how it would have felt to have lived in its shadow. The Wall is scattered in all directions. A few slabs stand before civic offices, but many more little chunks remain forgotten in desk drawers, or obscured on cluttered mantelpieces. And it is not just material fragments which linger in this way. Its legacy endures as books, letters, videos, and artwork, and all other manner of things. Yet perhaps most vividly what remains are the media pictures of the 'fall'. For these are not so obviously scattered and disconnected. In fact the history made instant by television, like many other iconic events captured on film, can be replayed again and again with relative ease. These images are continually quoted and adapted for all number of purposes, imbuing a collective memory which marks – in this case – the end of an ideological struggle.

Sadly, however, some lessons of the Berlin Wall have not seemingly been learnt. A stark battle has waged over the construction of a wall driving a wedge between Israel and Palestine. Not long ago one needed only go so far as Northern Ireland to witness another wall running straight through the middle of a neighbourhood. And this is to say little, of course, of the heavily fortified barrier that continues to stake out the border between North and South Korea; a genuine relic of Cold War division. Perhaps a degree of naivety in these cases need not be such a bad thing, not if it is put to critical use; if it is a step towards being open to new questions, or even older questions no longer being asked. As the French philosopher Jean-François Lyotard puts it: 'You cannot open up a question without leaving yourself open to it. You cannot scrutinise a "subject"...without being scrutinised by it.' Indeed, he suggests: 'You cannot do any of these things without renewing ties with the season of childhood, the season of the mind's possibilities' (Lyotard 1992: 116). The lesson to learn is that reading can never be finished, but is in fact always 'an exercise in listening,' an inquiry, that is, 'into what remains as yet unthought, even when it is already thought' (117). It is just such a procedure of critical enquiry and openness that I suggest might best be achieved from an engagement with images, to consider them as an integral resource for critical thinking in themselves.

*   *   *

At the heart of this book is the notion that the news media images of the fall of the Wall depict a moment of *instant history*; which is to suggest that history is witnessed as it happens, and recognised globally as being a defining moment of our times (whether marking a beginning, transition or finale). Perhaps the fall of the Wall is more accurately considered something of a precursor to the experience of 'living history' that is now such a condition of our 'wired' world. Nevertheless, as a pivotal moment in our history of experiencing history, there is a great deal to learn from it.

Throughout I find myself often needing to make bald references to 'the *fall* of the Berlin Wall' and, as is my primary focus, '*images* of the fall of the Berlin Wall'. I also refer to the East and the West, and to both East and eastern Germany, all as if uncontested designations. Added to which, there are German phrases *Wir sind das Volk* and later *Wir sind EIN Volk*, as well as the gnomic expression *die Wende* – which literally means the turning point, or change, a phrase which came into vogue shortly after the 'collapse of communism' (yet another common phrase). These must all be understood as rhetorical terms and phrases. There was no real 'fall' of the Berlin Wall, all articulations of 'the people' are likely to be hegemonizing, and there is no definitive agreement on any turn point, or *Wende*. Such phrases inevitably skip over a set of complex relations, contradictions and long-term processes (it took many months, for example, to 'decommission' the Berlin Wall, slabs of which to this day remain dotted about building sites or stacked up in dusty, forgotten yards). I refer, then, to these phrases and work *through* (or with) them, precisely because they are part of the way we frame our understanding of the events of the fall of the Wall. In choosing to write about any subject there is the need to invent a language that can best formulate and treat the object of enquiry. The words on the page will always attempt a correspondence of sorts, whether to the object of enquiry (a form of mimesis perhaps), or to the subject (as one might hail or send a letter to a friend). In choosing to write about *images* it surely complicates the relationship still further. By attempting to secure what I refer to in this study as *image critique*, there is a need not only to write and have something to say about images, but also to give them life, to let them write/illuminate for themselves.

Image critique relates, then, to a double procedure: of both presenting a critique of images (and visual culture), as well as allowing images in themselves to offer critical import. Thus, set against an impossibly large archive of images of the fall of the Berlin Wall (which must of course include the news footage emphatically *showing* the fall, or at least the scaling, of the Wall), I consider what it might mean to 're-scale' the pictures of such an event. In one sense this can involve looking again at the composition and nature of the images, as if to 'size them up' (or bring them back down to size!). Such a task can help make sense of their historical importance in terms of contemporary visual culture, but more importantly, I wish to consider what I will refer to as an 'ecology of images'. The phrase comes from Susan Sontag's final remarks in her seminal set of essays *On Photography* (1979: 180). In our 'image-world' of contemporary capitalist society, she argues, '[i]mages are more real than anyone could have supposed. And just because they are an unlimited resource, one that cannot be exhausted by consumerist waste, there is all the more reason to apply the conservationist remedy.' If there is perhaps something iconoclastic about her argument, it need not undermine the important assertion that images should hardly be considered so different from all other manner of *things* around us.

The idea (or image) of an eco-system of images brings with it a need for a system of care; a need to treat the flow of images with discernment, with concern for the impact of one image

on another. It is in this sense that I hope to direct attention away from the idea that images are merely to be interpreted or debunked (or 'solved' like clues in a murder mystery). Within the complex ebb and flow of everyday meanings and communications, I consider images to be more the *messengers* (i.e. more the *medium*) than the message. And like the angels which inhabit Wim Wender's Berlin in *Wings of Desire* (1987) and *Faraway So Close!* (1993), whose liminality allows them to move in and out of the human world, images can be thought of (though not necessarily always fully revealing themselves, or their significance) as conduits enabling us to think and maintain a vast reservoir of sharable and contested meanings and memories. Their 'ecology,' whilst needing constant upkeep, allows for topologies of thought, providing not necessarily a final evaluation, but nevertheless the means of a critical space in which to seek and assert critical points of view.

To take this idea a step further, the re-scaling of images of the fall of the Berlin Wall as an example of an image critique can be understood in terms of a notion of *Denkbilder*, or thought-images. It is Walter Benjamin who is most associated with this term, using it to refer to his short studies or meditations on objects, places, and people.[1] As Sigrid Weigel (1996: 51) describes, Benjamin's thought-images are intended to operate in a double sense: 'as images in relation to which his thoughts and theoretical reflections unfold, and also as images whose representations are translated into figures of thought (*Denkfiguren*).' The very act of thinking is 'performed' in the image-constellations he writes, and through which 'history, reality, and experience find their structure and expression' (51–2). Images for Benjamin are a primary mode and indeed material of thoughts and ideas. Furthermore, it is the primacy of images as a mode of 'writing', or connecting thought with the world around us, that forms the basis of his concept of *Aktualität*, by which he refers to a *materialization* of theory. As Weigel suggests, thinking and acting become one: 'This is not materialism *avant la lettre*, but quite literally a *re-reading* of the material' (4) – *the making of actuality itself*.

Re-scaling images in the form of thought-images (i.e. a re-reading or *writing* of the image) can perhaps be thought of as bearing relation – at least metaphorically – to the physical, tangible experience of scaling the heights of a wall. It involves an attempt to seize hold of the image, bringing it into a process or *figuring* of thinking itself; in some cases quite literally grabbing hold of the image through citation and montage. It is, as Benjamin acknowledges, a precarious, patient process, leading the researcher to wait and retrace steps 'until he sees details on which he can climb up, as one would using uneven places on a wall' (cited in Jennings 1987: 29). Significantly, Benjamin's philosophical method 'invalidates philosophical discourse as meta-discourse', and instead offers the insight 'that memory and action find articulation in images, that ideas are structured as images, and that what is at stake is therefore a praxis that can operate with images – a *politics of images*, not a figurative or metaphorical politics' (Weigel 1996: 9–10). As I hope to demonstrate, the *living*, active quality of Benjamin's 'politics of images' can help form a critical engagement with images of our contemporary instant history.

However, it is not my intention to simply apply Benjamin's theory of the image to the concerns of the present study; even if this were my aim it would hardly be possible. Benjamin's writings are well known for being opaque, and at times sketchy, giving only hints of portentous ideas in brief fragments. The result is that there is no definitive theory of the image to apply. One way of dealing with this problem I have found is to translate Benjamin's ideas and concepts across to other thinkers, and notably here Roland Barthes (whose writings are certainly much more lucid). If anything, it is insights from Barthes later 'novelistic' writings[2] that really underpin my approach to the image. In these late works, Barthes attempts to *write* about that which goes unwritten, and in doing so establishes an aesthetic which combines images with his text to formulate a unique mode of critique; such a relationship between word and image forms an important underlying theme for this study.

It is important to note, then, this book is not intended to be *about* Benjamin or Barthes (nor any other theorists as such). Neither of these cultural critics – both highly idiosyncratic in their work – can be said to leave us with a fully formed method for an image critique. Instead they provide a way of working, or a way of thinking that leaves open further possibilities. As Susan Buck-Morss suggests of Benjamin (and all of which could be said of Barthes): 'If it were purely a case of the genius Benjamin writing wonderful things, then we wouldn't be able to enact and re-enact the methodological possibilities that his work makes available' (2002: 328). There is no one specific Benjaminian approach. In fact, as Buck-Morss suggests, 'the visual metaphors he creates, that so impress us with his literary brilliance, are never simply metaphors. They are also objects in his world' (328). Buck-Morss's attempt to make her own such objects, to bring to fruition a materialist praxis, or living methodology, is an attempt (however faithful to Benjamin's own methods) attuned only to the on-going processes of the world around *herself*; not to any one specific commentary upon it. In other words it is an approach not to write like Benjamin, but rather to write as oneself, to handle (with care) the 'objects' in one's own world; one's own *Aktualität*.

Thus, it can be seen, image critique is not a simple form of image interpretation, nor the application of a single methodology, but rather an on-going construction of meaning and effect. It is *to be* an architectonic theory, building up and embodying an experience which relates directly, even *materially*, to the object itself under enquiry. At times it is itself a new image (adding to an ecology of images). But perhaps more importantly, at least, for the critic who invariably must resort to put pen to paper, it is also a *writing* about images, and *in* images – for, after all, 'literature' is itself an important medium for the formation and carrier of imagery. Perhaps where image critique in its written form comes face to face with aspects of a visual culture, it might well be considered a writing *beside the image*. As Benjamin (1999: 527) forewarns, where an 'illiteracy of the future' is 'not of reading or writing, but photography,' it is the *inscription* (or caption) that is evermore important. With respect to the contemporary conditions of academic and intellectual practice – still so bound up with the dominance of the word and the printing press – our inscriptions may indeed remain of prominent concern. But, I hope for a little more than that: *writing the image*, as I want to suppose here, need not necessarily be thought of as dissimilar to the way in which a photograph is a part of and yet equally 'set-out' from the reality it has captured.

*   *   *

In 1998 – almost a decade after the fall of the Wall – I left my home in London, and went to live for a year in a little town (or *Städtchen* as the Germans say) in former East Germany, not far from the Czech Republic border. It proved to be a very formative experience, eventually leading me back to study (and ultimately this particular study). What I came to understand by being away was that something had always been missing in the things I had learnt before.

Throughout my stay I lived and worked with people who had, up until only ten years previously, lived a wholly different kind of life. And though we never explicitly discussed the fall of the Wall and its implications, it was always there. It was always evident that our conversations were a direct result of *die Wende*.

Now sadly as only distant conversations, I nonetheless wish always to leave myself open to them; to find myself listening back each time I read and re-write these words. As the philosopher notes in his love letters, it is necessary we demonstrate a letter always, and therefore ought not ever arrive at its destination, 'it is not a misfortune, that's life, living life' (Derrida 1987: 33). In those loving postcards once sent from the Bodleian the philosopher was of course toying with the uncertainty of his own words; troubled by the origin and transmission of his text. Yet, whilst their destination might never finally have been reached, there was always the sense in which the centre from which they were composed held firm – their subject (and point of view) was never really in doubt. What I found when I went to live in eastern Germany was undoubtedly as much 'living life', yet bringing this into being in what follows must surely involve more than a reporting of words. The words and images offered here are most certainly not penned from within four walls of an established archive (– nor even maintained from within the bounds of a huge Wall and fortifications encircling an entire city). And it is not simply their arrival that is uncertain, but even their time and place of writing comes of no fixed abode; as if emitting from a persistent no-man's-land that, having once been defined by a clear dividing line, is now no longer certain or in clear view. Of course, it should never be forgotten, the *real* no-man's-land of a divided Berlin was on one side a lifeless non-space, on the other a forbidding and at times fatal place. Most importantly, then, whilst the images I turn attention to may never quite be pinned down (or written about), it is not to deny the need for a historical and politically informed critical purpose.

Having now returned (from being abroad, and being back at my study), rather than put faith in words alone, I suggest a form of criticism combined with creative writing and picturing, one with a 'living methodology' offering new constellations; a creative collision between things in the world and the human mind. As Benjamin remarks, '[i]n the fields in which we are concerned, knowledge comes only in lightning flashes. The Text is the long roll of thunder that follows' (1999: 456). With your hands now grasping many more pages than have so far been read, and with this Text being only a theoretical consideration of what must almost certainly be *another* kind of writing still to come, it is perhaps inevitable that that long roll of thunder will now follow...

*   *   *

This book was conceived and researched between the years 2000 and 2003 when I was based at the University of Nottingham. I express my deep gratitude for the financial support during this time of the Arts and Humanities Research Council, without which the book would most certainly never have existed. I would also like to acknowledge the support of the Freie Universität during the summer 2002 for enabling me to spend many intriguing hours in the streets of Berlin, as well as take cover from the heat of the city in the cool surrounds of their library.

Writing is generally a rather lonely journey, thus much of what finally appears here will be something of a surprise to those whose support I wish to acknowledge. My thanks go to Steve Giles, Ben Halligan, Anna Notaro, Steve Nugent, Arthur Piper, Catrin Schmid, Martin Jan Stepanek, Rodrigo Velasco and, of course, my parents and brother. I am also very grateful for the moral support of my colleagues at York St John University, particularly for the 'pastoral care' and friendship afforded to me by Stuart Page and Judy Giles. I extend a very special note of thanks to the Riechert family whose abounding hospitality changed everything for me and unknown to us all got me started on this book, as well as to Yve Lomax and Jonathan Hale, whose close and sympathetic reading (and indeed sanctioning) of my work as I brought it to its completion meant I could actually get on with preparing this book. Equally, I am very grateful to all those I have worked with at Intellect Books, in particular Sam King and Holly Spradling.

More than anyone, however, I am greatly indebted to Jon Simons whose acuity and tactfulness over the years when dealing with what were only ever a few bits of paper and unfinished sentences was quietly supreme. Finally, my deepest thanks and love to ky – the one person, other than myself, who lived through the maladies of this project on a daily basis; putting up tirelessly with a 'missing person' (lost to the other side of his Wall of writing). Her patience and insights have always demonstrated to me things far more profound and affirming than anything I could have hoped to have written (or pictured) here. As a little 'addendum' – if only to be read in the future – I should also like to thank my dearest little Luli who slept through all the long nights like a baby (I couldn't have asked for any better help!).

Notes

1. Walter Benjamin's most well-known collection is *One-Way Street* (1997), but the later *Arcades Project* (1999) and essays such as 'Images of Proust' (1992: 197–210) and 'Berlin Childhood ca 1900' (2002) engage more explicitly with a theory of thought-images.
2. Roland Barthes' novelistic mode is epitomized by one of his most popular books, *A Lover's Discourse* (1990), but also his 'autobiography', *Roland Barthes* (1994), as well as reflected in works such as *Camera Lucida* (1981) and *Empire of Signs* (1982).

BERLIN Besatzungszonen
Occupation Zones

- amerikanisch *American*
- britisch *British*
- französisch *French*
- sowjetisch *Soviet*

Dearest Sunil,

Thanks a lot for your nice letter. It is a real shame we are living so far from each other and our lives circle around so different things. But hopefully our lives are meant to be long so that there will be other times again, I am sure. Hope to see you 2004. Lots of love GHm

0.45 €

To
Sunil Manghani
Nightingate Hall
Univ. of Nottingham
Univ. Park Nottingham
NG7 2RD
ENGLAND

CHAPTER ONE

ON THE SIGHT OF THE BERLIN WALL

This book, above all else, is concerned with the role of images in critical thought, but takes as its focus *images of the fall of the Berlin Wall*. What I take to be revealing and indeed challenging about the Berlin Wall as a case study is its relationship to critical engagement, the way in which it *situates* questions of history, politics, human action and freedom, as well as the media, or more broadly visual culture. However, rather than simply develop and apply theory to this 'object' or case study, the intention is that both theoretical ideation and a thematic interest of the Berlin Wall interlace, and in the interstice between the two a critical perspective can emerge. Thus, to make clear from the outset, I do not offer here a straightforward hermeneutic or historical analysis of visual representations of the Wall. I am not concerned with working through specific images or sets of images of the Wall, nor overly concerned with what others have said about them; though inevitably many such materials are incorporated in one form or another into the discussions which follow.

My primary interest is to present an idea of what I term 'image critique': a double procedure of both a critique of images and their critical engagement. The aim, then, is to consider how images, and more specifically how a whole way of thinking with/through images, might bear upon the way we think critically about socio-political events and representations. In broad terms, I hope to remain faithful to traditions of emancipatory critique (informed as they are by the so-called grand theories of both Marxism and psychoanalysis), but more specifically, I engage with the contemporary issues and dilemmas that visual culture and image studies have helped bring to attention. My approach can be understood as being *thematic*, pondering over the case study of the fall of the Berlin Wall to explore issues relevant to debates of the image and visual culture. In this respect, I take on board a recommendation that in viewing philosophizing today we should not necessarily be looking to 'import the next grand Continental paradigm', for indeed, 'it is no longer a question of worshipping a series of proper names, but of *doing something* with what they left behind; doing creative, inventive thematic work' (Critchley 2001: 125). In part, then, I hope to *do* something here in the pages which follow, a consequence of which is that the book builds up an increasingly complex approach to the images in question and their theorizing. Hence, not the sort of study in which it is possible to lay out from the start a theoretical framework against which different bodies of material can be assessed. Instead, as suggested, it is through the *interaction* of both theme and theory that a critical approach is to be adjudicated. Realistically, I can perhaps only really put forward the *idea* of an image critique as an active, creative form of enquiry/writing; for this is a form of critique that I will suggest is more likely to come only in another *writerly* manifestation. Nevertheless, I hope something of the effects of an image critique can be felt in what follows, at least in that my 'line' of argument is rarely ever linear in fashion and that the various illustrations which accompany (and/or cut into) the text help keep our eyes open to all sorts of other possibilities.

It is actually only as a form of shorthand that I first began to describe my study as that of 'images of the fall of the Berlin Wall'. To my surprise, whenever I discussed the topic with others in this relatively ambiguous manner the response was almost always a genuine nod of understanding, even enthusiasm – 'what a good topic', many would suggest (without necessarily holding firm views as to why it might make such good subject matter). Frequently, these conversations prompted an anecdote of some sort, perhaps about how the person I was talking to had been 'there' in Berlin when it 'happened', or having known someone who was. All too often it transpired the person I was speaking to actually owned a piece of the Wall (however small), tucked away somewhere in their office or home. It is startling just how easy it is for the Wall (and its related images) to be conjured into conversation, seemingly to bear indisputable meaning for many different people.

Furthermore, after a minor blip in the conversation in which my interlocutor would invariably challenge me on what I meant by 'images' – how I intend to define or delimit the image (a 'small' matter to which I shall come to below) – the discussion would generally move quickly on to a specific interest (generally of *their* choice) regarding one of a whole host of image-types including, for example, photographs, paintings, film, installations, literature and, perhaps most frequent of all, graffiti. Of course, not all of these aspects necessarily relate directly to the actual *fall* of the Wall, nonetheless, it is by extension that they become components of it, for indeed all of these 'lost items' are what people want to talk about when broaching the topic of images of the fall of the Wall. It seems we are very well versed in *talking* (or writing) about visual culture and that we are clearly confident about what we take these things to be and mean. With respect specifically to images of the fall of the Berlin Wall, one reason for this confidence and awareness would seem to relate to the nature of the iconic image, which not only endures, but also enables further representations. It is as if there is something almost 'democratic' and transparent about the images of fall of the Berlin Wall, both as they first appeared (and continue to circulate) in the global media networks, as well as in our everyday conversations and incantations. I aim, however, to disrupt this confidence, though not as an iconoclastic gesture, but in order to assert a greater complexity in respect of these images. I do not want to interpret too soon, but instead find ways to keep the process of critical enquiry open longer. And I wish implicitly to keep coming back to the question of what is actually meant when we think of images, or 'image-events' such as the fall of the Wall. Overall, my point is not so much to find an answer or final definition to these images, but rather to keep the mind open to what we regard images to be, how we experience them in different ways and to what ends we can put them.

There are two important underlying concerns to mention from the outset. Firstly, this book has evolved following specific engagement in contemporary theoretical debates about visual

culture, the initial terms of which I stake out at length in chapter two. I acknowledge the importance of these debates in providing a suitable intellectual discourse in which to place my thoughts. Nevertheless, I have been somewhat disappointed overall with what has arisen by way of a 'visual critique' and in effect I seek a more urgent and creative form of enquiry attending to our visual culture(s). Thus, I think it is fair to say that in what follows I aim to put forward something of a 'supplement' to visual culture studies, both acknowledging the grounds upon which I develop my ideas, whilst equally displacing them by way of a critical evaluation. Ultimately, this leads to the recommendation for a form of image critique (a critical application of the image) that I am rather inclined to think sits to one side of current academic discourse.

Secondly – and as a practical implication of my critique of visual culture – there remains here an underlying interest in the relationship between word and image, in particular an interest in the potential for *writing the image*. The 'word' has, of course, long been the primary tool of academic enquiry, as well as being a subject of serious study. By contrast, images have more obviously been only an object of interest, to be written about and codified. What I have in mind with respect to an image critique is to unseat such an arrangement, to allow images to be as much a means of formulating critique, as they are an object of it. In part this relates to the use of visual images for critical purposes; however, it is not exclusively the case. Indeed, in 'writing the image,' I want to make sense of the image in broader terms and consider the important role that the image can play in critical *writing*, thus allowing for a more creative, figurative style of work.

The idea of 'writing the image' has for me been inspired by Roland Barthes' late writings. This includes, for example, Barthes' (1987: 84) notion of *écriture* (a term meaning writing or literature 'used for its own sake', which cannot be summarized as such, going beyond the mere transmission of information) and an associated *form* he often referred to as the 'novelistic'. In *A Lover's Discourse* (1990), for example, the novelistic mode enables Barthes to avoid any so-called scientific study or treatise on amorous discourse and instead write a 'fabricated' discourse of a lover. It is a text that creates an intertextual fictional character or 'lover' out of the very discourse of love (as it emerges from an array of literary, philosophical, psychological, religious, artistic and personal discourse), the purpose of which is to comment on how the *fiction* of the lover's self only leads to disappointment, frustration and loss. As Barthes (1985: 284–5) once explained in an interview, the book presents 'a composed feigned, or if you prefer, a "pieced-together" discourse (the result of montage)'. The text, then, is complex and layered. On one level it exposes the illusory nature of amorous discourse. Yet, simultaneously, it avoids the strictures of a demythologizing critique, for it treats its character (the discourse of love) with love and affirmation. Thus, the reader of *A Lover's Discourse* can both identify with an implicit critique of a cultural myth and still empathize with the 'I' (the character) who speaks the lover's discourse. Barthes' intention – as we find with all of his later writings – is that we are challenged in our own relation to the subject under scrutiny. Yet, this is without consolation of a definitive, objective theory, instead more a curious prompt (or writing) leading *us* (as 'reader') to a further critical reflection of our own.

Similarly, my hopes for an image critique is for a form or mode of enquiry that 'fabricates' (in every sense of the word) a complex site/sight for critical reflection. This is meant as an image equivalent to *écriture*, a construction 'used for its own sake'. Thus, not the development of a theory (that we might commonly suppose is set aside from that which it reflects upon), but rather a thought-piece, or even 'theory-product' as it were, an incident of writing and picturing that allows for a critical *experience*. Were this still to be defined in terms of a semiotics, it is one that is perhaps better characterized as a kind of painting. As Barthes (2000: 475) claimed in his late period, the semiologist needs be, in fact, 'an artist' playing with signs 'as with a conscious decoy, whose fascination he savours and wants to make others savour and understand'. The sign for this artist 'is always immediate, subject to the kind of evidence that leaps to the eyes, like a trigger of the imagination', which is why semiology in this case 'is not a hermeneutics: it paints more than it digs'.

In formulating this idea of an image critique and of 'writing the image', I am also indebted to Walter Benjamin's concept of the 'thought-image' – at the very least as a way of analytically describing the prospect of an image critique (see my note in the preface to this book). Similar in effect, though not necessarily in style, Benjamin's image 'constellations' are fabricated like Barthes' texts through the use of montage, citation, biography and aphorism; resulting in a singular, yet richly layered, text or inter-text. Further in this chapter, I draw upon Benjamin's (1992: 249) well-known passage on the Angel of History. This, I want to show, is a thought-image all of its own; one that provides a fitting emblem (to re-surface in subsequent chapters) for the poly-perspective nature of what I describe as image critique. Furthermore, it is also a pertinent motif for the complexity of the *historical* event of the fall of the Wall, which I frame below as a form of 'Instant History'. Before coming to this, however, let me first return more immediately to the 'image' of the Wall itself.

The Berlin Wall Today as *Image-text*

The fall of the Berlin Wall can be referred to as being simultaneously a *site* and a *sight* of critical importance. When it stood, the Wall obviously demarcated the site – through its physical imposition – of a fraught political dividing line. It was inevitably a place of much contention and angst, yet more than that it very *visibly* brought to life the tensions of the Cold War. The *fall* of the Wall is no less an important visual occasion. When civilians en masse first crossed over the formerly forbidden boundary between East and West Berlin all number of television (and newspaper) cameras were there on site to carry the images around the world. By and large, these are the images of the fall of the Berlin Wall that I take to be the subject of this study. As Susan Buck-Morss (1994: 11) puts it: '[t]hose television images *are* the historical event'. Yet, equally, the simple phrase 'the fall of the Wall' conjures up multiple meanings and associations, whether historically, politically or culturally. We need to accommodate a multifarious domain of images, symbols and myths, since it is only in a more holistic sense that we can really make sense of the symbolic weight of those memorable television pictures. Thus, with respect to defining and informing an image critique, I advocate *using* a wide variety of images as part of a critique, so raising the prospect of a kind of sighting/citing of various ideas, theories and problems. By its 'design' an image critique ought to provide a 'space' or site in which a critical engagement in images is fashioned. It is to afford us situations of writing or picturing, allowing critique to be a kind of thoughtful and thought-provoking *experience*. It is in this multiple sense that I describe images of the fall of the Wall as a site/sight of critical engagement.

To this day – despite its physical demise – the Berlin Wall remains to be found in all sorts of places and in all manner of forms, whether in oral history, photographs, novels and film, on television and as ornaments and tourist trinkets. It is frequently cited (or sighted) in countless books, magazines and journalistic writing and actual pieces of the Wall still exist, in some cases complete sections of it stand as monuments in German cities and before a number of civic buildings around the world. A notable example of which is a section that stands before the private library of the late Ronald Reagan. However, there are many other less significant sites, including, for example, a section located in front of a nondescript youth centre in the little known East German town of Reichenbach (Saxony) – of which I only know as I would walk past it (though without thinking much about it) most days during an extended stay there. Smaller pieces of the Wall are perhaps more readily located, having been something of a prize possession even for those who had no direct experience of the Wall. The tourist shops in Berlin are still cluttered with such pieces (though, by now, their authenticity is hard to vouch for). At an even more minuscule level, the Wall has even found its way into use as a homeopathic remedy, notably one considered to have a very high potency as a treatment/cause of trauma (Evans 2000: 22–26).

The *absence* of the Wall has meaning too; one might argue even a particular 'visuality'. Many visiting Berlin today do so in order simply to walk *freely* through the city and witness 'with one's own eyes' the Wall's disappearance. As one might expect, this is hardly without its complications. Nicolas Whybrow (2001: 41–42), for example, draws attention to an inconspicuous copper strip (engraved with 'Berliner Mauer 1961–1989') embedded in the road surface of Niederkirchner Strasse, running along the former course of the Wall. The strip acts as a 'monument' to the socio-political act of the Wall's rupture and removal. Yet, there is an odd paradox, for 'the strip is notable above all for the mildness of its impact', with most people failing to register it at all. Hence, Whybrow argues, 'it draws attention to the invisibility of the Wall – by *not* doing so, if you see what I mean – to its disappearance per se'. It is a fact supposedly bemoaned by some Berliners, or, at least, those who view the all too rapid vanishing of the Wall 'as indicative of a change that occurred too quickly and comprehensively'.[1]

Thus, overall, the site/sight of (the lack of) the Berlin Wall through a complex exchange of memories and associations continues to present various contradictions and paradoxes. It lies 'in a curious hinterland between memory and actuality' (Feversham and Schmidt 1999: 10) and, in this respect, in contrast to a supposedly 'static image engraved on the World's imagination', whether when standing or 'falling', the Wall as a (mental and/or architectural) structure and symbol can be said to be:

> a complex, multi-faceted entity representing many things to many people: for some it was a grossly-extended cinema screen on which the projected anxieties of the West flickered and danced, for others, a gallery of graffiti art, a locus of death and tragedy, a ruin, an absence, a memory, a void – the Berlin Wall is, in effect, a text: there is no single reading.
> (Feversham and Schmidt 1999: 14)

The idea of a 'static image engraved on the World's imagination' is plausible, indeed evident enough. As I discuss below (and in more detail in chapter three), the Wall became *the* signifier of the Cold War scenario. Yet, equally, there is an inconsistency in that such a static, singular image only really comes about because it is continually updated, modified and warped by an on-going proliferation of different images, image-types and contexts. Thus, the Berlin Wall was never simply a concrete edifice, but actually a panoply of symbols, myths and images; indeed, a textual and intertextual phenomenon. And these elements, I argue, can be put to work (or

re-directed) for critical purpose. Nevertheless, as an important point of difference, there is something distinct about understanding the Wall as 'image', rather than 'text' (albeit one with 'no single reading'). And if only because, in adhering to the codes and conventions of a 'media event' the fall of the Wall more than anything became *visible* to the wider world, manifesting as what I term 'Instant History'.

It is important not to get stuck in a rigid binary account of word and image. As already inferred with reference to Barthes' notion of the *writerly*, I am certainly more interested in understanding the relationship *between* words and images, to find a means to incorporate the one within the other. W. J. T. Mitchell (1994: 83–90) suggests the problematic of word and image – an infinitely unstable dialectic of translation – might best be understood as 'a symptom of the impossibility of a "theory of pictures" or a "science of representation"'. Traditionally, comparative method has been applied to bridge word and image, as a way of 'sorting out the differences and similarities'. However, the underlying presumption is a 'unifying, homogeneous concept' – this being, for example, the sign, the work of art, meaning, representation etc. In response to this problem, we might usefully consider the point of an image critique to ask not what the differences or similarities are between words and images, but what difference these differences (and similarities) actually make. This can only be asked by engaging with the materials themselves, to see what each offer different to other materials. Furthermore, the idea of an image critique is for images to *produce* their various effects for critical purposes – to let images play a role in bringing about an understanding (and complication) of meaning and representation, whether through composite, divisional or relational forms.

Crucially, image critique is not meant as some teleological procedure of interpretation. In fact, it may never provide resolute answers. Instead it keeps thought in motion, allowing other ways of seeing, helping us as it were to view from different angles. In this respect image critique is much more – as I describe above – a critical *space*, than a determined, fully-formed critique of something. The cultural critic and theorist Mieke Bal would perhaps take issue with such an approach, suggesting that an image critique is not critical *enough*, that it is lacking as a form of political critique. And not least because reliance upon the image or the 'visual' is to risk what she terms 'visual essentialism' (Bal 2003).[2] Bal's point of view is certainly not uncommon; in fact, as Martin Jay (2002: 269–275) remarks, 'the claim that images can be understood as natural or analogical signs with universal capacities to communicate has almost entirely come undone'. And, in place of this kind of claim, there has arisen what he calls 'the triumph of cultural relativism in visual terms'. He positions himself against such visual culturalism and here I take his remarks to underscore what I suggest an image critique needs to do. His argument also begins to help identify how an image-based methodology can be located with respect to the contemporary field of visual studies (more of which will be discussed in chapter two). Jay argues for the need to retain an understanding of an 'excess' of the image; an excess preventing figurality from being entirely reduced to discursivity. Thus, without wishing to override entirely a visual culturalism, he does nonetheless seek to question the predominant need to bring the visual into meaning through its translation. Drawing on work in the field of anthropology, Jays (2002: 275) describes how visual ethnography opens up 'more directly onto the sensorium than written texts and creates psychological and somatic forms of intersubjectivity between viewer and social actor'. It is this kind of visual 'knowledge' that I suggest an image critique can enable for new critical purpose.

Advocating an engagement with the image in all its excesses, as it relates to, fractures and combines with the text, may mean refusing to reconcile with any established critical framework. Yet, it does not mean the image can not be its *own* critical framework. As Régis Debray (1996: 149) remarks, 'every code does not have to be a language, just as every message does not have to be speech'. And, again, this is not to suggest that image and text need be considered as always separate entities, but instead, as Debray notes, as 'symbiotic' objects, the value of which is derived from their mixture. As Mitchell (1994: 95) puts it: 'all media are mixed media, combing different codes, discursive conventions, channels, sensory and cognitive modes'.

Thus, however much I may stress the importance of images and a purported image critique, I nonetheless understand the Berlin Wall in its multiplicity, not only as a visual image or picture, but a multimedia, multi-modal 'object'; to try and understand what kind of meanings the Wall, as an 'imagetext', generates and continues to enforce or enliven. In placing emphasis upon the image (for critique, or *as* critique), the immediate temptation is perhaps to privilege the *visual*, material image (or picture), over less tangible mental and verbal ones – or, indeed, their composites. The most common conclusion is that the image 'proper' is 'the graphic or optical representations we see displayed in an objective, publicly sharable space' (Mitchell 1986: 13). Following this logic, the obvious reaction to the rubric of *images of the fall of the Berlin Wall* would most readily (or 'properly') be to think of the wall as covered in graffiti, or conjure to one's mind the media footage, and/or photo-documentary images. This, however, is certainly to ignore an abundance of literary images of the Wall, and mental ones too; a good example of the latter being jokes relating to the Wall and East/West German relations (see Stein 1993;1996). It might be argued these images types somehow 'don't seem to be stable and permanent the way real images are, and they vary from one person to the next' (Mitchell 1986: 13). In fact, literary, dream and metaphoric images are oft deemed more open to doubt and instability. In addition, as Mitchell (1986: 13–14) notes, it is frequently argued that 'mental images don't seem to be exclusively visual the way real pictures are; they involve all the senses'. This only further alludes to the problem over definitions of the image. Indeed, to come at this a different way, we can soon find that even supposedly 'proper' images are 'not stable, static, or permanent in any metaphysical sense'. In one very obvious way, for example, the view of/from the Wall, depending on whether you were to the East or the West of it, made for stark differences of perspective, regardless of the fact it was still the same piece of concrete on either side.

Finally, however, in negotiating these difficulties over definition, the 'fundamental' meaning or concept of the image I employ here can be understood to relate to a notion of the image as 'likeness', or 'resemblance' – the image-type that Mitchell places at the very root of a suggested family tree of the image (Mitchell 1986: 31–35).[3] The idea of the image as 'likeness' might initially suggest a crude form of mimesis, of reflecting or mimicking an external reality. This, however, is not what is intended. Instead, 'likeness' is to be understood in terms of a *process of imaging* – or, for want of a better word, 'writing' – that is a perpetual motion of *thinking in images*. Akin, for example, to Walter Benjamin's notion of the mimetic faculty (1997: 160–163), which he describes with the child's ability to play 'at being not only a shopkeeper or teacher but also a windmill and a train'. The idea is of meanings being moved from one place to another, from an archive of what he calls *unsinnliche Ählichkeiten*. This is commonly translated as 'non-sensuous similarity', yet as Linda Rugg (1997: 141) notes this seems to imply 'not of the senses', when in fact it relates specifically to their use. Instead, she explains, *unsinnlich* broaches the idea of 'a way of reading' that in rejecting the ordinary sense-pathways of interpretation, 'goes beyond the normal reach of senses – perhaps even beyond sense'; to mean beyond a purely rational mode of thinking. Benjamin (1997: 162) would seem to suggest this is some kind of energy or medium of our thoughts which arises 'like a flame, manifests itself only through a bearer...like a flash, similarity appears'. And it is only limited to flashes – as it 'flits past' – that we are able to experience this *unsinnlichkeit*. Both word and image are party to this phenomenon, for whilst it is itself (as a mode of 'writing' or thinking) neither word nor image, it is contained or borne through them. As Benjamin notes, the graphologist 'has taught us to recognise in handwriting images that the unconscious of the writer conceals in it'. Some further clarification of this difficult concept might be made by noting the similarities with Barthes' (1977: 179–189) notion of the *grain* of the voice, or Kristeva's (1984: 25–30) use of the concept *Chora* – in both cases representing a material, bodily or sensual quality that carries meaning and makes 'writing' possible and distinct.

The point, in relation to an image critique, is that an engagement with images constitutes an *act* of production, offering a unique way of combining, distorting and replicating various elements. And, just as Barthes (1982: 164) suggests in his essay 'From Work to Text', that the text is a social space, 'where languages circulate (keeping the circular sense of the term)', the image can be considered here as an overarching term for a social 'imaging' (for want of a better word) – an imaging that can itself *locate* or designate 'image' phenomena. What is important in referring to the image in this manner, in locating the image in *writing*, is the re-assessment it makes of how we manifest and hold onto meanings in a less directed, linear fashion. Instead of a critical meta-language which looks upon an object from a critical distance, the incorporating of images into critique (as critique) has the effect of *embedding* (or at least inviting) the observer within a reflective, critical configuration.

By way of an introduction, then, this chapter attempts to 'set the scene' of what is undoubtedly a complex set of relations specific to the site/sight of the fall of the Berlin Wall; these being issues of social change, globalized media, the role and nature of images and new modes of critical intervention. The fall of the Wall can be framed as an instance of an instant history, which, as I will discuss below, has significant implications for how we relate to the event. I will begin by examining the fall of the Wall in terms of it being an 'image of our time' – as an event of international importance that manifests as an icon of the late twentieth century. However, not only is this an event of great historical significance, it is also, an important marker of a shift in our culture, asking us to re-consider the image we hold of our *own* times, as well as the image we hold of the critic and even criticism itself.

Instant History

Defining moments of history, at least since the advent of photography, circulate abundantly as a series of pictures, as icons of our past. In countless books we can pore over the twentieth century as a collection of images, whether of the burning Reichstag, the assassination of John F. Kennedy, the first man on the moon, a royal wedding, or Nelson Mandela's 'walk to freedom' and so on.[4] It is not only that we watch these scenes, but that they can be *shared* as reference points in and for our discussions. Included in this collection will almost certainly be the images captured on the 9th November 1989 of East and West Germans criss-crossing the various checkpoints along the Berlin Wall, or chipping away at it with chisels and hammers.

As a general rule, all these 'images of history' can be considered in varying degrees to be 'random, unscripted, unofficial, and unauthorised images' (Mitchell 1994: 369); qualities which imbue them with a sense of immediacy and reality. It is the unaccounted details of a recorded image which have the ability to punctuate media codes and awaken us to the fact that what we are seeing is based in a reality; a phenomenon that 'which-has-been' – or, with the 'fact' of television, it would appear 'that-which-*is*' (Cavell 1984). Even with highly orchestrated events, such as the landing on the moon or a royal wedding, there will be elements of the transmission which cannot be scripted or contained. These elements are part of the live experience. Just how Princess Diana smiles before the camera as her carriage takes her to the cathedral, or how the astronaut's voice crackles across the radio as he takes his first steps on the lunar surface, are each moments, however slight, of unpredictability. To parallel Barthes's (1977: 179–189) notion of the 'grain of the voice' referring to the 'body' which *carries* the spoken word, these unofficial, unscripted elements of images are the material evidence, or *grain* of the historical event. Yet, there is perhaps something still further and more distinct that can be gleaned from the relatively recent events such as the fall of the Berlin Wall. The images that circulate our media networks today are not only key moments of history, but what I term here as images of an *Instant History*. By this I mean a form of history that would seem to take place all of a sudden, instantly relayed to a wide audience, becoming instantly recognizable, instantly historicized.

Technological progress is undoubtedly a part of this developing trend. Images such as the fall of the Berlin Wall are instant, in the first case, by virtue of the fact that they are (or at least we believe them to be) delivered to us on our television sets simultaneous to their actual passing as an event. The history seen to be unfolding before those 'on-location' is immediately the very same scene of history seen to unfold for audiences many miles away. It is the nature of the 'transmission' that this image seems not to be distorting the 'original' view. Inevitably, it is a view that is contained in some way, if only because the operation of the camera limits what we get to see and for how long we see it (it cannot afford us the luxury, for example, of being able to move about at will, as, for example, we have become accustomed to with the virtual domains of 3-D computer landscapes). Nevertheless there is little sense in which the image we receive has in someway first been translated; it appears instantly relayed. Secondly, these images are instant in that history is made all of a sudden and so not subject to a practice of periodization that has the benefit of hindsight. Instead, the images immediately mark some new period in which we live. Thus, instant history can be characterized by two quite specific qualifiers – being *instantly relayed* and *instantly immortalizing* or historicizing.

Given today's vast array of media dissemination, it is fair to say that countless images fulfil these principles. A third qualifier, however, is that these eventful images are ones that become *instantly recognizable*, and in two senses: they are instantly understandable at the time of their transmission, as well as being highly communicable. In other words, they are instantly recognizable, or 'iterable' (regardless of what they might stand for), being introduced in all manner of citation and conversation, often in contexts going far beyond their origination. This would seem broadly to bring me to a definition of the iconic image, yet what is particular to an image of instant of history is its *impact*, not only on all future iteration of its history, but also on the circumstance of the event itself.

In his reflections on the events of May 1968 in Paris, Barthes (1989: 149–150) provides an interesting commentary on the nature and impact of a somewhat earlier instance of instant history, or as he terms it 'hot' history: 'history in the course of being made'. He suggests the transistor radio (then a new technology) played a pivotal role in re-defining the way in which the events were both experienced and orchestrated. He recalls 'streets filled with motionless people seeing nothing, looking at nothing, their eyes down, but their ears glued to transistor radios'. The radio as 'auditory prosthesis' not only informed participants of the actions they were immediately involved in but, also, 'by the compression of time, by the immediate resonance of the act, it inflected, modified the event'. In the case of the Berlin Wall, it was of course television which played a pivotal role. So, instead of 'their eyes being down', the 'people' on this occasion looked straight ahead, their eyes glued to the 'box.' Not only did television help East Germans realize the full significance of the unfolding events, it prompted yet more to move out onto the streets and join in with the mass demonstrations. At the time of my writing similar kinds of broadcast images were again in circulation from other parts of the world. Today, however, it appears protest groups are ever more quickly harnessing the power of their own 'spectacle' image. With the public protests in the Ukraine, for example, following alleged corruption during the 2004 elections, the demonstrations in favour of the challenger, Viktor Yushchenko, had – at strikingly short notice – 'laser lights, plasma screens, sophisticated sound systems, rock concerts, tents to camp in and huge quantities of orange clothing' (The Guardian 27.11.04, p. 22). DeLuca and Peeples (2002: 134) suggest that in light of the new kinds of contemporary forms of social organization and modes of perception/reception, public debate, scrutiny and opinion-making no longer takes place only within the bounds of a (Habermasian) public sphere, but rather more through a 'public screen', meaning an aggregate of all the various means of mass communications (i.e. the 'screens' of television, the Internet, newspapers and advertising). The power of media events in rearticulating hegemonic discourse has proven to be, as in this case of the Ukraine, quite considerable. I shall come back to arguments of the 'public screen' in chapter five, when looking at the public art of two German film-makers, whose films effectively re-stage the event of the fall of the Berlin Wall.

Returning again to Barthes' (1989: 150) account of the events of May 1968, he notes how the reporters were as much ensconced in the confused atmosphere of the events as were the 'people' who took to the streets. The reporters' 'informative word', he remarks, 'was so closely involved in the event...as to become its immediate and consubstantial meaning, its way of acceding to an instantaneous intelligibility.' In fact he goes as far to say, 'it was the event itself'. In certain respects these remarks pre-empt the nature of commentary regarding the Gulf War in 1991, epitomized by Baudrillard's (1995) polemic in which he suggests the war never took place, but was instead a media event of war. Similarly the televised images of Germans on both sides of the Wall a few feet away from the reporters speaking to cameras equally became the event itself. We remember this event, whether or not we know or remember much else that transpired from its occasion.

The impact of an instant history is potentially profound and far-reaching, changing how we relate to major events in the world, but also, how we remember (and study) them. There are three, inter-related aspects to any definition of Instant History that warrant exploration. Firstly, as an Image of our Times, instant history events reflect a new immediacy of knowledge and information, which have a levelling effect – the critic and expert becoming as much a spectator to events as any one else. The effect is to alter the situation of the critic; arguably, in fact, placing responsibility upon us all as potential critics and experts. Secondly, the consumption of instant history events might be said to *Screen (out) History* in various ways, which relates particularly to a new kind of transparency of the media; evident, for example, with the rise in televisual 24–hour news reporting, which in turn has led to the very mechanisms and logistics of live reporting itself becoming newsworthy. There is a potential flattening out of ideological differences in contemporary journalistic practice, but this does not necessarily lead to a more complex reporting or picturing of events. Thirdly, we can consider an event such as the fall of the Wall as a form of *Instant Replay* – not only is its form of history to be thought of as a specific moment in time, as an *event*, but it also refers to an inherent repetition and circulation of meaning, the event being instantly available for citation and re-circulation. In effect, this creates an ever-present and malleable continuum of history; a formation of history ever ready for new configurations (if all too often only in bite-size, CNN-styled 'factoids').

An Image of Our Times

The Berlin Wall makes for one of the most incredible stories of the twentieth century, with its symbolic weight having far exceeded that of its physical intimidation. Not only did it divide up a city and its inhabitants, and not only was it to become the symbol of post-war German division, but also it was 'positioned within the symbolic order as the cornerstone of the Cold-War discourse' (Buck-Morss 1994: 11). From the time of its construction in 1961 until its 'fall' in 1989 the Wall was a key resource for political rhetoric, revealing several different phases in its symbolic use over the three decades in which it existed. So, for example, in only the first few weeks 'the newly-erected Berlin Wall was for the West a source of anger toward the East, a cause of great sorrow, and a sign of failure of the West' (Bruner 1989: 319). Yet, the Wall proved to be a more malleable and significant symbol still. In only a couple of years and particularly following US President Kennedy's visit to West Berlin in 1963 (when he famously expressed his affinity with the 'free' city of Berlin), the rhetoric relating to the Wall shifted emphasis, appealing to ideas of 'solidarity in the West rather than the failures'. Much later, in 1987, US President Ronald Reagan's speech, given directly in front of the Brandenburg Gate, pronounced a rhetoric of challenge, when he famously urged: 'Mr Gorbachev, tear down this Wall.'

Bruner published his study in the month prior to the final events of the fall of the Wall, giving him just enough time to include a brief note on the forced resignation of the East German leader Erich Honecker (in October 1989). He was, however, to be unaware of the dramatic images of the fall of the Wall that would soon follow. In fact, whilst Bruner does actually predict the end of the Wall, he misjudges the impact the event was to have. The Wall in its final years appeared as a symbol of ennui for the whole 'theatre' of the Cold War. And debates at the time were never quite aware of just what a compelling symbol the Wall would become with its demise. A dispassionate, rational note on the public discussion of German reunification during this period is revealing of just how misplaced the debates were:

> It appears there is more rhetorical momentum for the removal of the Wall than for the reunification of the two Germanies...Apparently the solution is to treat the Wall and reunification as two separate issues. We may predict that the Wall will fall long before there is any substantial movement on the reunification issue.

(Bruner 1989: 326)

So, whilst there was growing acceptance (on all sides) that the Wall was now largely redundant; increasingly less critical attention was given to it and its effects on the lives of people living in its shadow now dissipated. Paradoxically, then, when the Wall did actually fall, it appeared to have happened all of a sudden, a dramatic surprise for everyone.

For over a week prior to the event, western news outlets had been reporting on the growing public demonstrations, the faltering government body, as well as the huge number of refugees fleeing the country. Yet, equally these reports made no prediction of the entire collapse of the German Democratic Republic (GDR), only its re-organization and stabilization. Even following the surprising announcement by a GDR official, on the fateful day of Thursday 9th November 1989, that travel restrictions were to be suspended with immediate effect, reporters on the evening news programmes maintained a cautious brief. On the UK's Channel Four evening news programme, for example, their 'diplomatic editor' on-the-spot in Berlin was asked to give 'a sense of the atmosphere in East Berlin', to which he replied: '...there certainly isn't anything like dancing on the street. I think everyone who watched the evening news tonight will be viewing it with a degree of caution' (*Channel Four News* 09.11.89, 7pm).

A couple of hours later, the BBC's *Nine O'Clock News* closed with a summary by a reporter who stood in front of the Brandenburg Gate, suggesting calmly: '...it won't be until tomorrow that East Berliners can apply to local offices and obtain travel permits, and even then it is not entirely clear when they will be able to cross' (BBC News 09.11.89, 9pm). Yet, in less than an hour, East Germans – albeit slowly at first – were crossing through to the West. An hour on from the BBC's broadcast, ITN's *News at Ten* was at least able to break the 'real' news story halfway through its programme: 'We've just heard that 100 people have crossed through the Berlin Wall tonight.' (ITN News, 09.11.89, 10pm). Nevertheless, the programme then proceeded to air pre-recorded reports discussing the broader significance for the international political scene of ending travel restrictions in the GDR.

It is perhaps fair to say, none of the reports aired on the day (or indeed over the first few days) were able to explain very much. The following day's news and extended weekend news programmes in the main simply repeated scenes of East Germans crossing over into (and later shopping in) the West. To paraphrase those stopped in the street to comment on the situation, it all seemed somewhat 'unbelievable', 'incredible', and 'like a dream'. To take these words as emblematic of the event, the fall of the Berlin Wall (and the endemic 'collapse of communism') not only overtook commentaries predicting its demise, but also exceeded all prior frames of reference. The various reporters and experts brought into news studios to discuss the unfolding scenes appeared unable to speak with genuine authority on the subject and more often than not (despite the palpable mood of joy) continued to frame everything in the negative terms of Cold War politicking. So, for example, even after the Russian Foreign Spokesman, Gennadi Gerasimov, casually and rather humorously described the Soviet response by way of reference to Frank Sinatra's signature tune 'I did it my way' – suggesting that each country within the Warsaw Pact would need now to sing its own tune – he was still generally regarded as being cagey.

Channel Four's main newsreader, Jon Snow, for example, noted in his headline statement on the Friday evening show: 'The opening of the Wall is welcomed from Washington to Moscow', followed immediately with the caveat, 'Though from the Kremlin there is a warning that the Soviets will not tolerate the abolition of the border between the Germanies' (*Channel*

Four News 10.11.89, 7pm). Later in the same programme their correspondent in Moscow reported a 'mixture of relief and anxiety': relief that the flood of refugees would now hopefully soon ease; but anxiety for 'the kind of instability that the Kremlin has always feared'. It was a sense of anxiety further compounded by extensive studio debate with primarily western political officials, including the former American Defence Secretary Casper Weinberger (a key player during Reagan's administration). Yet, despite the same editorial line running throughout the programme, there was no firm quote from any Soviet officials. In a brief interview with Gennadi Gerasimov, the Moscow correspondent asked whether there was concern over the speed of change. Gerasimov replied in a cautious and relatively ambiguous way, saying, 'Not about the speed, but about the possible instability'. It is really of little surprise that there may have been some concern, especially given Russia's close proximity (and direct relationship) to the situation, along with the very real practical implications that would follow with any possible instability. Yet, Gerasimov's tone by no means portrayed a sense of an immediate threat of the kind the Kremlin had supposedly 'always feared'. This was certainly more an effect of a style of journalism still tethered to the (usefully dramatic) suspicions of Cold War rhetoric. And, furthermore, it was simply to ignore the fact – reported by the same correspondent in Moscow – that not only had the Soviets encouraged East Germans to press for change, but were also willing to 'let the story tell itself', with images, that same night, openly broadcast on Soviet television: 'pictures from the Berlin Wall. Images of freedom that touch emotions not just in the West, but in the Soviet Union as well' (*Channel Four News* 10.11.89, 7pm).

It is these *same* images found on Soviet (as well as East German) television that we most remember. In fact, the prevailing interpretation of the event of the fall of the Wall coalesce around a rather basic, generative 'theme of celebration,' which, in turn – as I will explore in chapter three – comes to underscore a neo-conservative discourse of political and economic liberalism encapsulated by Francis Fukuyama's (1989) much cited 'end of history' thesis. It is almost as if, as the prominent symbolism of the Wall was 'emptied' out by its fall, it as much opened itself up to a new grand significance. Somewhat ironically, then, despite the fraught history of the Cold War and the prominence that the Wall took as a symbol within it, it is the *fall* of the Wall (as opposed to the sheer inhumanity of its design and steadfastness) that would have seemed in the end to have caused the greater cultural and political rupture. It is a moment prompting many such comments, as, for example, with anthropologist John Borneman's (1991: 10) remarks when he describes the fall as 'a great chiasmus, a peripateia, a classical moment of reversal, changing the look of things and established discourses almost beyond recognition'. An interpretation echoed by the cultural critic Dick Hebdige, who notes:

> when the Berlin Wall/mirror shattered, suddenly a lot of other things smashed too. The most important thing that got obliterated was the cast-iron reality of the postwar bipolar order which had been literally cast in concrete since 1961 – secured, and guaranteed, symbolized, reflected, held in place in the terrible mirage of the wall. All those ideological investments, all those ideological and geopolitical maps inscribed as if in stone around it. All melted into air.
>
> (Hebdige 1993: 270)

Hebdige's point is that somehow 'we' knew where we stood when the Wall was in place, yet with its demise the 'security' of all that had existed suddenly collapsed along with it. The resulting state of affairs became known by many – at least many on the left – as 'a crisis in cognitive mapping'. Scott Lash (1990), for example, notes how this was a turning point for those previously invested in a Marxist tradition, for it supposedly now became a stern fact that socialism – thought, or at least hoped to be the *next* form of society – was *not* going to follow on from that of capitalism (indeed, if anything it was the other way round). When the Wall fell in real time and space, it as much fell upon the credibility of the intellectual community to keep up with events:

> If daily life in the East gave signals of impending collapse, its tremors were sensed more accurately by average citizens than by intellectual elites. While experts and scholars were busy predicating more of the same, the Cold War system imploded. Without war, without revolution, without cultural renaissance, it simply came to an end.
>
> (Buck-Morss 1994: 11)

Academics, critics and experts all over the world had been caught napping in their armchairs; a sentiment Dirk Philipsen (1993: ix), a German historian working in America at the time, neatly describes when he remarks: 'Like so many other people I vividly remember where I was the day the Berlin Wall came down: at home in Durham, North Carolina, sitting with incredulous awe in front of my television set'. Philipsen, along with many others, had sat watching the television news reports in the weeks preceding, learning of the demonstrations, the popular demands and the faltering Party leadership. Yet crucially, he notes: '[the] sudden turn of events I had certainly not expected – nor, it is now clear, had anyone else'.

Is it all but mandatory to respond to the fall of the Wall in terms of surprise and bewilderment? Today the event continues to signify a sense of rupture, or turnaround; both an end and a beginning. And with everyone privy to the same scenes – with everything, as it were, laid bare to be seen – the cultural critic is as much an 'average citizen', no doubt finding themselves, like Philipsen, 'sitting with incredulous awe' in front of the television set. This is the 'new' status of the critic, which does not need to be denied or shunned in any particular way; in fact, if critical engagement is to be maintained and strengthened, it is perhaps more appropriate for it to be accepted and understood. It is a line of argument Susan Bordo (1997) takes when she describes herself as a cultural critic living in a world of images; as being a consumer, enjoying those images, not impervious to their appeal. To explain her point, she revises Plato's allegory of the cave, arguing that whilst for Plato 'the artificial images cast on the wall of the cave are a metaphor for the world of sense perception...For us, bedazzlement by created images...is the actual condition of our lives' (2). And, whilst she is concerned about the illusionary nature of cultural images (that supposedly maintain false ideas of gender, race etc.), suggesting that we need to 'learn to see with something other than bedazzled eyes' (15), she is equally of the opinion that 'cultural criticism does not so much ask that we leave the cave as turn a light on *in* it' (14).

Bordo's interest in her own 'bedazzlement' relates, then, to the concept of an image critique. Her strategy is to accept the role and importance of images in the social and cultural production of meaning (to remain *in situ*, but nonetheless to shed more 'critical' light on matters). Potentially, this would appear to mean reaching for a collection of somehow better, or more 'truthful', images, with Bordo arguing for the contextualizing and complicating of otherwise simplified, reductive images. This obviously fits in with her view of both consumer/critic living (and taking pleasure) in a world of images. Yet, the main criticism that can be made of her approach is that ultimately it represents a fairly straightforward mode of demystification with the idea that the more complex image or narrative about the world is the more truthful. And so whilst Bordo removes any former distance between the critic and the consumer of the image, at root she is still committed to the idea that images (at least the uncomplicated ones) are somehow dangerous or manipulative. Arguably, this would make her critical of Philipsen's awe-inspired time sat watching television, so potentially undermining the uncontested 'truth' of the images of the joy and celebration witnessed with the fall of the Wall. Thus, to make sense of Bordo's approach with respect to an idea of an image critique, there is evidently a shared interest in attempting to further contextualize and complicate the image, but the difference is that it is not about attempting to secure a particular image, or collection of better, more truthful ones. Instead, even if perhaps at the risk of being unstable, an image critique requires its 'picture' be rendered anew each and every time it is viewed or read – just as we will see is the case with Benjamin's thought-image of the Angel of History, which we are invited to read/write anew with each and every encounter of its passage. Thus, it is not necessarily important that an image critique is likely to be complex and layered by nature, but more important that it is designed for a cognitive experience; 'thought-images' being, as Benjamin has it, flashes of inspiration, not forms of interpretation or assessment.

Thus, in describing the fall of the Berlin Wall as an 'image of our times' I mean to suggest, in the usual sense of the phrase, that it is an icon of a specific moment in contemporary history – the sort of image, for example, that we are accustomed to seeing in magazines or on television as part of a review of the year and so forth. However, it is also the fact that this particular image engenders, or at least brings to attention, a change of emphasis in terms of our situation (our position and status) in viewing and commenting upon it. It is, after all, an image which changes, even ruptures a political landscape. It is also an image, as I discuss below, that reaches a mass audience, presented in what would seem a new 'transparent' way, as if it were a 'democratic' image of nascent democratic change. It is an image, then, of a more quotidian time, an image of our time. As such, we are all engulfed one way or another by its resonance.

Screening (Out) History – A New 'Transparency' of the Media

The images portraying the scenes of jubilant East (and West) Germans clambering up onto the once formidable Wall and pouring through the checkpoints into the West were televised live around the world within hours of having occurred. The camera crews (having already been present in the period leading up to the fall of the Wall) stayed on for days afterwards to collect up as much of the atmosphere as possible. And – though it would not be uncommon today – news programmes across all channels unusually devoted most, if not all, of their airtime to the pictures coming out of Berlin. In the main these were live, often hastily edited transmissions, incorporating countless 'vox pop' sequences and point-of-view camera shots winding through the jubilant crowds. Generally, there was minimal editing involved, often the quality was quite poor and content at times perhaps even a little dull, or at least unclear. For example, as the 'story' broke over night, the stark contrast of border spotlights bleached out much of the filmed image, leaving often only grainy silhouettes of people gathering in the streets. And these pictures continued to be replayed for a number of days filling extended weekend news broadcasts.

For the media theorists Daniel Dayan and Elihu Katz (1992: 1), the televising of the fall of the Wall can be characterized as a 'media event,' a facet of which is that it makes for a kind of festive viewing, whereby audiences recognize 'an invitation – even a command – to stop their daily routines and join in a holiday experience'.[5] Not only were people amassing in large numbers around the Wall, they were also gathering to watch the scenes as they unfolded on the television screens in living rooms, kitchens, bars and clubs. For East Germans it was also, of course, a vital means of finding out what was going on around them, as well as a prompt to join with their fellow citizens. Of course, it is worth noting that, as important as it was, the television news did not *initiate* 'revolution', though it did accelerate the process and enable its dramatic visual representation. Not only, then, did the media screen the world in its metamorphosis, they also played a significant part in helping to bring about political change in the first place.

Television – from its inception – has always played a key role in public debate and not least because it can bring a 'public' together, or at least invent an imaginary public sphere. The very uniqueness of television's 'small screen', which enables pictures to be brought directly into the living room, fosters an intimate though nonetheless prosaic style unlike any other mass media (except perhaps radio). This has made television a medium much criticized for its banality, but equally known for its far-reaching cultural resonance. Subsequently television is considered a primary ideological tool. In divided Germany there existed a very unusual circumstance, a fraught imbalance in terms of what was considered 'required viewing' of its 'public.' It goes without saying, East German television was centrally managed by the government, yet what could never come under control was the 'intrusion' of the airwaves from western broadcast media – or, as the East German authorities termed it, the 'electronic imperialism' of the West. In West Germany, however, the state never worried about their citizens watching GDR television, not least perhaps because, as the anthropologist John Borneman (1991: 136) puts it, 'GDR programs were too boring to compete'. By contrast, the watching of western television by East Germans was from the beginning a covert activity, taking on a 'peculiar additional *frisson*, of the forbidden, the Other, the "free"'. According to one study, by 1989, 95 per cent of all East German households owned a television set, with most able to receive broadcasts from the West. In this way West German television provided East Germans 'with authentic information about how people in the West lived...[o]n their screens they could watch the image of a society which was completely different from their own, free and prosperous' (Buhl 1990: 3). There were many attempts to control the situation and even numerous programmes made specifically to critique or counter the claims of the western programmes. Nevertheless western television, and in particular its news service, was highly regarded by ordinary East Germans.[6]

In the time leading up to the fall of the Wall, western journalists in the GDR were strictly controlled. They were shadowed by the secret police and required to travel with official observers. Nevertheless they were consistently able to bring to light the contradictions of the government or simply give airtime to otherwise ignored activities, including, for example, the important church meetings which later developed a whole cluster of protest groups. As West German television increasingly came to record public protest, the political agenda was more difficult to control in any credible fashion. Subsequently, however much functionaries of the ruling party tried to pacify its people by assuring future change, the ordinary citizens were equally able to watch West German news each evening, where they could gauge how many of their fellow countrymen were as much unimpressed by the late promises. Crucially, then, it was through television that East Germans were their own witnesses to the 'most open humiliation of the Communist system' (Buhl 1990: 7). A particularly symbolic moment came with the GDR's 40th anniversary held in October 1989, just weeks away from the then unimaginable event of the fall of the Wall. While the regime celebrated with the usual parades and portentous speeches, 'Western cameras captured the less festive mood of the people', and from this point on 'East Germans were able to observe in their own living rooms how dramatically their oppressors were losing power' (Buhl 1990: 7).

Whilst commentators are quick to acknowledge the role West German television played in bringing about change, it is generally to ignore the important role of East German television too. It is, of course, very difficult now to ascertain just how much the various media outlets, East and West, were involved in the events. At the time it was only really western academics who were in a credible position to conduct research, hence, a focus on the role of western media (see: Buhl 1990; Franz 1996; Hesse 1988). Without any extensive surveys,[7] the only real information comes by hearsay or in ethnographic reports (see: Borneman 1991; Darnton 1991). Nonetheless, tucked away on the arts page of *The Guardian* several days after the fall of the Wall, the paper's television correspondent includes a brief note on the East Berliner's view of western television, which he notes, 'was not always what you might expect'. In fact, according to the individuals spoken to, many switched channels in the month leading up to the fall of the Wall, because 'suddenly their own television was telling them what was going on as fast as the western service' (*The Guardian* 13.11.9, p. 37). The government had indeed come round to the idea of greater media transparency, again as a measure to calm its growing number of dissenters. In the end, perhaps, it proved to be even more important than the many years of western media supremacy. The fact that their own television news was giving them the news 'as it was' no doubt gave greater confidence to those seeking change, since change was indeed appearing before their own eyes on their home television channels. As one respondent to *The Guardian's* reporter put it: 'For once we know our news is really current, we know what is happening in the West. We didn't before, or at least only the negative stuff' (*The Guardian* 13.11.89, p. 37).

Without dwelling on what is no doubt a circular debate over whether it was East or West German media outlets that played the more significant role, the overriding fact is that television as a *whole* played a pivotal role in the events leading up to the fall of the Wall, as well as making the 'event' itself a televisual one. In fact, in this double sense, the fall of the Wall can be placed in the broader context of the development and expansion of global, twenty-four hour news services, which have had a huge impact on the internationalization of current affairs. Mitchell (1994: 367) describes the live-streaming of world events in terms of a new 'transparency' of the media, the significance of which is notable not only for the way in which history and politics unfolds and are *seen* to unfold, but also for the way in which we might need to re-think forms of critical enquiry and debate. The new transparency of the media relates to an increased frequency and availability of forms of dramatic televisual spectacle. Images from events such as the Tiananmen Square protests, the fall of the Wall and the Gulf War, as well as episodes such as the Rodney King beating or, indeed, the footage of fearful hostages held in Iraq as 'broadcast' across the Internet, present us with 'moments of breakthrough' (Mitchell 1994: 365–8), overtaking the codes and conventions of the programmes in which they appear. In one respect such images give the audience the clear sense that what they are watching is indeed the 'truth', even if there is little resource to deal with them or know what they really mean. It is as if these images and messages are not tempered or transformed in any way by the 'usual' manipulations of the media – whether by structural, technological means or creative, journalistic decisions. In other words, these are nominally 'pure' representations, not re-presentations. In the case of the fall of the Berlin Wall, the occasionally awkward camera work, the poor visibility, the somewhat bleary vox pop interviews (conducted in broken English), and the people pushing past reporters as they attempt to speak to camera, all are elements which count towards the break in media codes and conventions. And even if some images are later proved to be inaccurate, or mis-placed in some way, this does not undermine the 'scene' of showing these images, of their being a constituent part of the events in the world being reported. Such is the pace of global 24-hour news broadcasting, by the time any inaccuracy is noted the 'story' has always moved on to something else.

What adds to the effect of transparency is the fact that increasingly the 'new transparency of the image is also visible in the foregrounding of mediation itself' (Mitchell 1994: 368). The media apparatus in itself becomes evermore visible, with the technical and logistical tensions incurred becoming important to what is being reported, even itself becoming what is newsworthy. So, for example, during the Gulf War in 1991, '[m]edia "personalities" were everywhere, and the institutions of mediation (cameras, control rooms, telestrators, intertitles, framing, scheduling) were placed on display as never before' (Mitchell 1994: 368; see also Zelizer 1992). In this way the 'smooth illusionism' of professional media production had become transparent, making the news as much the 'showing' of how the media works to respond to the incoming 'randomness, improvisation, and accident' of the eventful spectacle. In the case of the fall of the Wall such foregrounding occurs when, for example, the newsreaders back in the studio interact with the correspondents *in situ*, perhaps asking how they are managing to find a secure spot from which to make their report, along with the various anomalies which occur due to hurriedly prepared reports and the experiencing of technical difficulties with sound or images.

The result of this 'new transparency' has tended to move debate on from why particular information is being 'fed' to us and by whom, to questions about the kind of 'televised' world we live in (whether real or virtually experienced), and what position we can take up in it (see Lewis 1991; Morley 1999; Robins 1996). Furthermore, the changing political landscape that results from the collapse of communism, and the end of the Cold War, has further compounded a new media style and agenda. Polarized ideological viewpoints have generally been swept aside, replaced by an opportunity to picture the world from a single, encompassing liberal democratic viewpoint. As a result there has been less need to make sense of the different competing sides, but more concern to bring the information together as quickly as possible, to make as much 'sense' of what is unfolding; a clear shift, as it were, from political society to information society. Thus, during the Cold War era, as Mitchell (1994: 366) contends, the 'metapicture of visual media evolved within narratives of paranoia and melodrama. The critical unveiling of "hidden persuaders," subliminal messages, and ideological codes was (and remains) a primary task of critical theory.' Yet, now he continues, 'what do we make of an era when the persuaders are not hidden, the messages are overt, and ideology is both everywhere and nowhere?' This is the new 'landscape' we now inhabit and need respond to.

Of course, it is hardly that the old inequities have been entirely superseded by a new condition of the media and its global context. As Buck-Morss (2000: 254) argues, the important factor in the politics of the image of the Gulf War was not 'high technology'; instead it was government censorship, 'as old as mass media itself. It was the same politics that prevailed in the Soviet Union during the Lithuanian crackdown and the August coup – except that George Bush did not need to storm the TV station to gain their compliance'. And what is lost with the fall of the Berlin Wall is a fuller representation of East Germans, even despite the event being all about them. So, whilst it is important to note that the perception of the media as being manipulative and ideological in its purview has significantly changed, there remains a stubborn paradox: when all of the information is ever more at our disposal, there is still, in all this 'transparency', much that we would seem to be missing. It is as if the headlines are blaring out the news, yet there is less by way of sufficient detail from which to read between the lines. In such a situation, how do we take up a critical perspective? The media is our window on the world, it formulates what we see, and lets us see it too, but how are we to open it? How can the likes of Philipsen, for example – our Germanist sitting attentively in front of his television screen, thousands of miles away from the events of the fall of the Wall – manage to find his voice, let alone the voice of others?

Or, as Mitchell (2005: 207) puts it: 'What does it mean to "address media" today, at the threshold of the 21st century?' It is a question he poses, not to seek ways of 'understanding' the media pace McLuhan, but 'in order to foreground the way media address us or "call out" to us, and the ways in which we imagine ourselves talking back to or addressing media.' The assumption is all too often that a critical, meta-analysis, such as semiotics or psychoanalysis, can take an external position and make sense of what is going on in a dispassionate, even scientific manner. Take, for example, John Ellis' (1999: 55) idea of television viewing as an experience on a par with the psychoanalytic process of 'working-through'; with television being 'a vast mechanism for processing the raw data of news reality into more narrativised, explained forms'. His point is that, like the form of the soap operas that it airs, television would seem to come to no firm conclusions. Instead, as a medium able to reach a wide public audience, it provides a complex, vibrant context for ongoing public debate, innovation and experimentation. It is not a completely unattractive idea, but how can this 'working through' be raised to the level of critical, reflective practice? If you simply write up your 'notes' from a day's working-through, it is really only to draw out from the experience itself; you leave behind precisely that which you wish to understand. Mitchell (2005: 210) approaches the problem in a slightly different way. He assumes 'no theory of media can rise above media themselves, and that what is required are forms of vernacular theory, embedded in media practice.' These he suggests are to be what he refers to as metapictures: 'media objects that reflect on their own constitution, or (to recall Robert Morris's wonderful object of Minimalist Dadaism), boxes with the sound of their own making'. (I shall return to this concept of the metapicture in more detail in chapter five, examining its effects in relation to two films that specifically deal with images of the fall of the Wall.)

Mitchell (1994: 425) takes the view that whilst we probably cannot change the world in any 'big' political sense, 'we can continue to describe it critically and interpret it accurately'. In doing so, he suggests, there is a need not just to interpret pictures, but also 'to change them' (369). Thus, whilst the idea of a metapicture, or 'box with the sound of its own making', might only be a hypothetical model (or 'vision'), it suggests a *design*, more than a concept, for the kind of critical theories needed; theories, which, arguably, 'are themselves visual, that show rather than argue' (Buck-Morss 1996: 30). In the chapter which follows, I will discuss in more detail this 'design' of a visual critical theory, which I suggest indicates a potentially new departure in critical writing or picturing. Certainly, it is a procedure to which attention can and ought be paid even *after* the event. Whilst we may be unable to change the world, especially at the moment when we sit bedazzled before our TV screens, that does not and must not mean an end to critical engagement. Those same images of the fall of the Berlin Wall witnessed at the time of the event, we continue to share to this day (in one way or another) through cultural exchange and new representations. It does not mean these images must somehow mask or suppress other better, more truthful images; nor, however, should we avert a critical gaze. The greater 'transparency' of the media – the ever-present screening of history (as it happens) – invites us *into* the media in unprecedented ways. The task now is to adequately respond.

Instant Replay – Re-Citing/Sighting History

We come now to a slightly deeper question: Why is it we remember this event of the fall of the Berlin Wall, and what (or how) exactly do we remember? Let me approach this question by supposing the television pictures of the fall of the Berlin Wall are *moving images* – and by that I mean not merely that they are images captured by the temporal mediums of film (or video), but that their quality and content varies from report to report. It is easy to forget that pictures generated and disseminated by broadcast media are by their very nature ephemeral. Day and night, television presents a host of visual material, little of which is viewed on later occasions. Thus, apart from a period of initial dissemination (when pictures can often seem to be replayed endlessly) news footage is seldom repeated. Nevertheless, the images of the fall of the Berlin Wall, along with images of many other global events, do in fact continue to reappear on numerous occasions, even if on an ad hoc basis. For whatever reasons these images have become significant and enduring, forming lasting memories for many different people. These are *moving* images at an emotional level too. This might seem an obvious point to make (and perhaps after the horrifying 'spectacle' of 9/11 it is common enough to think this way), but, just as Susan Sontag (1979: 180) finds it necessary to suggest, '[i]mages are more real than anyone could have supposed', I am inclined to think we easily forget the 'reality' of these images, how they relate to us culturally in the everyday. Perhaps because we tend to regard images from news reports as capturing a reality existing *elsewhere* in the world we overlook the fact that these pictures do become deeply embedded in our own lives, so forming part of a fragmented, but collective memory both local and global.

What follows from this line of thought is that the image of the fall of the Berlin Wall has never actually gone away – indeed, it just keeps *moving* on. There is no single definable picture to refer to, only a multi-faceted phenomenon of its image. To put this another way, if there is an aura to this image, it is not an 'originary' one, but an aura as much of its ephemerality. As Benjamin (1992: 211–244) is noted for saying, with technical reproducibility the very concept of authenticity changes. The reproduction is independent of the original, able to show aspects otherwise unattainable and able to place the 'copy' into new situations, new constellations; the reproduction 'substitutes a plurality of copies for a unique existence'. In this way the reproduction (as a phenomenon itself) is able to open up new perspectives or even new spaces within the same (a suggestion that may be better understood with reference to the multiple views of cubist and surrealist art fashionable at the time Benjamin was writing). Whilst this presents problems – not least the fact that Benjamin can be read as lamenting the demise of a so-called original – there is a critical purpose to be gained from this technical flexibility. As Benjamin argues, 'in permitting the reproduction to meet the beholder or listener in his own particular situation, it reactivates the object reproduced'.

One way of making sense of Benjamin's observations is to (re)frame what underlies his understanding of reproduction and associated concept of history with reference to Deleuze's (1994: 1) discussion of repetition and difference. 'To repeat', Deleuze suggests, 'is to behave in a certain manner, but in relation to something unique or singular which has no equal or equivalent'. Repetition, he goes on to suggest, might be thought to echo, 'a more secret vibration which animates it, a more profound, internal repetition within the singular'. Whilst this 'singular' may never actually be secured, its repetition at least continues to allude to it; and this, he goes on to argue, makes for the apparent paradox of festivals:

> they repeat an "unrepeatable". They do not add a second and a third time to the first, but carry the first time to the "nth" power. With respect to this power, repetition interiorizes and thereby reverses itself...it is not Federation Day which commemorates or represents the fall of the Bastille, but the fall of the Bastille which celebrates and repeats in advance all the Federation Days; or Monet's first water lily which repeats in advance all the others.
>
> (Deleuze 1994: 1)

Thus, what Deleuze refers to as repetition is not something we can truly locate, but is instead only made available in relation to other versions of itself. The result being, if we see 'it,' we are seeing an *instance* of 'it': we are seeing, for example, a version of Monet's lilies, but not all of them as one singular repetition. Repetition is perhaps better thought of as a 'medium', or a form. An example Deleuze (1994: 21) gives is of rhyme, which he notes, 'is indeed verbal repetition, but repetition which includes the difference between two words and inscribes that difference at the heart of a poetic Idea, in a space which it determines'. If there can be a similarly central Idea of images of the fall of the Berlin Wall, it is manifested by all the different cases of its reappearance; its continued reverberation 'which repeats in advance all the others'.

There are, of course, always tangible examples of images of the Berlin Wall that get repeated (made possible not least by forms of mechanical reproducibility). And, these images continually circulate, whether in books, on television screens, on postcards or even in the mind. 'We are right', Delueze argues, 'to speak of repetition when we find ourselves confronted by identical elements with exactly the same concept'. Yet what he suggests, is that there is always something further to discern; thus, 'we must distinguish between these discrete elements, these repeated objects, and a secret subject, the real subject of repetition, which repeats itself *through* them' (1994: 23, emphasis added). In other words, repetition is observed (or cited) through a series of differences, a series of particulars. Yet, it is its 'secret subject' that is always repeatable;

always available just as the writing through a stick of rock is available at each and every cross section, with each and every bite.

If we are to view the 'image' of the fall of the Wall in terms of its underlying repetition then we need to focus upon it more as a continuum, rather than a series of discrete, empirical occurrences. It is to be examined as a vibration that rings out over time and space, altering in pitch, but not in its overall timbre. In this case, the 'secret vibration' or subject – as this book attempts to chart – is all about a sense of (western) liberation and victory. It is a resonance or afterimage that persists, not a specific image in itself. My contention is the need to take up a stand *within* this continuum, rather than to attempt to pass judgement from an imaginary sideline. It is *through* its repetition that this image gains its meaning, so it needs to be through its movement of meaning that a critique is made. To take Siegfried Kracauer's (1995: 86) enigmatic recommendation for the treatment of a so-called 'Mass Ornament', if critique is to properly engage with society, it must necessarily lead 'directly through the mass ornament, not away from it'. What this means in practical terms in producing an image critique is not laid out in any particularly clear or instructive way. However, Benjamin (a contemporary and, indeed, friend of Kracauer) does provide us with some possibilities; notably with his eloquent passage on the Angel of History (1992: 249),[8] which offers a very pertinent description or emblem of a philosophy of history to suit what I have considered here as our (post)modern experience of Instant History.

The Angel of History is said to be able to see always in terms of a critical realization that Benjamin suggests we too ought attain; for '[w]here we perceive a chain of events, he sees one single catastrophe which keeps piling wreckage upon wreckage'. The angel, we are told, is caught up in a storm of 'progress'; a storm that we ourselves can be said to experience. However, whilst the storm 'irresistibly propels' the angel into the future, his back is turned: 'The angel would like to stay, awaken the dead, and make whole what has been smashed.' It is a compelling picture that Benjamin conjures up, as much as it is a picture of compulsion itself. Benjamin is alerting us to the need to be vigilant, even to 'turn back' and awaken the dead – to remain aware, that is, of the whole continuum of history. Crucially, this is not meant as some sentimental, nostalgic reading of history, but something far more immediate and tense. It is in the 'irresistible' present – and always in the present – that Benjamin wants us to be alive to our condition. The 'turning back' means to inflect a 'dialectic'. Thus, as we move onwards, we are to maintain an oppositional stance – to 'hold back' – in order to be aware of how meaning is made, and at what cost. Sigrid Weigel (1996: 59) explains this well:

> The turn back organises a form of perception which – positioned in the flow of time, but adopting a stance opposed to it – directs the gaze towards what had disappeared in that flow, towards what has been destroyed in history, the elements that have been used...in short, towards "what passes away in the becoming".

This, then, is to make current that precise moment in which the 'reproduction' (of the continuum) re-activates or repeats its meaning. Yet, there is still more to this image of an Angel of History than mere description of an alleged critical, re-activating procedure. As Weigel points out, Benjamin's image of the angel should not, as is so often the case, be understood simply as a metaphorical image of the progression of history (indeed, it would surely account for little –

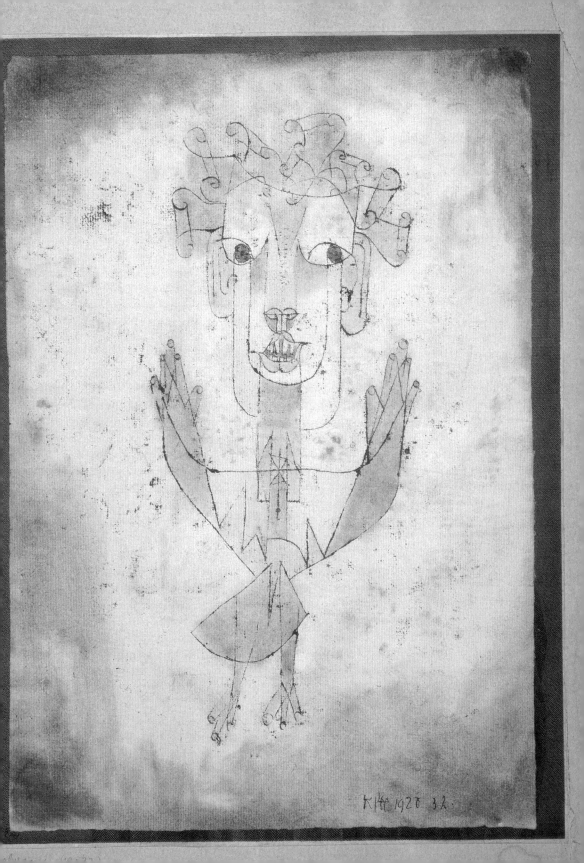

and hardly warrant the attention it receives – if that were all it was). Instead we can look at this short entry as more of a constellation of ideas or openings, a thought-image even, which in itself poses the idea of Benjamin's (seemingly unwritten) theory of this instance of the 'turn back', of the dialectical image. In other words, the Angel of History can be taken as an emblem or, indeed, a working model for a 'theory' of image critique.

In order to explicate this (again following Weigel's account), it is worth keeping in mind Benjamin's double procedure of the thought-image, as being 'images in relation to which his thoughts and theoretical reflections unfold, and also as images whose representations are translated into figures of thought' (Weigel 1996: 51). In this way, the dialectical image can be understood as a cognitive experience, images being for Benjamin both the primary mode *and* material for the production or re-reading of thought and ideas in themselves. A consequence of which is to invalidate philosophical discourse as meta-discourse; for Benjamin does not examine what is before him, rather he works his way *in*. The crux of this approach is the insight 'that memory and action find articulation in images, that ideas are structured as images, and that what is at stake is therefore a praxis that can operate with images – a *politics of images*, not a figurative or metaphorical politics' (Weigel 1996: 9–10). Images, then, even mental images, need to be thought of as 'things' in the world.

Weigel (1996: 46-60) develops the idea of a 'politics of images' through a close analysis of the Angel of History. In her reading, she demonstrates a 'polyperspective' constellation of three discrete elements, or 'views' of the angel, each a different moment in its *movement*. First, and easily overlooked, are the opening four lines of a poem by Scholem. In these lines we hear the voice of the angel itself ('*I* would like to turn back'), which then contrasts with the second view, the mute, frozen figure of Paul Klee's painting *Angelus Novus* (1920). As with the first point of view, the figure in Klee's painting is suggestive of a forward movement, whilst looking backwards – *as if* 'he is about to move away from something he is fixedly contemplating' (Benjamin 1992: 249). However, the look or movement towards the future ('This storm drives...irresistibly into the future') brings *us* – the reader – out to a third view upon this angel, a view from afar, a viewpoint of the angel of history (or perhaps the author himself). Like the flats of a theatre stage we can look into and out of the image: our point of view leads us towards a painting of an angel; and beyond that (or inside that even) its interior voice.

What, then, is this complex, layered image of the Angel of History? What does it really show or perform for us? In this case, the thought-image can be said to centre about Benjamin's fascination with Klee's painting, *Angelus Novus* (a painting he once briefly owned). Rather than distance himself from that fascination, to adjudge it as false consciousness, he describes the process of transforming conventional images, traditional metaphors and his own linguistic figures into thought-images or reflections in 'moments of awakening'. As Weigel (1996: 59) explains:

> ...it is a reflection that does not neutralise or rationally resolve the desire condensed in these pre-existing images. Rather, the desire is incorporated into the thought-image, so that it becomes both allegorical practice and redeeming critique (rettende Kritik) in one.

Thus, Benjamin's Angel of History not only foretells a philosophy of history pertinent to the concerns here of an instant history, but also establishes something of the principles for *writing the image.* In this case, literally a text-based image critique, a form of writing and reading of the image that creates a certain mental space (or puzzle) in which to contemplate the image of an angel (as a philosophy of history), as well as providing critical contemplation (of sorts) over Paul Klee's painting. However, it is vital to point out that whilst the 'textual movement' of this passage is, as shown above, 'tripartite in structure' (which might suggest a dialectic of meaning), 'it does not culminate in a synthesis, but in a constellation of non-synchronicity' (Weigel 1996: 58). The three images or perspectives of the angel are not intended to produce any specific meaning, but rather to jostle with one another, whether to join up, rub against or simply stand in difference. This is a feature one might regard as being most significant, distinctive and, undoubtedly, challenging about any purported image critique. As a constitution of meaning, it is 'quite different from a "grammatology" orientated around the modern conceptualisation of the sign. It is not a *différance*...operating with a range of linguistic material', but rather, 'the origin of ideas and their crystallisation in linguistic figurations' (52–3). In other words, the 'thought-image' is a figuration that does not get to be 'translated into conceptual terminology or meta-discourse' (58) – instead its construction *makes happen* a 'moment' of critical thought, your *own* critical thought, as it lifts off the page. As such it is hardly an image of resolution, but instead – through a set of configurations of non-synchronicity – an image which keeps open a moment for ongoing critical reflection.

Having briefly been swept aside (or, hopefully, *along*) by examining Benjamin's Angel of History, let me now return to an example of the image of the fall of the Berlin Wall and make some sense – a little more concretely, if perhaps less eloquently – of how this conception of history as repetition and continuum is entered into, or, as it were, 'entertained' (to reflect something of the fascination Benjamin held for the Klee painting). The recurrences of images of the fall of the Berlin Wall certainly appear in different contexts, though no doubt most frequently within current affairs. Images are usually employed as a form of 'shorthand' by media professionals. Studies show, for example, that the iconic status of news images can have the effect of a catalyst with regard to news agendas. Images are appropriated not only by media professionals, but also interest groups perhaps seeking to change political agendas (Bennett and Lawrence 1995; DeLuca 1999). Arguably, the iconic images of our twentieth century 'are moments of visual eloquence that acquire exceptional importance within public life' and importantly play a role in the 'performance of public judgement' (Hariman and Lucaites 2003: 38). However, in the case of the fall of the Berlin Wall, it is perhaps fair to say that the use of its imagery tends not to be used for critical purpose, but rather – as I will examine in more detail in subsequent chapters – the securing and maintaining of a dominant interpretation of political and economic liberation, which in turn has become an overarching narrative of much recent political history.

These arguments can be followed through by turning attention to the reporting of the toppling of Saddam Hussein's statue in the early summer of 2003. The pulling down of this statue in Baghdad's Firdoos Square was broadcast live and then immediately replayed by the media as a defining, 'victorious' moment in the 'War on Iraq' – indeed yet another example of an image of instant history. After the networks had 'patiently' watched live on air for the statue to be yanked from its pedestal, the footage of the toppling of Saddam's statue was quickly edited down into smaller iconic 'image-bites.' It is typical of twenty-four-hour news broadcasting to air various looped sequences over which presenters in the studio and correspondents on location can pontificate (or stall for time!). This footage was, of course, no exception, replayed obsessively throughout the day. Subsequently, it recurred in varying forms on many other occasions, cited as much by media professionals as by protestors in the street (the latter, for example, replacing the toppling of Saddam Hussein with the toppling of a George Bush figure!) – in this respect another 'image of our times'. I first saw these images as reported for *BBC 24* by the then feted BBC journalist Rageh Omaar. I happened to be abroad at the time, it was late at night with no one around to witness the scenes with me. To my great surprise, edited into the sequence of the statue falling was – even if only for a few seconds – library footage of the fall of the Berlin Wall – this being an example of one of the many 'sights' of the fall of the Berlin Wall that I have been alluding to. It really was only a very brief sequence, but, nonetheless, there spliced into the report from Baghdad in 2003 were the events of Berlin in 1989. What could be the purpose of this montage sequence?

As Rageh Omaar (2004: 193) explains, this particular statue of Saddam Hussein was not an especially important one (indeed, it had been erected only a year before). And it was not that its removal had a direct connection to the ousting of Saddam from power. The reason that the 'toppling' of the statue came to be such a key reference point was at least partly due to the fact that its removal 'took place under the gaze of the television cameras'. But more than that, this event was immediately referenced as a historic moment, which in turn fuelled the need to explain or rather simply *show* this event as being historic. It is in this respect that the fall of the Berlin Wall helps to further fashion, or 'fabricate', the visual editorial or rhetoric. Thus, the imagery of the fall of the Wall is, as Omaar understands it, a specific reference point or snapshot of history, that in this case comes to stand for liberation. And it is not strictly that it operates as a signifier of liberation that can be applied to other events as a lens that colours in a specific way, but more that it sits well within a broader and growing collection of news icons that represent celebratory events of liberation. Each, then, compounds the other, maintaining and strengthening a pattern of liberation footage. Matthew Gilbert and Suzanne Ryan (2003), for example, point out, '[t]his kind of "liberation" footage...is almost a convention of TV war imagery', highlighting the fact that numerous newscasters and experts (even the US Defence Secretary Donald Rumsfeld) have made the link that 'scenes of the statue's fall recalled similarly high-profile moments after the fall of the Berlin Wall and the collapse of the Soviet Union', along with 'visual vestiges of the mayhem in Tiananmen Square'.

The iteration of these image-events becomes as if, to use Benjamin's phrase, 'one single catastrophe which keeps piling wreckage upon wreckage.' In this case, liberation is *the* key meaning attributed to (and so repeated with) the images of the Berlin Wall, a meaning or interpretation which gathers such momentum as to bracket out many other interpretations. In fact, the fall of the Wall becomes an *icon* of liberation and celebration; when used in conjunction with the footage of the 'fall' of Saddam Hussein's statue, it is itself *only* this meaning, this reference point of liberation.

As a high-profile, professional TV journalist, Rageh Omaar is, of course, duty bound to produce the kinds of reports (using a stock of images) expected of him; to put together the conventional packets of information that are the norm of news production. Yet, on his return to the UK, immediately following his time reporting the siege of Baghdad, Omaar attempts to make sense of, even re-frame, his work as a journalist. During a public address for the Huw Wheldon Lecture 2003 (and later included in his autobiographical account of reporting in

Iraq), Omaar (2004: 193) reflects critically on the significance of what he calls the 'imagery of events of our history'. As a journalist he readily acknowledges that the imagery of these historic events each provide us with 'a snapshot, a reference point of complex, dangerous and uncertain historical process that has changed the world'. Equally, however, he accepts that this is the case despite the fact they can 'never give us the whole or, in some cases, the real story'. He observes:

> The image of Nelson Mandela emerging from prison to walk to freedom did not inform us about the long and painful process of burying apartheid. The fall of the Berlin Wall, which involved hundreds of thousands more people than the pulling down of Saddam Hussein's statue in Firdoos Square, was not an accurate reflection of the difficulties of reuniting Germany.
>
> (Omaar, 2004:193)

This clearly poses a dilemma. The report Omaar filed on the toppling of the statue is, he acknowledges, *the* report most people remember. Yet, in his opinion it should not necessarily have been the snapshot to be *seen* to change the world. In fact, from his point of view, there were many other reports of his which were far more thoughtful, poignant and complex (including, he suggests, reports on the rising chaos and anarchy at the local hospitals). Hence, in his lecture, *looking back* on his 'moment' in Firdoos square, reporting live on the falling statue, he poses a question: 'what would have happened if the picture that day had shown a wide shot of the statue, revealing the banks of photographers and cameramen trying to capture the image of the ordinary Iraqis jumping up and down on the face of the toppled dictator?' It would still have been a meaningful image, he suggests, but its significance would not have been what it is today; instead, 'many people would have said the whole event was just a media circus' (Omaar 2004: 242).[9]

The real dilemma of whether or not to pan out from the scene as the statue was toppled is not a dilemma Omaar would have concerned himself with at the time. As he notes, he had more practical concerns, 'I tried to cling to the phone as I was pushed and crushed in the mêlée, shouting descriptions of the wild ecstasy around me' (2004: 192). Indeed, like the reporters of the events of May 1968 whom Barthes describes, Omaar is ensconced in the charged atmosphere, his harried words (distorted over the satellite phone) melding with the action, becoming their 'immediate and consubstantial meaning' (Barthes 1989: 150). It is a dilemma that I suggest is nonetheless inscribed within the image itself, but which perhaps can best be drawn out with an image critique. In other words, I want to argue that it is by working with/in the image itself that we can best ascertain how it is made, how it functions and what dilemmas it contends with. An image critique of a news event, such as the toppling of Saddam's statue, would need to preserve the 'reality' of journalists in their necessity and desire to partake in the drama of historical snapshot images; to engage with the very energy that drives the stories of historical change (just as Benjamin, for example, in his allegory of the Angel of History attempts to retain something of his fascination for Klee's painting of the angel).

In a small way the combining here of a commentary on both Rageh Omaar's original report and his later presentation for the Hue Wheldon lecture suggests perhaps something of the bare ingredients of a critical image. Although, this surely lacks the layering and intrigue of a singular critical image(-space) as found with Benjamin's passage on the Angel of History. Inevitably, we can not get around the fact that instant history is made all of an instant (without time, for example, to make the decision to pull the camera out to a wide view picture). However, that need not undermine our ability and commitment to maintain a dialogue with the *continuum* of instant history – the kind of history that is not only made of an instant at a specific point in time, but which is continually reiterated, so shaping our future thoughts and discussions. The need, then – as I have already stated and will go on to examine in terms of current intellectual debate over visual culture – is to *create* a variety of image effects, rather than piece together a collection of acceptable, 'truthful' ones. It is to make new 'metapictures' (as Mitchell describes) – with the sound of their own making – that keep present the very kind of dilemmas that Rageh Omaar, here, can only share with us from a safe critical distance. The critical image, then, ought itself to zing with the crackle of the satellite phone, as if it too were coming to us live...To be timely – or *moving* – like the emotive images themselves of events such as the fall of the Berlin Wall.

Towards an Image Critique...

I have tried to give the sense of a proliferating image domain of the site/sight of the fall of the Wall, and with particular emphasis upon a phenomenon I term Instant History. The impact of which I describe as threefold. Firstly, it gives rise to images of our times, pictures of our world which we use to orientate ourselves and our critical understanding of events and history. In turn this prompts the need for new critical methodologies – potentially a whole new manner of criticism and expertise. Secondly, the advent of instant history has brought with it a new kind of transparency of the media. In part this reflects a devolution of ideological tensions (as had been rife in the period of the Cold War), yet, does not necessarily aid us in a complex understanding of events in the world. Finally, instant history is not only about events at specific moments in time, but also relates to an *instant accessibility* of historiography, which places the experience of events such as the fall of the Berlin Wall within a constant continuum. This continuum of the historic event of the fall of the Wall resounds with a singular repetition, which relates, in this case, to a pervading western celebration of political and economic liberalism, an end even to ideological history. In chapters three and four, I explore these ideas, with reference specifically to Fukuyama's (1989) 'End of History' thesis and as described through a more elaborate spectacle or imaginary of Berlin (as it stretches back into the city's Cold War past). Taken in this way, the fall of the Berlin Wall can be seen to be predicated upon a discourse of western ownership of the Wall, which in turn allows for its fall to be a victory owned/celebrated by the West. Thus, rising out of the well-known scenes of revelry at the foot of the Wall during the night of its 'fall' is a dominant neo-liberalist discourse of ideological supremacy. This circumstance leads to a significant dilemma, which Zygmunt Bauman (1992: 175–186) describes as 'living without an alternative'; living without recourse to a richer political spectrum, out of which one might hope would come the prospects to exchange alternative political futures. In chapter five, turning to two German films that re-frame the event of the fall of the Wall, I consider how an image critique might work to undo such limited prospects. Thus, I examine processes in which the actual media images of the fall of the Wall (as incorporated into the films) can be re-staged for new critical effect, allowing for a complex public screening

or 'working through' of multiple perspectives on the event and its aftermath, so undoing the singular, euphoric narrative of victory for western liberalism.

An image critique is not something that we should want to be neatly formulated or prescribed. It must always relate to a specific engagement with things and ideas in the world, at a specific time. An image critique, then, is not intended as a means to an end, but a means to think on further, to enrich what we know, to complicate what we might otherwise all too blithely come to accept. And, most importantly, though an image critique may appear a somewhat elusive and open-ended form of engagement, it ought to be understood always to relate to very real and difficult matters in the world. So, whilst the case I make for a critique on a theoretical and formalist level is of some in-between or adjacent position, it is not only a response to normative academic procedures and assumptions. In fact, all along, I wish to respond as much to the kind of *real* divisions of which the Wall is itself an emblem.

I began this study way before I knowingly started work on it. I remember the occasion vividly. Almost ten years on from the fall of the Wall, I found myself standing before the broad, oval steps of the *Runde Ecke* building, the former *Stasi* headquarters in Leipzig and the scene of the Monday night demonstrations through the autumn of 1989 (see Maier 1997: 135–146). At the time when I visited the building, it had been turned into a makeshift museum documenting the banality of the state surveillance system. In glass cabinets the primitive spy 'technologies' of the *Stasi* were on display and hundreds of seemingly innocuous photographs, of ordinary citizens (as ordinary suspects) living out their quotidian lives, were displayed in room after room of this grand building. In all honesty, I can not say I was deeply affected by these formal exhibits, instead, standing outside on the steps of the building I felt a tremendous awakening and sense of connection to the past.

Engrained on the stone steps remains the residue of the wax that melted down from all the hundreds of candles placed there during the weekly protest vigils. There is little perhaps that I can say in a scholarly manner about this moment, except to say that it was here that the lightning really did strike, when I had a sense of 'what passes away in the becoming'. I have since spent a great deal of time trying to find some means to explain what it is I came to realize there, this study being the culmination of that process. Yet, I hardly think I will ever fully satisfy the curiosity and thoughtfulness inspired at the time. To evoke something of Descartes' (2000: 27–28) meditations on the changing states of a piece of wax, I can at least understand the possibility of all number of states of thoughts as would have occurred for me in this scene, but it does not then follow that I can articulate them in words alone.

Of course, for Descartes it is in the mind that we can come to understand the true nature of the wax. By contrast, an image critique need not accord to any such idealism, but rather seek to engage with the very *materials* that inspire these kinds of meditations in the first place. And so, whilst I do not wish here to put into words the revelation I had standing on the steps of the *Runde Ecke* building in Leipzig, I will at least note that it was precisely because I was *there* that I have gone on to want to write a book such as this. If anything, then, it is this kind of commitment to thinking in (and with) the world that I hope an image critique can evoke. As Benjamin tells us, it is for the historical materialist to remain 'in control of his powers, man enough to blast open the continuum of history' (1992: 254); a duty never completed, but equally never to be deferred. The 'Angel of History' offers us a poetic account of this dutiful historian and critic. By suggesting the angel sees not a chain of events, but rather 'one single catastrophe' we are brought to realize that in the 'here and now', we stand in a blizzard of mosaic pieces, a single accumulation of history refusing teleology and progress. Benjamin's aversion to 'anchor' these pieces of history in narratives and explication, but rather to construct 'out of them' – to formulate dialectical images that awaken us to the impact one thing has on another – makes for a challenging approach to history. As he laments, 'every image of the past that is not recognised by the present as one of its own concerns threatens to disappear irretrievably' (Benjamin 1992: 247). There is a pervading theme of redemption in Benjamin's work, but, as with the image critique I describe here, it is only ever a *process* of saving, never the final recovery that he urges upon us. It is a notion of redemption that relates well to Nietzsche's (2003: §56) principle of Eternal Recurrence, which, as a critical method, perpetually plays out attention to the appropriateness of each and every action undertaken. Benjamin encourages this vigil of critical awareness, raising it to a political (Marxist) test of human justice. In looking towards an image critique, it is my intention only to build upon such critical, though always Sisyphean, 'foundations'...

Notes

1. A later development has been the memorial at Bernauer Strasse, the design of which integrates surviving materials from the original border area of the Berlin Wall to maintain a sense of austerity and even prohibition in the overall effect. The memorial was officially inaugurated on 13 August 1998 and entrusted to the State of Berlin by the Federal Republic of Germany. In addition to this, on 9 November 1999 – the 10th anniversary of the fall of the Wall – the Berlin Wall Documentation Center on Bernauer Strasse opened its doors to the public.

2. By 'visual essentialism' Mieke Bal (2003: 12) refers to 'the unexamined isolation of 'the visual' as an object of study'. It is visual essentialism, for example, that she suggests allows for the cliché 'a picture is worth a thousand words' to perpetuate. Her overriding objection to this is that it actually has the effect of turning us away from the visual itself. For the idea, she argues, 'that visual things withstand language, that visuality is ineffable, has been used as an excuse to spend lengthy, wordy but unverifiable discourses on this unspeakable thing'. As such she contends, 'the notion that visual (art) is unspeakable harbours an anti-visualist sentiment'.

3. In designing a family tree of the image, W. J. T. Mitchell (1986: 10) designates the specific types of imagery central to particular intellectual disciplines, with, for example, 'mental imagery belong[ing] to psychology and epistemology; optical imagery to physics; graphic, sculptural, and architectural imagery to the art historian; verbal imagery to the literary critic', as well as perceptual images occupying 'a kind of border region where physiologists, neurologists, psychologists, art historians, and students of optics find themselves collaborating with philosophers and literary critics'.

4. See, for example, Peter Stepan's (ed.) *Photos That Changed the World* (2000); Peter Barnard's *We Interrupt This Programme...20 News Stories that Marked The Century* (1999); as well as the various *Life Magazine* books, which include *100 Photographs That Changed the World* (2003) and the annually published 'The Year in Pictures' series.

5. It is worth pointing out that Daniel Dayan and Elihu Katz (1992) themselves place the fall of the Wall within their list of 'media events' – being a new genre of television, the live broadcasting of history. Yet, this is despite the fact that it would seem not to adhere to one of their key defining criteria of events as being *pre-planned*.

6. The western newscasts presented the East German authorities with the most significant problem, for whilst drama series and other entertainment shows were equally informative of a western way of life they did not carry the same authenticity and honesty of the news programmes (the hugely popular shows *Dallas* and *Dynasty*, for example, were hardly any more real for those in the West than those in the East!). According to one study (Hesse 1988), conducted in 1985, 80 per cent of the East Germans sampled judged West German news services to be more or much more credible than East Berlin's state television. It was this belief that 'helped Western TV news to become the outstanding source of information', in fact, '[t]he main news programmes, *Tagesschau* (ARD) and *Heute* (ZDF), enjoyed much higher relative ratings in the East than in the West' (Buhl 1990: 4).

7. Of note is Peter Ludes' (1994) edited volume *Visualizing the Public Spheres*. Having gained access and collaboration with partners of East German broadcast media, the collection of articles and interviews provide some insight into an East German perspective on the media. However, even in this case, all the interviews with media journalists which make up the bulk of the book are with those working in the context of either the USA or the former Federal Republic of (West) Germany.

8. As my analysis of Walter Benjamin's text (1992: 249) goes on to show, it is not really appropriate to call this so straightforwardly his 'Angel of History' text. To start with, there is more than one angel, and not all of these are angels of history as such. Nonetheless, for the sake of clarity, I will continue to refer to the passage in this way, but always to keep in mind the fractured complexity of the identity of the said Angel of History.

9. Interestingly, with Saddam Hussein's later dramatic capture, international media crews filmed again in the Firdoos Square a crowd of some 200 Iraqis. This time, however, '[t]here was no mass outpouring of joy, no seething crowds of thousands of people thronging the streets, no scenes like those that occurred in the cities of Eastern Europe as Communism collapsed' (Omaar 2004: 242).

CHAPTER TWO

THE PROBLEM OF VISUAL CULTURE

Having introduced 'images of the fall of the Berlin Wall' within the framework of what I term 'instant history', which makes for a complex 'object' of interest, it is evident any purported image critique as a means to respond or interrogate its phenomena is equally not easily explained (more likely best *performed* or put to affect). To help further sharpen and contextualize the problematics inherent of this subject matter, this chapter examines the contemporary intellectual context of visual culture studies; a field of research which has undoubtedly helped initiate and situate my approach. However, I do not take visual culture to be without its problems, instead I propose image critique as something of a supplement to current debates. I am interested in the potential for a different kind of critical analysis, one that is not necessarily easily placed within an academic framework. I want to take 'critique' to be an object of intrigue (all of its own), as well as to mean being critically engaged – just as the allure of Klee's painting, for example, is woven into an intriguing 'critical space' when Benjamin writes of his Angel of History. With respect to the contemporary debates of visual culture, I take my cue from an eminent scholar of Walter Benjamin, Susan Buck-Morss (1996: 30), who urges (if not laments) the need for a 'visual critical theory', by which she means 'theories that are themselves visual, that show rather than argue'. Whilst I readily accept that the discourses of visual culture studies have initiated an important new intellectual paradigm, I am generally of the opinion that the debates and theories have not gone far enough; or put another way, as *only* debates and theories the result in most cases has been a faltered, perpetually new 'problem' of the visual always up for further (theoretical) negotiation.

A short anecdote is perhaps illustrative of the problem. At a seminar event I attended for a project dealing with the practice of writing for art and design students, one member of the panel recommended a selection of 'interesting' books on visual culture that he had bought for the project members (using the project funds no less!). He held each book up to view as he spoke, inviting the group to browse during the coffee break. As he held up Nicholas Mirzoeff's (1998) *The Visual Culture Reader*, he made light of the fact that this rather 'hefty volume' of the *visual* barely bore a single image in all its pages. Although he spoke in jest, the tone I thought was a little reminiscent of a petulant Alice, in *Alice in Wonderland*, when noting of her disdain for a book without pictures (for 'what is the use of a book without pictures or conversation?'). It was significant how well the comment went down with those gathered at the meeting, seeming to encapsulate in an instant a simple, yet oft-ignored response to the study of visual culture. So, whilst there is a genuine interest in reading and writing about the subject (as well as having procedural meetings about it too!), there is perhaps a longing for something different to 'happen' or manifest when engaging with the visual – whatever this might be, at the very least it is to have some pictures sit alongside the words!

To take this a little further, Mirzoeff (2005: 1–4) – in a later book – offers his own anecdote in which he tells of the failings of his visual culture theory. In a New York gym on the day of the invasion of Iraq, in 2003, he finds himself next to a man kitted out in military-style garb cheering loudly as they watch (on the multiple TV screens of the gym) the first explosions of the so-called 'shock and awe' operation: 'As I watched him watching, I became aware that I had nothing to say back to him that might deflate his bombast'. This, he suggests, 'was literally the exercise of power...[for] all the deconstructive, feminist, anti-racist, visual culture theory that I have at my disposal, there was no way to counter the sweating, exulting triumph of the war watcher'. We can understand the book to be some kind of response Mirzoeff offers back to this particular episode. Importantly, however, given the 'epiphany' in the gym, Mirzoeff does not aim with this book to perform the usual 'ritual "exposure" of media images', to unmask their bias or demonstrate their lack of representation etc. In concentrating on 'questions of watching, the status of the visual event, and the visualised model of power in global culture', Mirzoeff instead attempts a more creative, layered analysis framed around the figure of Babylon. This, he suggests, 'plays the role...that the Arcades of nineteenth-century Paris performed for the critic Walter Benjamin'; which as he goes on to explain, is to propose 'a physical and historical space that is nonetheless profoundly disjunctured and ambiguous, interspersing the contemporary and the future it is trying to dream with the primal past'.

Different figurations of 'Babylon' (old and new) provide a very rich set of mythological, historical and oneiric associations, which Mirzoeff draws upon to construct a complex arena of analysis. Fundamentally, he does not seek to 'provide some lofty and probably unattainable overview of the war', but rather seeks merely to 'provoke debate and discussion on the intersected place of the viewer and the image in the visual event' (2005: 11). In explaining here what he means by 'event', Mirzoeff makes reference to Foucault's theory of the event as a nexus or node within which subjects operate and condition their freedom of action. In particular, he takes his cue from the suggestion that the study of events is to work 'by constructing around the singular event, analysed as process, a 'polygon' or, rather, 'polyhedron' of intelligibility, the number of whose faces is not given in advance and never properly be taken as finite' (Foucault cited in Mirzoeff 2005: 11). Mirzoeff applies his critique of such a networked, layered 'event' by constructing a series of viewpoints, which, more specifically, work as 'three intersected layers to be prised apart...the locality of the viewer, the contents and contexts of the image, and the global imaginary within which the viewer attempts to make sense of the screen-images' (12). Not unlike, then, the three intersected layers, or 'polyperspective' vista of Benjamin's thought-image of the Angel of History described previously, Mirzoeff attempts to elaborate a more creative style of critique.

Mirzoeff's book would seem to represent something like the kind of critical commentary – potentially open to both an academic and non-specialist audience – that I believe needs to be

risked. It is in the (creative) writing that this book attempts to define a different kind of critical approach; its intersected layers, or 'polyperspective' vista working like an extended version of Benjamin's notion of the dialectical image, which in turn is to embody some of the principles of construction that I advocate with the form of an image critique. However, as will become evident below, such an approach to writing/thinking is hardly common or well founded. Susan Buck-Morss is perhaps one of the few theorists to have seriously and consistently experimented with a new role of images in critical writing. It is her work that I refer to in the closing section of this chapter as a beacon of what might yet become of visual culture studies.

In an interview with the editors of the *Journal of Visual Culture*, Buck-Morss (2002: 328) acknowledges her debt (over a long period) to Walter Benjamin but, importantly, notes it is not his method that one applies; rather, one develops a method out of a dialogue with his work, with emphasis always upon the creation of 'things' (in this case thought-images) in the world. Her interviewers suggest her working method be described as a 'living methodology' to which Buck-Morss adds, 'or a materialist praxis, a way of working – a way of thinking'. This living methodology includes both bringing into view 'the material remains of life stored – rescued – in libraries, museums, second-hand stores, flea-markets', as well as bringing into *being* new objects and metaphors that lead us to think anew (just as we find with Mirzoeff's figures of Babylon). In the first instance, it is a matter of being alert to 'all of one's senses to do justice to material reality'. In the second, it is about finding ways to manipulate and present the materials found. This, then, is how I would like us to begin to imagine what an image critique might actually *look* like. In opening out the debates of visual culture in this chapter, it is certainly the case that any determined critical approaches remain purposefully unsettled. Yet, equally, it is because of the 'open-space' of a visual culture paradigm that there exists the potential to allow for a new style of criticism.

The Pictorial Turn – (un)Setting the Scene

The proliferation of debates on visual culture represents a relatively new (inter)disciplinary departure; but one, it would seem, that opens up more questions than it answers. In fact there is a great deal of confusion over just what visual culture really means and entails. Is it, for example, the name of a field of study? Does it refer to a domain of culture, or is it a new academic discipline or, of course, all of these things rolled into one? Inevitably, it has been difficult to establish any core foundation or direction. And it is certainly the case that public debates about visual culture, stemming from the mid-1990s, have hardly reached any decisive conclusions. In fact, in some cases these have only resulted in stark contested positions.[1]

What does unite those engaged in the subject, however, is the assertion of – or at least the acceptance of a debate over – a distinction between image and text. Whilst a theory of the image can hardly be said to have found any definitive articulation, the 'text' and 'textuality' (even 'intertextuality') are concepts deeply embedded in the practices of the human sciences, as well as extending into wider popular discourse. Models of textual analysis (which include linguistics, rhetoric, semiotics, psychoanalysis etc.) have come to be at the centre of critical methodologies within the arts and humanities, allowing, for example, for the analysis of film, performance and even sports as cultural texts. In fact, everything and anything has become subject to analysis by way of being a *text*, or held within *discourse*. As W. J. T Mitchell (1994: 11) reminds us, the belief has been: 'Society is a text. Nature and its scientific representations are "discourses." Even the unconscious is structured like a language'. The 'text,' then, has come to underpin a whole way of thinking and interpreting our world, situating us in what Richard Rorty (1979) describes, in his account of the history of philosophy, as the 'linguistic turn'.[2] In response to this (and in light of the evident interest in visual culture) Mitchell (1994: 11) reflects upon what can be considered a new challenge to this history, suggesting 'that once again a complexly related transformation is occurring in other disciplines of the human sciences and in the sphere of public culture' leading to a shift towards what he calls a visual or 'pictorial turn'. The full implication of which is that 'visual experience or "visual literacy" might not be fully explicable on the model of textuality' (16); if anything, it is this principle that can be taken to be the 'foundational postulate to visual culture' (Mitchell 1995: 543).

However, unlike the 'linguistic turn', the pictorial turn does not mean we now have 'some powerful account of visual representation that is dictating the terms of cultural theory' (Mitchell 1994: 13). In fact, it is rather the opposite; there is no single theory of the image, no underlying terms. Despite key critical terms such as the gaze, spectacle and surveillance, we still do not know exactly what to think about pictures. We do not know about their relation to language, nor 'how they operate on observers and on the world, how their history is to be understood, and what is to be done with or about them'. Mitchell's (1994: 417) own professed 'economy' on theory is the result of a conviction (borne out by the very 'logic' of the pictorial turn) 'that we already have an overabundance of metalanguages for representation and that no "neutral" or "scientific" vocabulary (semiotics, linguistics, discourse analysis) can transcend or master the field of representation' – indeed, each of these metalanguages are in themselves a *medium*, like any other mode of representation. Thus, Mitchell's 'picture theory' is, then, not meant to finalize a particular understanding, but rather allow the *scene* of academic, interpretative engagement to be recognized for what it is, in hope of keeping open a critical awareness of the exchanges and translations being made in the name of visual culture/studies. This is what he describes as a de-disciplinary exercise whereby focus on the 'visual' helps illuminate what is left out by one disciplinary mode of analysis or another, and how specific interpretative frameworks codify and articulate the visual in relation to what is otherwise passed over or bracketed out.

A particular problem that arises from this so-called de-disciplinary exercise (and one Mitchell himself alerts us to), is that clarification with respect to methodology is made only in terms of what is *not* achievable. It is suggested, for example, that what is *not* meant is 'a return to naïve mimesis, copy of correspondence theories of representation, or a renewed metaphysics of pictorial "presence"'. Instead the pictorial turn is supposedly 'a postlinguistic, postsemiotic rediscovery of the picture as a complex interplay between visuality, apparatus, institutions, discourse, bodies, and figurality' (Mitchell 1994: 16). As we know from the earlier postmodernism debates, such a 'post-' definition is by default a negative one, either folding back in upon itself (critically or not), or simply unwilling to posit future direction. Of course – whether we like(d) them or not – the postmodern debates have been extremely significant and far-reaching, just as in this case it would seem so are the current debates with respect to a pictorial turn. It is certainly the case that the growing theoretical interest in visual culture has signalled a move towards a more subtle engagement with the visual, which, at the very least, works to remind us of a continual presence of 'something' we take to be the visual and understood, for example, to be 'as important as language in mediating social relations'

(Mitchell 1996: 82). It is certainly with respect to this level of engagement that I seek to develop an understanding of images of the fall of the Berlin Wall.

In accepting the potentially far-reaching consequences of a so-called 'pictorial turn', we are seemingly left with an unsettled, or unhinged, site (or sight) of inquiry. As Mitchell (1994: 418) himself notes, the outcome of his efforts to formulate an image theory has 'yet to be pictured'; though, he suggests, were he to give it some shape, 'it would have a thoroughly dialogical and dialectical structure, not in the Hegelian sense of achieving a stable synthesis, but in Blake's and Adorno's sense of working through contradiction interminably'. This, of course, is how in the preceding chapter I sought to describe an image critique, as an interminable working through, of a polyperspectival, dialogical structure. So, on the one hand, suggestive of an image critique, there is the potential in visual culture studies to enable a radical critique (in both form and content). On the other hand, of course, it remains the case that without knowing what might come *after* (or even besides) the 'text', we can not easily determine any specific new approach. The difficulty in defining visual culture has repercussions for academic discourse, not least the re-evaluation of scholarly expectations. Whilst we may recognize the importance of the de-disciplinary operation of visual culture (certainly politically in devolving boundaries and calling for genuine collaboration, even outside of the humanities), the obvious, yet oft-neglected, criticism is that there is a lack of responsibility for getting involved more directly with the visual, for allowing the visual to contribute critically as a form of knowledge or intelligence in itself. The interest (and interdisciplinary curiosity) is no doubt there, but visual culture has, to date, really only been swamped by internal debate, with arguments over who lays most legitimate claim over it, or what its true objects of analysis should be. In what follows here, in order in to try to make a little more sense of the dilemmas at stake in adopting (or at least working out from) a visual culture paradigm, I suggest it pertinent to pose a layered interrogation of just what the 'object' of visual culture might be. To ask: not simply what objects visual culture might seek to analyse, but also what objective(s) visual culture might be said to hold. Furthermore, and perhaps most importantly, to consider what object, or *form* visual culture research might itself take; that is, how it might best be realized as image critique. Although intricately inter-related, I take these three points of departure each in turn.[3]

Objects of Visual Culture

The 'object' of analysis for visual culture studies would seem obvious enough, being supposedly *all* that which is related to the 'visual'. Yet, of course, such a definition opens up a massive, even unmanageable arena of research interests (and poses all number of methodological quandaries). In his sceptical introduction to the subject, James Elkins (2003) cites a list of things scholars of visual culture have been found to take to be of interest. The list runs over a whole page and includes many things one might well predict (such as photography, advertisements, new media, contemporary fine art etc.), but also all number of other weird and wonderful things, not least of which include: international airports, Barbie, Eastern European Christmas decorations, pink flamingos and other lawn ornaments, fin-de-siècle gay pornography, and so on. Within such a heterogeneous list it is simple enough to add here a study of the Berlin Wall.

Of course, a charge frequently made of visual culture is that there is nothing particularly new about it, with much of the same having been (and continuing to be) explored through the disciplines of film, media and cultural studies, as well as sociology and anthropology. One significant point of difference, however, is the new field's potentially obsessive interest in the 'visual' – to the point where a more complex experience is bracketed out. In other words, the visual is disproportionably foregrounded, leading in some cases to a form of visual determinism. As Elkins (2003: 83) argues, '[v]isual images might not always be the optimal place to look for signs of gender, identity, politics, and the other questions that are of interest to scholars'. One example he gives are the analyses of the media treatment of the death of Princess Diana, which often sought to demonstrate the media's complicity in the creation of a global media network. The question he raises is whether or not these kinds of pictures are really in *themselves* important in our understanding of globalism or, simply, instances of this phenomena, otherwise equally (if not better) handled by non-visual theories of globalization. On occasion, then, it would seem 'the images are there just because the writers are invested in them, not because images are needed to make the arguments work' (Elkins 2003: 82–83).

By extension, it can be argued that all too often visual culture analysis is too self-evident. Why, for example, is it necessary to unpack and unmask the 'visual' when it is also argued that the visual is a very immediate, intuitive 'system' of meaning? Elkins wonders, for example, whether students really need 'to be coached' in order to make sense of the Rodney King video or, as above, the media coverage of Diana's death. And similarly with advertising, how much needs decoding, when 'decoding' (ironic or otherwise) is as much part of advertising viewership itself? (Elkins 2003: 75–6). It is precisely because my focus here of images of the fall of the Berlin Wall is indeed an 'object' fitting easily into the category of contemporary transnational media *and* is potentially overstated as a visual event that I have wanted both to acknowledge these criticisms, as well as assert my own reservations about a visual culture approach. Again, this is a reason why from the outset I have wanted to make clear I am not advocating any straightforward hermeneutic or historical analysis of visual representations of the Wall. Instead, I want to understand how the *use* of images of the fall of the Berlin Wall can contribute in themselves to a critical approach to its event and spectatorship; to make them intricately bound up with an image critique.

Image critique – I want to suppose – is to provide a more complex and *creative* approach to visual analysis and cultural criticism. However, such 'good' intentions cannot simply be posed as antithetical to the approach of visual culture, for whilst the criticism made of Mirzoeff (and others) in maintaining too narrow an object domain can be substantiated in certain respects, it is equally in other ways inaccurate. In fact, as a consequence of visual culture's particular predilection for interdisciplinarity, the 'object' of analysis is frequently described in terms far more complex than a mere inexhaustible treasure trove of visual objects. So, for example, Mirzoeff (1998) and his collaborator, Irit Rogoff (1998), both stake out what they describe as a tactical, post-structural visual culture, which emphatically does not seek to delimit the objects of visual culture, but instead advocates a supposedly new (even virtual) 'object'. This is not an object as 'thing' but instead the *process* of visual experience and interpretation – a process which has come to be encapsulated by the term 'visuality'; a concept which fuses both vision and the visual with respect to their social and culture dimensions (see Foster 1988; Mirzoeff 2006).

The two most significant (and inter-related) implications that follow from the concept of visuality are the way in which it makes vision historical and the emphasis it places upon a visual *subject* (rather than object) – both having the effect of opening up the field of visual culture to novel attempts at cultural interrogation and interpretation. The concept gives rise to a fluid

(Foucaultian) genealogy of visual culture, of multiple sites of meaning and perspective, each depending on the current social and cultural matrix surrounding the viewer and viewed. So, for example, what is made apparent by historicizing vision is the nature and unfolding of hegemonies of seeing (and of being seen), each considered to be up for contest over time (Jay 1993; Crary 1988).[4] Again, however, as we find with respect to the pictorial turn more broadly, an important implication is that 'in place of the traditional goal of encyclopaedic knowledge, visual culture has to accept its provisional and changing status' (Mirzoeff 1998: 13). In chapter three I attempt to explore the unfolding hegemony of vision, when I introduce the idea of a 'Berlin Imaginary'. This I intend as a way of situating the Wall (and the fall of the Wall) in a complex visual history. When examined in terms of its visuality, the fall of the Berlin Wall has many different ways of being seen and pictured. On the one hand, following Elkins concerns over visual determinism, it was arguably an event simply caught on camera, an event that politically means little as such with respect to its visualization. Yet, on the other hand, it is also an event that provides us with an enduring 'picture of the world' at the end point in the Cold War. And, critically, with the field of vision quite different depending on which side of the Wall you are placed, I argue there is a distinct 'view' of the demise from only one side of the Wall, a perspective which only maintains East-West inequalities.

It is the function of opening up new possibilities and considering the relationship between and across modes of seeing that makes the concept of visuality important as a critical 'tool' for visual culture studies and, significantly, helps mark its approach out from other disciplines which otherwise remain defined by their respective object domains (as is the case, for example, with art history, literary and media studies, philosophy etc.). In fact, in this way, visual culture is taken to be an 'interdiscipline', supposedly because it is defined by the 'death of the object' – a phrase (resonant of Barthes' (1977) seminal post-structural statements of 'the death of the author' and 'from work to text') that Mieke Bal (2003) and Mirzoeff (1998) use to signal a radical shift incurred by the study of visual culture.[5] In place of a clearly demarcated object domain, visual culture is argued to *create* its 'object' as an interdisciplinary object, one '*that belongs to no one*' (Bal 2003: 7). In this way, the 'visual' is to be understood as 'impure', by which Bal suggests it is always more broadly placed, either synaesthetically, discursively or pragmatically (19). Mirzoeff (1998: 7), for example, describes everyday experiences of visual culture as being, more often than not, set apart from the 'formally structured moments of looking'. Thus 'visual events', as he labels them, operate as much *outside* of the more obvious sites of spectatorship such as the cinema, the gallery or even the domestic sphere of the television. And images, as Rogoff (1998: 16) argues, 'do not stay within discrete disciplinary fields such as "documentary film" or "Renaissance painting," since neither the eye nor the psyche operates along or recognises such divisions'. Thus, she suggest, visual culture is experienced in a far more fluid and complex manner; like a 'scrap of an image', for example, which 'connects with a sequence of a film and with the corner of a billboard or the window display of a shop we have passed by, to produce a new narrative formed out of both our experienced journey and our unconscious'. It is this kind of 'interactive' phenomena that the post-structuralist strand of visual culture studies seeks to understand and describe and which has undoubtedly influenced my understanding of the fall of the Berlin Wall as a complex visual 'object' and/or event.

Nevertheless, an important criticism levied against a post-structural visual culture is that its overall effect conflates a number of important concerns, crucially to privilege an *abstract* interest in the visual for self-contained critical importance. As Carol Armstrong (1996: 27) has argued, the objects of study in this respect are 'viewed not as particularized *things* made for particular historical uses, but as exchanges circulating in some great boundless and often curiously ahistorical economy of images, subjects, and other representations'. In other words, the tendency for a visual culture conceived in this way is to place a pre-determined structure, albeit a 'fluid interpretive structure' (Mirzoeff 1998: 11), *before* the visual object, and so potentially thwart any considered ontology of pictures themselves. Rogoff's (1998: 15) response would be that there is produced (as least potentially) 'a field of vision version of Derrida's concept of *différance* and its achievement has had a twofold effect both on the structures of meaning and interpretation and on the epistemic and institutional frameworks that attempt to organise them'. However, this perhaps only raises further concern, for although a 'vision version' of deconstruction, or *différance*, would seem to make some kind of sense, when taking on board the insights of a pictorial turn there is surely lurking here a dilemma or tension with respect to the relationship between text and image. Thus, whilst I may certainly remain sympathetic to deconstruction (no doubt with image critique even playing its part in such a procedure), I am wary of a visual *equivalent*. In fact, if – like Martin Jay (2002) – I am to assert that the image remains somehow in excess of language, then I am led to argue there are always 'elements' of the image that actually obviate a deconstruction. A symptom of which, is a sense of the immediacy of the image (that spark of significance, for example, that Benjamin takes to underpin the critical function of *denkbilden*) – an immediacy from which there is no elaboration or elongation (as in duration or *différance*).

Barthes (1982), in his book *Empire of Signs*, offers a useful way of understanding this point of difference. The book – which, like *Camera Lucida* (1981) is a book of both personal writing and photographs - opens with a neat 'methodological' statement: 'The text does not "gloss" the images, which do not "illustrate" the text. For me, each has been no more than the onset of a kind of visual uncertainty, analogous perhaps to that *loss of meaning* Zen calls a *satori*' (1982: no pg). He goes on to take the Japanese *haiku* poetry form as emblematic of this critical 'visual uncertainty', noting that 'the brevity of the haiku is not formal; the haiku is not a rich thought reduced to a brief form, but a brief event which immediately finds its proper form' (75). Thus, quite apart from all the 'talk' (or 'talking over') of a deconstruction as a means to achieving dialogue with the subaltern, in *Empire of Signs*, Barthes attempts to give us situations of writing as 'spaces' (or even pauses) in which another voice might be heard, in which images do not reduce rich thoughts to a brief form, but immediately finds it proper form. Situations, then, in which we encounter another writing entirely – a visual writing as it were, or at least a writing *with* images (and not about them).

To put this another way, any worded analysis of visuality can too easily become a mere circular exchange of visual *meanings* (i.e. the visual reduced to a brief form). Thus, what I criticize Mirzoeff (and others) for is in not taking visuality far enough. It is not enough, for example, to simply account for the visual event, rather I consider it necessary to *create* visual events, to create thought-images or, as above, to write *with* images. Such constellations will no doubt then become situated within an interdisciplinary, intertextual 'world' as suggested by visual culturists such as Rogoff and others. What I am arguing is that it is surely better to be creating, or *writing the image* for critical affect, rather than be 'creating' a supposed new object of visual culture that would appear really only to be an academic object, the *theoretical occupation* of the visual event. Thus, image critique as I define it, is not an attempt to *apply* theory but rather to *let in* images themselves, to offer up their own critical perspective; not as a determined account or engagement with the visual, but acceptance of the image as and for itself, a *thing* – a 'subject' as it were – of its own.

Objectives of Visual Culture

The (political) objectives or motivations of visual culture are variable and often contested, but it has been with its more prevalent cultural studies guise that social and political interests have prevailed as the mainstay of visual culture studies. Following Foster's (1988: ix) discussion of visuality, at the heart of visual culture is perceived the need to socialize vision, 'to indicate its part in the production of subjectivity...and its own production as a part of intersubjectivity'. Thus, like cultural studies, which 'sought to understand the ways in which people create meaning from the consumption of mass culture', so visual culture can be said to 'prioritize the everyday experience of the visual from the snapshot to the VCR and even the blockbuster art exhibition' (Mirzoeff 1998: 7). Yet, as I have outlined thus far, visual culture – through the 'lens' of the pictorial turn – establishes a new problematic or de-disciplinary exercise. It examines not just visual cultural objects and events, but also the visuality of enquiry itself. In other words, that which is *framed* (or pictured) by cultural criticism is also placed under scrutiny. In light of this, in 'coming after cultural studies', as Bal (2003: 20) puts it, visual culture studies should not necessarily be seen to endorse its predecessor without first questioning the problems raised in and about cultural studies itself.

Cultural studies has always held an interest in cultural politics, though, arguably, *only* 'from a theoretical perspective'; being, for example, much less willing 'to engage in a politics of culture, including policy formation and analysis' (Hooper-Greenhill *in* Bal 2003: 20). How, then, might visual culture fare, especially when, in general terms, it is seemingly 'less Marxist, further from the kind of analysis that might be aimed at social action, more haunted by art history, and more in debt to Roland Barthes and Walter Benjamin than the original English cultural studies'? (Elkins 2003: 2) Bal (2003: 20–21) is of the opinion that it has the potential to be *more* political, arguing that 'a political *tone* is less instrumental than analyses that expose politics within the object', and adds, 'knowledge does not automatically make a difference'.

Central to Bal's argument is the idea that 'seeing is an act of interpreting', which in turn, she suggests, means 'interpretation can influence ways of seeing, hence, of imaging possibilities of change.' Drawing on Homi Bhabba's notion of 'seriating', her idea is for objects to be brought together 'in specific ways', to make new series, which then 'facilitates their making and reiterating statements'. Analysis of these specific series, as well as crucially 'the grounds that bring the objects together', enables a critical, de-naturalizing intervention. Mirzoeff's (2005) study of the war in Iraq is again a useful example to keep in mind. He does not refer explicitly to 'seriating', but he describes his thematic approach (with its layered imagery of Babylon) in terms of creating – or intervening with – new series of meaning and interpretation. As he suggests, in order to make sense of the 'potentially infinite number of viewpoints' of the event of watching the war, it is necessary they are 'framed within a series to be intelligible' (Mirzoeff 2005: 11). Importantly, this is more about exposing (and experimenting with) knowledge than *applying* it for political ends.

To take 'exposure' rather than the application of ideas and knowledge as a motivating principle of method, visual culture (at least in the form I propose here of an image critique) can be said to allow for an 'encounter between object and analyst' that means transforming 'the analysis from an instrumentalist "application" into a performative interaction between object...theory and analyst' (Bal 2003: 24).[6] A result of this interaction is not only an analysis of the 'object', but also the creation of a new, second object. In which case knowledge is not so much under control, but instead made to be experienced. As Barbara Stafford (1996: 76) suggests, in connection with new digital technologies, this interaction means 'we remain the producers and directors of knowledge. Nuggets of visual data endlessly and enticingly summon us to collaborate in their restaging'. Arguably, at stake is a kind of critically engaged *visual curiosity*, which is to imply, as Rogoff (1998: 18) argues, 'a certain unsettling; a notion of things outside the realm of the known, of things not yet quite understood or articulated', even an optimism 'of finding out something one had not known or been able to conceive before'. It is this unsettled and unsettling prospect of the visual that forms (for want of a better word) the very 'foundation' or, more appropriately, the motivation of much visual culture studies, asserting for visual culture its political possibilities or, more accurately perhaps, an ethics of seeing (see Bal 2005).

Understanding the writing-up of visual culture as a *performed* relationship between object, analyst and theory also helps clarify the relationship between historical analysis and visual culture studies. For Bal (2003: 25), the role of visual culture studies is clearly to make an 'historical-analytical examination of visual-cultural regimes'. Nevertheless, the perspective, she maintains, is always one of the *present*. In this respect, visual culture works not to 'reify one historical state in the past but looks at the present situation as a starting point and searchlight'. This equates, for example, with Mirzoeff's (2005: 4) attempt to look at the present and future, whilst, as he puts it, 'trying to dream with the primal past'. And, as I have stated with my layered account of images of the fall of the Berlin Wall, I too wish to assert a similar 'historical perspective' of the *present*. I seek to treat the remnants of the Wall as they implicate our thoughts and actions *today* (though, equally, not to exclude how they affected 'on the day' the actual event of the fall of the Wall and subsequent media reaction). With respect to the 'continuum' of instant history this is a *perpetual* critical task. Moreover, by defining images of the fall of the Berlin Wall in terms of an open dialogic 'object' there is the sense in which current theoretical, interpretative approaches are not adequate; if only because they all too quickly close down or delimit this open dynamic and end up explaining images by turning away from them. It is for this reason I advocate a performative, creative approach to formulating critique. Image critique is performative in the sense that in issuing a critique of images, it is also the action of making those images themselves appear for the purpose of critical reflection. Benjamin's Angel of History, as discussed in chapter one, is a specific example of this idea, since our very experience of reading his passage on the Angel is intended to be something like the experience of a multiple 'time' or set of perspectives he is writing about.

The only problem, of course, is that any 'actually existing' pursuit of visual culture studies has so far generally been diverted from such laudable aims. What is evident in reading Bal's polemical account of visual culture, for example, is that her liberated kind of visual culture studies is somehow always *still to come*. Similarly, Elkins (2003: 7) makes a point of distinguishing between the already existing field of 'visual culture' and 'visual studies' as the field he thinks or at least hopes visual culture might eventually 'grow to be'. In terms of what is actually disseminated, visual culture (like cultural studies) remains fairly ineffectual in political terms and, as I will discuss below, has proven to be relatively conservative in form. As a whole, it is an enterprise that has become 'considerably demanding intellectually' (Chaney 2000: 112), with debate often only circular and internal. To parallel Stephen Connor's (1994: 129) remarks on postmodern theorizing, there is frequently the mistake 'of only attending to the manifest *content* of that theory, rather than assessing its discursive effects: looking at what it says, rather than at what it does'. In this respect, Michael Holly (2003: 238) wonders why, in fact, the original energy and vibrancy evident in the early days of the subject's development has apparently withered. It was an energy derived, he remarks, 'not from its seriousness, but from it playfulness', and goes on to point out how everyone involved shared in the liberating view that *anything* was possible, noting 'so many of us yearned to do something else'.

Of course, all the talk of refining disciplines and interdisciplinarity is perhaps all but 'academic' anyhow. We might well do better to simply recognize the difference between, firstly, visual culture as phenomena with which we can all engage and, secondly, the *study* – the scholarly pursuit – of visual culture which appears to be bound to the (relatively conservative) domain of academic debate and publication.[7] It is the former, I believe, remains important, but which I suggest we can *add* to in critical and creative terms. Image critique, albeit defined in imaginary terms, exists in a somewhat in-between state, re-capturing, I hope, something of the initial hopes for doing 'something else' as Holly puts it. At the very least it is to suggest a more creative, 'playful', but no less critical kind of research and/or political engagement.

Towards a Visual Critical Theory

It is significant and indeed surprising that despite its professed interdisciplinary make-up and direct critique of textual analysis, visual culture has to date prompted little actual innovation in terms of its form(s) of writing, production and dissemination. Elkins (2003: 120–123) makes the argument that visual culture studies, as it currently stands, has proved to be *too easy*. Hence, he urges it to become 'more ambitious about its purview, more demanding in its analyses, and above all more difficult'. As a part of which, he poses a challenge for those engaged in visual culture studies to write more 'ambitiously' – to write authoritatively and insightfully about the field, but also simply to 'write as well as you can'. The problem of good writing he suggests is well highlighted by considering the work of John Berger, who emerges as one of the most widely cited inspirations to the field. What makes this fact particularly strange is that 'no art historian or specialist in visual culture writes anything like Berger.' Indeed, no one seems willing to experiment in the same way with the form and style of writing and production. Art historians and other specialists of visual culture seldom work closely with an image-maker (such as in Berger's case, the photographer Jean Mohr) and would never, for example, interrupt their prose with poetry, permit themselves long parenthetic remarks or personal reminiscences. Yet, 'why not', Elkins asks, 'when those signs of the engaged writer are part and parcel of the philosophy of the engaged viewer that Berger himself helped bring into art history?'[8]

Elkins (2003: 157–158) offers an analogy with that of the music historian who generally is expected to have some competence in playing and reading music. This same kind of competence, he argues, is rare in art history and visual culture, suggesting as the subject of visual studies develops, 'it should consider ways of bringing image-making into the classroom

– not just in theory but in actual practice'. In fact, he suggests the making of images (from drawing and painting to video editing) ought to be practiced in the *same* seminar rooms where historical and interpretative work also takes place, arguing that only then 'will it become apparent just how difficult it is to knit the two kinds of experience together and how tremendously important it is to try'. Mitchell (2002: 178) provides a revealing 'illustration' of what is at stake when theory and practice meet (in the same room) when recounting a classroom session in which he asks students to conduct a practical exercise to show 'seeing itself'. One presentation he singles out is of a woman whose 'prop' is her nine-month-old baby, who begins to show off to the audience, so disrupting the mother's presentation. The overall effect Mitchell suggests is 'a contrapuntal, mixed media performance' that underlines 'the dissonance or lack of suturing between vision and voice, showing and telling'. On the one hand, this performance highlights the particular problem of reconciling the visual (as irreducibly visual) with a satisfactory critical framework, or mode of critique. However, the more ambitious aim of the 'Showing Seeing' exercise, he argues, is 'its potential as a reflection on theory and method in themselves [...] to *picture theory* and *perform theory* as a visible, embodied, communal practice, not as the solitary introspection of a disembodied intelligence' (emphasis added). Again, Mitchell seeks to make sense of this exercise in terms of his de-disciplinary concerns. So, whilst he does at least allow this 'contrapuntal, mixed media performance' to become something of an object of thought in his writing, in the end it is perhaps rather of only limited effect; we really only have Mitchell's *word* on the performance.[9] The problem is, with respect to the norms of academic writing, we just can not quite get over the unassailable quality of this exercise, of its contrapuntal, mixed-media nature. Indeed, short of having a three-dimensional pen and paper, it is not possible to (studiously) harness its true import.

So, how might this relate to the kind of visual critical theory that, for example, Susan Buck-Morss advocates? Not unlike the mother's presentation of Mitchell's Showing Seeing, perhaps, Buck-Morss (1996: 30–31) makes the case for a form of critical theory to be in itself visual, to 'show rather than argue'. In which case, we need to believe '[a]esthetic experience (sensory experience) is not reducible to information'. Interestingly, she wonders whether this is too old-fashioned an idea to suggest, and goes on to remind us that visual culture is in fact in the hands of its 'producers' of tomorrow; these being, she notes: 'the camera-women, video/film editors, city planners, set designers for rock stars, tourism packagers, marketing consultants, political consultants, television producers, commodity designers, layout persons, and cosmetic surgeons'. Of course, whilst the democratic potential for 'thinking in images' is perhaps a genuinely new circumstance, the problems of *writing* and theorizing the visual object are far from new. Hans Sedlmayr (2000), for example, a member of the formalist Vienna School writing in the 1930s, posed searching questions about the relation of object to its interpretation, advocating an alternative perspective for picturing (or indeed performing) theory. In his view, art history was to make imaginative, creative interpretations and aesthetic constructions akin to the work of artists themselves. It is an idea later echoed provocatively by Susan Sontag (1994: 14) in her famous essay 'Against Interpretation', where she argues that in 'place of a hermeneutics we need an erotics of art'. Arguably, then, in lieu of *framing* an exercise in Showing Seeing as de-disciplinary there is a need simply to show seeing itself – to let such a 'picture theory' *stand for itself* as 'a visible, embodied, communal practice.' Ultimately, the critic, or 'imagologist', might then join with the ranks of tomorrow's producers of the image.

Yet, we are brought back to the question as to why so few seem willing or able to engage in the kinds of writing that Sontag might propose with an erotics of art, or as has been canonized following the idiosyncratic writings of Walter Benjamin, Roland Barthes and John Berger. Perhaps the contemporary scholarly community have too much invested in the subject matter to enable them to break free of its constraints. Ironically, perhaps, the texts of those wandering thinkers and *ur*-imagologists, of the likes of Benjamin, Barthes and Berger, are the very texts we continue to dwell upon precisely because these thinkers were *not* specifically scholars of the visual, but rather writers *interested in what interested them*. Indeed, perhaps it is more often those outside (or at least on the fringes) of academia who provide a richer engagement with visual culture and visuality. We might consider, for example, that the huge success of Berger's *Ways of Seeing* (1972) was as much related to the fact that it was a television series reaching a mass audience. A more contemporary example that comes to mind is the author W. G. Sebald, whose acclaimed books such as *The Emigrants* (1996), *The Rings of Saturn* (1998) and *Austerlitz* (2001) have provoked huge interest in a relatively short period of time.[10]

Although Sebald's books are generally classified as works of fiction, they also have a documentary feel, incorporating and juxtaposing photographs and documents with the writing; the effect of which more often than not prompts a sense of critical uncertainty. Sebald himself describes his aesthetic as being 'the opposite of suspending disbelief and being swept along by the action.' Instead, he wants his readers to find out more about the characters and situations in his 'novels', to be constantly asking: 'What happened to these people, what might they have felt like?' His technique, to 'generate a similar state of mind', is to make his reader feel always 'uncertain' (*The Guardian Saturday Review*, 22.09.01). The use of the visual is again here an example of how visual culture as critical inquiry may evoke a certain ethical or political form of questioning. Buck-Morss's more explicitly scholarly work is very similar in approach. She describes her book *Dreamworlds and Catastrophe* (2000: xv) as 'an experiment in methods of visual culture. It attempts to use images *as* philosophy, presenting, literally, a way of seeing the past that challenges common conceptions', and so providing the general reader 'with a cognitive experience that surprises present understandings, and subverts them'. In this case, instead of reasserting the idea that the ideological split of the Cold War meant two very unique ways of living, and two very divergent ways of projecting a collective future, she highlights the similarities (her approach, thus, nicely chimes with the concerns of this book, certainly as will become more apparent in the chapters which follow). The images Buck-Morss uses throughout the book are in one respect a visual 'compendium of historical data', but they also provide a means to achieve the cognitive experience she intends, leading to new constellations and ways of thinking critically about the past. All of the above is combined with a layered, montage text, written, as Buck-Morss herself states, in fragments.

A question that needs to be asked, however, is why a *writer* such as Sebald (and *despite* also having been an academic too) can be praised for his writings, yet a scholar such as Buck-Morss is quickly criticized for an 'ambiguous' approach? In one review of *Dreamworlds and Catastrophe* she is lauded for her attempts to 'salvage the revolutionary critique of capitalism'; but nonetheless her arguments are heavily criticized for being ambiguous and 'not quite sustained' (Stone 2001: 48–50). The reviewer, whilst acknowledging the fragmentary writing style, proceeds to state 'it does not, therefore, cohere'. Furthermore, at no point in the review is there any comment on the book's analytical use of images (and this despite their importance as a philosophical method being explained explicitly in the book's introduction). More telling, perhaps and regardless of his plea for a more innovative enquiry and a more ambitious approach to writing academically, Elkins too is rather unsupportive of Buck-Morss's work. In commenting, for example, on the visual sequences in her earlier book, *Dialectics of Seeing* (1989), he suggests they portray 'the weakness of any series of images largely unsupported by text: it can be read in so many different ways that it tends not to attract discussion.' Similarly, in commenting on *Dreamworld and Catastrophe*, he argues that the images, whilst inserted into an extensive text, 'are still susceptible to being read as signs of nostalgia for failed modernist utopias, and I think they would be read in that way if they had been printed in a photography magazine' (Elkins 2003: 100–101).

What Elkins and others seem unable to accept is the fact that Buck-Morss actually wants to incorporate the unreliable nature of images into her critique. She wishes to allow for the fascination of the image (as we found with Benjamin's fascination of Klee's painting) to enable and complicate the kind of cognitive, critical experience of which Benjamin was an advocate. In this case, Buck-Morss undoubtedly 'entertains' the possible nostalgic meaning of the images she uses as a means to comment upon the comparative role of modernist utopian narratives. What is interesting about Buck-Morss's work is that she allows her critique to run in different directions, before coming to 'completion' as fashioned by her particular scholarly engagement. This, then, is the very 'art' of her living methodology (as noted at the start of this chapter). To my mind, Buck-Morss's call for and practice of a visual critical theory provides the most credible starting point from which to pursue any purported idea for an image critique. It is markedly different to the kind of visual culture studies that I have discussed here at length. That is not to say there can be no crossover or relationship, but that presently there is significant deviation, specifically in what results as the 'output' of research.

Thus, rather than taking the 'visual event' (the fluid relationship between viewer and viewed) as the focal interest of research and critique, Buck-Morss inhabits its very 'logic' (if such a word can be used) as a means to create a new critical method. In this way, she is willing to engage with and incorporate images in order to *form* her critique. And, significantly, the object of analysis does *not necessarily have to be a specifically visual interest*, but rather comes under visual or pictured scrutiny following her methodological interest for the critical import that images offer. In so doing, she maintains the specificities of the ontology and materiality of an image, placing the image 'as is' in a critical writing so as to affect a change in one's thinking. In other words, she intends to initiate both critical speculation and evaluation through cognitive experience. For Buck-Morss, then, it is the 'risk' of visuality that underpins her experiments with a visual critical theory. This means her critique is not necessarily stable, but generally through a layered and sustained use of various images (and dialogue with those images) she is able to frame a specific argument whilst also accepting various routes of difference and even contradiction. It is despite (or because of) the problems that images pose, that they contribute to a sophisticated kind of critical inquiry, less concerned with asserting final conclusions, but more readily able to keep in view the process itself of critical and historical thinking, and so offering a kind of visual ethical questioning. And, crucially, it is precisely this kind of open, critical visual inquiry that I suggest can usefully be applied to (or found in) images of the fall of the Berlin Wall. As a form of critique, not only might a certain instability of the image be harnessed to affect change in political perspectives (to revive, perhaps, a revolutionary critique of neo-liberalism and/or re-examine the status of East Germany after the Wall), but also – as I attempt to show in chapter five – to help understand how the various images of the fall of the Wall can in themselves provide a means to and be incorporated into their own critique.

Re-Scaling Images of the Fall of the Berlin Wall

The media images of the fall of the Berlin Wall undoubtedly helped visualize a fundamental moment in global affairs. As I will discuss in the following chapter, these images are remembered as marking a celebration, a victory, an end of an era (even the end of history itself!). Yet, surprisingly, given their iconic status, very little attention has actually been given to them specifically as images. In part this is perhaps due to the difficulty of bringing images into a critical discourse. Recent debates in visual culture have gone some way to correct this but, as I have argued, there is still the need to accept a different kind of critical knowledge that images can offer. This, I have tried to argue, requires finding ways of 'writing the image' as different to writing about them. Thus, in seeking to re-scale images of the fall of the Wall, there are two significant factors at stake. Firstly, the need to engage with a more creative kind of critical writing that incorporates images in a dynamic way in the process of critique itself. Secondly, the need to adjust expectations, in order not to obtain critical resolutions, but rather to seek critical spaces in which greater complexity and polyphony of thoughts and voices can be screened. To draw this chapter to a close, I will offer a few further images to illuminate (or, as it were, visually summarize) what I mean. In the first case, these are images of visual apparatus as a means to distinguish image critique as a form of writing different to visual culture. In the second case, two images or configurations of walls (one artistic, the other literary), which bring to attention the critical, open-architectural spaces I intend.

The contrast I have sought to highlight between visual culture and a purported image critique can be brought to light through the visual metaphors of two distinct optical devices. Visual culture, I suggest, operates something like a kaleidoscope (which employs a set of mirrors to make a seemingly infinite array of patterns). This device lets us look as a signifier moves eternally onward, as with the beads of a necklace knocking one onto the next. Image critique, however, might better be thought like the zoetrope (or its successor the kinetoscope) which combines a succession of images to form a single animated one. Physically (by the nature of its viewing slits) this foregrounds the relationship of the visual apparatus and the experience of being engaged with 'moving' images. It also allows us to consider an active role in making the image move, which in our case, hopefully, is to get them to do certain (critical) work.

With the metaphor of the kaleidoscope, I mean purposely to suggest visual culture is in itself a visualizing apparatus, a very specific kind of lens which when held over its subject (and subject discipline) enables everything to take on a different set of patterns. An illustration of this kind can be found in Meiling Cheng's (2003: 30–31) commentary on the relationship between feminism and visual culture, which she describes with an analogy of colour pigments on the surface of a pond. Feminism, she suggests, is represented by the paint itself suspended in the water. As the history of feminism has developed from being a direct (perhaps crude) challenge to the patriarchal status quo to a more subtle and complex set of debates, so the colours on the pond have changed from stark primary colours to a more diffuse and varied palette. Visual

MARIBEL

VAYA CIEGO NOS
PILLAMOS AYER
NOSOTROS HOY

culture, however, is represented by the water itself. Thus, as a supposedly transparent medium, visual culture 'triggers the interest in finding ways of comprehending and deciphering the existing images manufactured by contemporary culture'. There is perhaps something fragile about visual culture's 'suspension' whereby '[w]e allow the heavy to impinge upon the light, not to deaden the light, but to turn it into a certain illuminating matter'. Visual culture undoubtedly offers a great deal of potential in critically approaching the image. It is open, as it were, to all the kinds of beautiful chaos that a kaleidoscope can offer. Nevertheless, it should be remembered, this 'chaos' is of an orchestrated optical mechanism – once you have played with a kaleidoscope enough times you realize the collision of shapes and colours actually do repeat themselves. Or, as with Cheng's example, 'a certain liquidity distances our act of seeing from the seen; we approach visible sights as if through a watery screen, a pond of visions that keep undulating'.

Of course, the indeterminacy of the image, through such undulating visions, is not necessarily overcome with an image critique. Nevertheless, the difference I wish to emphasize is an idea of constructing or *situating* images for their own critical meaning (which equally respects critical agendas beyond those of purely visual concerns). To this end, I take the zoetrope as its metaphor; a contraption which issues as Rosalind Krauss (1988: 51–58) describes a 'rhythm, or beat, or pulse'.[11] In reference to Max Ernst's picturing of the zoetrope in his collage *A Little Girl Dreams of Taking the Veil* (1930), Krauss notes the acknowledgement of two places occupied simultaneously: 'One is the imaginary identification or closure with the illusion', whilst the second position, 'is a connection to the optical machine in question, an insistent reminder of its presence, of its mechanism, of its form of constituting piecemeal the only seemingly unified spectacle'. This 'double effect' she notes, produces 'a sense of being captured not so much by the visual as by what one could call the visuality-effect'. This ability to be both inside and outside the constructed image, to have the means of production of a 'visuality-effect', is what, I argue, an image critique needs to achieve. It is not simply a process of foregrounding the form, or mechanism of meaning, but also of putting in place the 'hallucinatory' effect of the unified image; to retain its luminance and allow its particular rhythm or beat to enter into our critical engagement.

Thus, in contrast to visual culture, which provides a specific view or filtering of an image, the point about an image critique is to make the image *itself* the context of viewing. This is certainly intended as a complex, polyperspectival mechanism of viewing, which, equally, is to suggest a context that itself brings into being a visuality-effect, rather than its mere consideration or interpretation. In the case of Ernst's picture, for example, from outside the revolving drum as we peer through the slits as they pass rhythmically in front of our eyes, we witness a succession of stationary birds 'performing the majestic flexing of their wings in what would appear to be the unified image of a single fowl' (Krauss 1988: 59). Conversely, from inside the drum, 'the experience would be broken and multiplied, analysed into its discrete, serial components, the result of chronophotography's record of a mechanical segmentation of the continuity of motion' (59). And what unites the experience of both inside and outside is:

> the beat or pulse that courses through the zoetrope field, the flicker of its successive images acting as the structural equivalent of the flapping wings of the interior illusion, the beat both constructing the gestalt and undoing at the same time – both positioning us within the scene as its active viewer and outside it as its passive witness (59–60).

In formulating an image critique it is necessary then to manage both the inside and the outside of its construction. In other words, the image formed by its writing/picturing must have a means of 'flight' both to reflect the spinning of the zoetrope and its unified visual spectacle, but also to keep present a view from *within* its own construction. As such, image critique will never be a simple, stable form, but nonetheless, it is one that perhaps has a more genuine chance of challenging (even changing) hearts and minds – getting us (as readers or viewers) to do the work of critique, engaging us cognitively, making us *feel* something of what is shown before us. It is, then, surely the beat or pulse – as Krauss terms it – that must become the very artistry of the visual culture critic

*   *   *

The idea of an image critique is not about making final, resolute arguments through pictures – nor about advocating a collection of better, more 'truthful' ones. Instead it refers to a more open-ended and ongoing critical reflection; a thought-image to be, as it were, a critical space in which to discover and wrestle with the full complexity of ideas, things and events. Fitting with the theme of this book, I will finally illustrate its concept with reference to two different depictions of famous walls. The first is of an installation artwork specific to the fall of the Berlin Wall; the second a literary image (or 'construction') of the Great Wall of China.

Ten years after the fall of the Berlin Wall, the Moderna Museet in Stockholm organized an extensive collaborative research project and art exhibition. The project, entitled *After The Wall*, brought together academics, artists and critics to examine and debate art and culture in 'post-Communist Europe' (with the majority of participants from the 22 countries involved having actually experienced communism at first hand). In conjunction with the artworks exhibited at the museum, an impressive two volume book was published, which includes photographs of the artworks, information on the participating artists and over 30 articles on art, communism, visual theory and politics (Pejiç and Elliot 1999). However, leafing through this hefty exhibition catalogue, I felt it was the one contribution that could not be reproduced on the page in any way that was seemingly the most interesting. The work in question was an installation, a sound sculpture by the artist Lutz Becker, which is given a very brief mention at the front of the book. In the corner of a double-spread photograph depicting a crowd at the Berlin Wall (with a man in the centre about to swing a sledgehammer into the Wall), there is a short paragraph, as if offering the 'small print' before one works one's way through the rest of the book:

> Lutz Becker has made a montage from sounds recorded at the Berlin Wall in the weeks directly after 9 November 1989 when it was first opened. These record, in particular, the eerie sound of its gradual erosion by hundreds of people attacking the concrete with hammers and chisels. The so-called Mauerspechte (wall-peckers as opposed to woodpeckers) worked on the Wall day and night, the sounds of their hammering, knocking and breaking travelled along its length as the concrete edifice worked like a gigantic resonating body. Walls are normally silent, mute; at the moment of its destruction the Berlin Wall gained a voice. The public approaching After The Wall will hear this montage of sound, invisible, but intensely present.
>
> (Pejiç and Elliot 1999: [no pg])

What would seem to be important about this work is not simply its 'eerie' quality, nor the idea of it giving voice to the disappearance of the Wall – though both aspects are of course significant. Instead, with respect to the idea of constructing an image critique, what is perhaps most revealing about this work is the way in which it enabled visitors to the exhibition to view all the other *visual* artworks in the gallery. As its description notes, this installation was invisible yet, nonetheless, intensely present. As you are invited to wander the gallery and see all the other pieces of work, a specific context is constantly being reiterated through the ambient noise of the Wall as it was brought down. And whilst most of the artworks – to look at – actually bore little direct relevance to the Wall, such aural immersion provided a particular mental and emotional dimension, always bringing you back to the very event that was the *raison d'être* of the exhibition in the first place. In other words, the *event* through its 'repetition' gave the prospect of a time (of an exhibition) after communism, a time *After the Wall*. Thus, whilst galleries are usually subdued, even silent spaces, Becker's montage of sound made the *whole* gallery – like the hammered down Wall – one 'gigantic resonating body', like a complex thought-space to reflect upon the multiple meanings of and responses to the fall of the Wall.

Just as with all the variety – its 'resonating body' – of the collected works displayed at the Moderna Museet, an image critique should be thought of usefully as a piecemeal construction. It is a thought-image or theory-product that can never be said to be complete, nor, indeed, to resolve matters as such, but rather persists in opening up a rich and complex view upon those matters held under scrutiny. In so doing, it cannot help but maintain (even collude with) a myth of what it is engaged with. Yet, importantly, an image critique does not seek to present only one point of view, rather a dialogue of many – or at least to leave strategic gaps in which *other* thoughts may be welcomed, if not entertained. In this way, it is intended as an architectonic theory, perhaps best illustrated more than explained. And so, finally, I give the last 'word' to the image of yet another wall; though no ordinary wall, instead Franz Kafka's description of a jigsaw construction of a wall every bit as famous as the Berlin Wall, if not more so (being most certainly of greater standing):

> *The Great Wall of China was finished off at its northern-most corner. From the south-east and the south-west it came up in two sections that finally converged. This principle of piecemeal construction was also applied on a smaller scale by both of the two great armies of labour, the eastern and the western. It was done in this way: gangs of some twenty workers were formed who had to accomplish a length, say, of five hundred yards of wall, while a similar gang built another stretch of the same length to meet the first. But after the junction had been made the construction of the wall was not carried on from the point, let us say, where this thousand yards ended; instead the two groups of workers were transferred to begin building again in quite different neighbourhoods. Naturally in this way many great gaps were left, which were only filled in gradually and bit by bit, some, indeed, not till after the official announcement that the wall was finished. In fact it is said that there are gaps which have never been filled in at all, an assertion, however, which is probably merely one of the many legends to which the building of the wall gave rise, and which cannot be verified, at least by any single man with his own eyes and judgement, on account of the extent of the structure (Kafka 1961: 67).*[12]

Notes

1. See the Visual Culture Questionnaire (1996) as a key document which brought out into the open a number of tensions and anxieties regarding the scope and definition of visual culture (particularly with respect to the discipline of art history, considered by some its natural 'home' and by others a somewhat out-of-date predecessor). In addition the discrepancies and uncertainties surrounding the subject area are highlighted by W. J. T. Mitchell's (2002) set of ten myths and counter myths of visual culture as apparently propagated, wittingly or otherwise, by various notable scholars in the field.

2. Rorty's history of philosophy portrays a series of 'turns', starting with medieval philosophy being concerned with *things*, to enlightenment philosophy with *ideas*, and, finally, contemporary philosophy with *words* (Rorty 1979: 263).

3. I have explored this layered inquiry of the objects, objectives and form of visual culture in an earlier, embryonic account of a particular debate over the nature of semiotic marks in painting (Manghani 2003a). Separate to my argument, though in some respects paralleling it, Mieke Bal (2003) has posed a similarly layered question of the 'object' of visual culture – I draw upon her discussion frequently here.

4. A good example of the changing state of hegemonies of vision can be given of the challenge to Cartesian perspectivalism (which separates object and subject in vision) from modernist art, which brings attention to the distracted viewer, the optical unconscious (Benjamin 1992: 211–244) and an embodied field of vision (Merleau-Ponty 1962). And, even *within* a single 'scopic regime' there are the possibilities of change and contest. Svetlana Alpers (1983), for example, in her study *The Art of Describing*, examines visuality in terms of specialist visual knowledge, pertaining to a particular cultural or social sphere. Thus, visuality does not simply denote historical shifts in the hegemony of vision, but equally the tensions underpinning these changes.

5. For my criticism of what I regard as a mis-appropriation of Barthes' statement about a new object of interdisciplinarity, see Manghani (2003a: 25–27).

6. The concept of visuality helps us move away from an uncontested interpretative notion of enquiry, towards a more reflexive, interactive one, with 'knowledge' 'constituted, or rather, *performed*, in the same acts of looking that it describes, analyses and critiques' (Bal 2003: 11). In a similar vein, Barbara Stafford (1996: 4) makes the case for a more complex engagement and proficiency of imaging, what she calls an 'intelligence of sight'. She explains, for example, that premodern graphics were not amenable to quick reading and so took time to be viewed and appreciated. As James Elkins notes, Stafford's central idea 'is not so much to "read" or "decode" the image as it is to ponder and return repeatedly, without hoping to ever understand once and for all' (Elkins 2003: 14). Stafford illustrates this principle with the arrangement of artefacts in 'curiosity cabinets' (fashionable in the eighteenth century). Today, she notes, we may select a computer icon with the touch of a button, whilst 'eighteenth-century beholders of polymathic diversity mentally clicked on a theatrical roster of automata, watchworks, and decorative arts accumulated in a fantastic case.' This 'performative gesture'. she suggests, served to extend oneself 'intellectually, psychologically, and emotionally outward to a strange "other" served to bridge the gap between known and unknown experiences' (Stafford 1996: 75–6).

7. In finding myself wanting to move away from many of the internal debates of visual culture, I am more in favour of designating a field of study (and mode of critique) that might more appropriately be labelled 'image studies'. This, I contend, allows for a field of study which can be obviously more inclusive and extensive than simply the 'visual' – a criticism that has plagued visual culture. James

Elkins (1999), for example, advocates a extremely broad 'image domain', yet is still very much attached to what he describes as 'a love for the visual world' (Elkins 2003: viii). Subsequently, what can appear missing is a 'love' of other kinds of images taken from a broader 'family of images' (Mitchell 1986: 9–14); including, for example, literary and mental images. Image studies, then, would seek to examine the variety of image-types in terms of their own specific differences. This is one reason why, perhaps, it might make for a more appropriate and inclusive umbrella term – and significantly allows for a kind of 'unconstricted, unanthropological interest in vision' that Elkins (2003: 7) suggests 'needs to be risked if the field is to move beyond its niche in the humanities'. For more on this subject, see the introduction in Manghani et al. (2006).

8. Notable exceptions include: Yve Lomax (2000); Rosalind Krauss (1993); and Susan Buck-Morss (1989; 2000). Also worth mentioning are the books in the Reaktion Books' *Topographics* series. The titles included in the series represent a mixture of both well-known critics such as Victor Burgin (1996) and, indeed, Jean Mohr and John Berger (1999), as well as interesting new writers such as Stephen Barber (1995). For further discussion on this series, see my review article (Manghani 2003b).

9. It is important to note: whilst I may criticize the impact W. J. T. Mitchell's Showing Seeing exercise has had on research, as a 'classroom exercise', it undoubtedly represents high-level commitment to a dynamic and challenging visual culture pedagogy. For further reflections on this classroom exercise and its significance for visual culture studies, see the special issue of the *Journal of Visual Culture*, vol. 4, no. 2, August 2005, 'The Current State of Visual Culture Studies', ed. by Martin Jay.

10. In addition to many favourable reviews of his books and accolades from notables such as Susan Sontag (as well as being seen by many – before his untimely death – as likely to win the Nobel Prize for Literature), W. G. Sebald's novels and essays have gained much scholarly interest, including a whole conference dedicated to his work held at University College Cork in July 2005.

11. The context in which Rosalind Krauss (1988) is writing, she takes this rhythm to act 'against the stability of visual space in a way that is destructive and devolutionary' (51). She is concerned specifically with the contestation (through artworks) of a modernist idea of grounding the visual arts in a particular notion of the autonomy of vision. However, in a broader sense, she can be understood to refer to this rhythm, beat or pulse, as a critical, creative force.

12. Franz Kafka's short story 'The Great Wall of China' was first published in the original German, *Beim Bau der Chinesichen Mauer*, in 1931.

It is photographed in black and white, always a sign of sincerity [...] But is it realism to show the Berlin Wall as a wall? The Berlin Wall is not a wall. It is a seam. It is a seam that binds the world

E. L. Doctorow
The Book of Daniel

CHAPTER THREE

THE END OF HISTORY?

...Three o'clock in the morning
It's quiet and there's no one around
Just the bang and the clatter
As an angel runs to ground
U2
'Stay, Faraway So Close!'

To begin with a brief tale of two 'ends', for strangely enough the story of the Berlin Wall illustrates an end of history twice over – once when it was built and then, again, when it falls. But whilst the first case draws a tragic end to a topography and way of life, as well as a cordoning off of socialism from the western world, the latter, in observing the resolution of a divided nation (and world), supposedly marks a philosophical end point of humankind. An end point that, arguably, is more about a future secured than of what had come to pass. Indeed, the fall of the Berlin Wall as a 'sign of history', shorn of the weight of its prior significance, is recognized as a celebratory image, a symbol of an unabashed victory of economic and political liberalism.

Checkpoint Charlie, 1961: Hagen Koch, an East German border guard,[1] was handed a brush and a bucket of white paint and told to paint a line along the road, thus marking out visibly and very precisely the borderline between East and West Berlin. A thin, but nonetheless defining line, '[i]t was, maybe, 6 inches wide but it held apart the equivalent of two tectonic plates: precisely this side was where the power of the United States and its allies ended, precisely that where it ended for the Soviet Union and its allies' (Hilton 2001: 3). As the unfolding Cold War was to prove both sides were indeed very powerful, and together they shaped the global political, economic and military conditions for the next half of a century. And whilst the Cold War is not generally thought of as a physical conflict, but rather a series of threats and counter-threats, it was nevertheless all too real. This was arguably a war about modern technology: the ultimate technology, nuclear capability.

Equally, however, it was one of the oldest forms of technologies, architecture, which came to stand between the atomic forces – the harsh logic of war put on hold by the absurdity of building a concrete wall straight through the heart of a real, living and breathing capital city.

It was in the early hours of Sunday 13th August 1961 that Berliners were rudely awoken by the bang and the clatter of one the most incredible building projects ever likely to take place. In an operation that involved many thousands of police and military personnel, the entire 103-mile perimeter of West Berlin was sealed off from the East in less than twenty-four hours, using mostly just concrete posts and barbed wire. And whilst protests were made through the 'appropriate channels,' the thin white line demarcating the East and West border now became a very real and formidable architectural contour. This act of ultra-rationalism resulted in many cruel and surreal situations, 'the division zigged and zagged through sixty-two major roads, over tram tracks, round a church and through its cemetery, across the frontage of a railway station and, stretching the credulity to its absolute limits, clean through the middle of one house' (Hilton 2001: 1). Berliners could only look on in shock; within hours, their lives altered irrevocably, suddenly unable to get to their place of work, or facing the fact that by evening would be unable to return home. Family members and friends became separated, able only to wave across to one another from opposite sides. The wall that was built at this time was nothing like the final construction of what most would commonly relate to as the Berlin Wall (a structure that came to stand some twelve feet tall and would always inevitably need to be torn-down), but nonetheless it was to be its ominous foundation.[2]

The construction of the Wall brought about a significant hiatus in Germany's united history (dating back to Bismarck's defeat over Napoleon III in 1871). But it did more than that, for it stood at the epicentre of a global theatre wherein the Cold War was played out. The division visibly marked out by the Wall froze world history, which became ideologically polarised between capitalism in the 'West' and socialism in the 'East.' For the nation-states of the Western world the divide was convenient, spatially isolating socialism 'in order to prevent its spread to the "free world"' (Buck-Morss 2000: 35). For the East, it made for 'a temporal bulwark, protecting the nascent socialist societies so that they could develop in history uncontaminated by the economic and social distortions of capitalism' (36). Isolation meant the regime could 'remain autarchic and hence masters of their fate, providing time to catch up with the capitalist West in terms of production, while not falling back from the historical level that the political revolution had achieved' (36). However, as time was to tell, in this state of suspended animation the regime only faltered and slowly decayed. In Berlin specifically, the effect was such that, like the overgrown garden that wraps its way around Sleeping Beauty, the heart of the city – formerly one of Europe's busiest – lay in ruins, a stranglehold on no-man's land; its prime real estate lost to the hardy shrubs sprouting up between the landmines and debris. And there in the shadow of the Wall all lay dormant for the next 28 years...

*   *   *

There are a number of factors leading to the final demise of the Berlin Wall, including a shift in macro-political dynamics (affecting international politics and diplomacy) as well as

localised changes affected by opposition groups and well-known members of the intelligentsia. But at the heart of this event of global importance is also a simple administrative bungle. On the morning of the 9th November 1989 – the day the Wall 'fell' – two Ministry officials had been ordered to draft a proposal for a new law to allow East Germans the unconditional right to visit West Germany. A public announcement was scheduled for early the next day, though the plans were read out to members of the Central Committee on the same afternoon. Crucially, Günter Schabowski (a member of the Politburo responsible for media relations) was not present at the meeting, yet, later that same day was required to hold a press conference about the impending changes. An unprecedented move in itself the press conference was to prove a sensation, leading directly to the demise of the Wall itself. It was towards the end of the session that 'a rather tired Schabowski dealt with the travel issue in a rather confused reply to an Italian journalist,' suggesting that the Party wanted to 'liberate the people from a situation of psychological pressure by legalising and simplifying migration' (Childs 2001: 86). Until the new law was passed there would be an interim regulation allowing those wishing to leave to do so. This however caused the confusion. Pressed as to when these regulations would come into force, Schabowski replied 'immediately,' and 'without delay.' But he meant by this only those who wanted to migrate, to turn their backs on the GDR for good (Childs 2001: 87). The evening news programmes reported Shabowski's press conference, but made little sense of the true implications of his announcement, only really adding to the confusion it had caused.

A member of the opposition group New Forum, appearing as a guest on various news programmes, said he was 'flabbergasted' by the announcement, but believed the new regulations to be 'too little too late' to satisfy the people, adding: 'You can't just walk across the border, but it's very easy to travel now' (cited in Childs 2001: 87).[3] East Germans, however, sitting at home watching the evening news were under the illusion that to travel they simply needed to have their identity cards stamped. Huge crowds began to gather outside the various police stations and checkpoints. 'The collection of humanity at the Wall,' as one historian describes it, 'was wonderful to behold – there were people carrying shopping, people carrying young children, people still dressed in their work clothes' (Richie 1999: 835). These gathering crowds gradually grew more and more restless, loudly chanting 'Open the gate! Open the gate! The Wall must go! The Wall must go!' (835). News of this 'revolution' quickly spread. All those sitting in session in the West German Bundestag, in Bonn, rose to their feet on hearing of the announcement and gave a round of applause. In West Berlin the city Mayor described it 'an historic hour,' as many rushed to the Western side of the Wall to chant in unison with their counterparts in the East (Childs 2001: 87). Late night news programmes began with reports of crossings of a few hundred citizens and nearing midnight it was apparent border guards had acquiesced entirely, enabling many thousands of East German citizens to cross over to West Berlin that very night. The scenes captured live by television networks both East and West were ones of celebration and joy, in turn having the effect of bringing yet more people out onto the streets. It was a party atmosphere, with an open invitation.

The spontaneous festivities of the night continued through until the next day and over the weekend. This time the only bang and clatter to be heard was of hundreds of people *chipping away at the Wall with implements of all kinds, from door-keys to sledgehammers, each taking away pieces of the Wall as trophies. By the morning the East German authorities were using cranes to remove whole slabs of the Wall in order to create more crossing points to cope with the numbers waiting their turn to visit the West. Over that first weekend some '800,000 East German shoppers and revellers crossed into West Berlin to go on an impromptu spending spree.' And by the end of the first four days a reported 4.3 million East German citizens throughout the whole of the GDR had crossed over into the West (Richie 1999: 837). On arrival they were entitled to 100 DM 'welcome money' and were able to enjoy free food, drink, transport, souvenirs, accommodation, and even free street maps printed especially for the occasion.*

These two 'ends' of history could hardly be more different. One, a planned event, conducted under the cover of darkness. The other, seemingly accidental, an occasion of euphoria and celebration caught by the full glare of the media lights. Unlike the first end of history that split East and West apart, leaving each to their own histories, the second ending of this story – the end of the Wall itself – marks the collapse of former categories and the melding of a new kind of history. The clock starts up anew for East Germans and for a reunited Germany as a new chapter in its history unfolds. Yet, this is a different sort of ending, for with socialism being brought in 'from the cold' by the buoyancy of its capitalist alter ego, it is an apparent end to history that is marked; defined by some as 'the end point of mankind's ideological evolution' (Fukuyama 1989: 4). On the ground, despite the obvious strained political and economic circumstance leading to the event, the end of the Wall was seen to be motivated less by ideology or political will and more by human agency (and error). Indeed, it was an event interpreted much more in terms of emotional resonance, than of political significance. And it is this part of the complete(d) story of the Wall that we remember now the most. The morning after the event, for example, the British Prime Minister Margaret Thatcher gave her reaction to the press, saying: 'Oh I think it is a great day for freedom...you can see the joy on people's faces and you see what freedom means to them, it make you realise that you can't stifle or suppress people's desire for liberty.'[4] It is this part of the story, which now comes before any other, that presents to us a 'theme of celebration'. It is as if the removal of the Wall leaves us open to new possibilities, denoting the finality of change (for the better). We are ever aware we now live in a post-Wall world, left open (and unhindered) to a progressive political paradigm of 'choice', competition and free trade.

Set side by side, these two stories of the Wall offer us a powerful narrative of human plight and perseverance in the face of dogmatic political wills; with the final emotional 'presence' of the fall of the Wall making for a very neat ending indeed. Yet, bringing these two ends to meet so neatly – snapping them shut like interlocking building blocks – is to *tell a tale* of the Wall. Unlike Benjamin's (1992: 249) Angel of History who 'sees one single catastrophe', we perceive only 'a chain of events' – as such, it is as if the whole complexity of our recent history is distilled into simple pivotal moments, potentially leading us to disengage from the critical state that Benjamin suggests is the catastrophe. All too easily, then, our own view of history gets snagged by the debris and quickly 'runs to ground'. As with the angels, Damiel and Cassiel, in Wim Wender's fantastical films set in Berlin who each eschew their omnipresent perception in order to be a part of our world, we too risk a heavy fall – to lie slumped before monuments (whether the Wall or other such political icons), vulnerable to the run of a 'local' – all too human – symbolic order.

*   *   *

The photographer and theorist Victor Burgin (1996: 184) describes the phenomena of joining or (mis)layering histories as 'the assembly of simultaneously present events, but whose separate origins and durations are out of phase, historically overlapping'. This, he suggests, is the 'imbricated time of our global lived space'. He takes the metaphor from Freud, who used it as a warning against explaining one part of the manifest dream by another 'as though the dream had been coherently conceived and was a logically arranged narrative' when, on the contrary, 'it is as a rule like a piece of breccia, composed of various fragments of rock held together by a binding medium, so that the designs that appear on it do not belong to the original rocks imbedded in it' (cited in Burgin 1996: 178). Imbricated time is another way of alerting us to the dilemmas of an instant history, whereby history forms a continuum out of which key historic moments are re-iterated and re-circulated again and again. In order to better understand our history, we need to get past the narratives that pull things together and instead get in amongst the original 'rocks', to dislodge what so readily binds them. Benjamin's description of a 'dialectics at a standstill' is applicable here (with the aforementioned "rocks" being equivalent to his reference to the 'image'):

> It's not that what is past casts its light on what is present, or what is present its light on what is past; rather, image is that wherein what has been comes together in a flash with the now to form a constellation. In other words, image is dialectics at a standstill. For while the relation of the present to the past is a purely temporal, continuous one, the relation of what-has-been to the now is dialectical: is not progression but image, suddenly emergent.
>
> (Benjamin, 1999: 462)

This is how – albeit obliquely – Benjamin suggests we might achieve (or at least understand) a critical awakening, or what I have begun to describe as an image critique. As part of which, it is also necessary to understand something more of the binding agent, tethering what otherwise may come to us in a flash. In this chapter, I intend to pull out from the debris...to extract various image elements relating to the Berlin Wall for historical and political analysis and with a view to inform the practice of an image critique of the fall of the Wall. Thus, where in chapter one I referred to the layering of Benjamin's thought-image of the Angel of History with an analogy of the flats of a theatre stage (each discreet component combining to form one entire scene), in this chapter, I want to get in amongst the spaces that lie between those screens (and understand what they are made up of). The overriding aim is to show how the dominant interpretation of a supposed 'end of history' (combined with the prevalent 'theme of celebration' which surrounds the story of the fall of the Wall) shapes the symbolic landscape as a kind of one-way street, within which all critique comes to be situated (with our good old Angel of History as it were running to ground). It is in light of this circumstance that, in chapter five, I want to go on to show how a purported image critique might appropriately renew a spirit of critical inquiry by making new constellations of images of the fall of the Wall.

Thus, keeping in mind the concept of instant history, I consider here in more detail the actual framing, or rather – in keeping with the metaphor of breccia – the patterns of this history.[5] Surely an important task, for although an image critique might well suggest a more *immediate* form of knowledge (as some kind of illumination or spark of insight), it equally should not be confused with an ahistorical approach. In fact, in order to successfully layer an image critique, to construct a polyperspective thought-image, a broader awareness of the complexity and currency of the images concerned is vital. Overall, then, this chapter aims to provide an analysis of some of the political and historical context relating to the fall of the Wall, as well as a consideration of an associated 'economy' of images from which as I will consider in chapter five new critical constellations might be told and illustrated. As I explore various aspects which underpin the historiography specific to the 'story' of the *fall* of the Wall, what comes to light is not only how the writing of the history of the fall of the Wall has shaped the way we think about it, but also how the Wall itself (and its location in Berlin) has informed the process of writing and thinking about the events of 1989.

Beginning with the End – A 'World Picture'

The global significance and spectatorship of the fall of the Berlin Wall has made it a key historical marker. Noam Chomsky, for example, in his *World Orders, Old and New* (1997: 1), suggests that the fall of the Berlin Wall, 'can be taken as the symbolic end of an era in world affairs'. However, he goes on to argue that whilst such a 'conventional picture' is not necessarily false, 'it is nevertheless misleading'. His point is that by 'uncritically adopting' this picture, not only do we misunderstand our recent past, we are also not 'well-situated to comprehend what lies ahead'. His comment points to the critical task sitting at the heart of this study in two ways. Most obviously, Chomsky highlights a 'critical' problem, in terms both of the need for a political, historical critique of the fall of the Wall and the inherent difficulty in achieving this due to the weighted symbolism of its prevailing, conventional picture. However, Chomsky also, if inadvertently, brings to the fore the significance in itself of 'picturing' the world. It is important to acknowledge that Chomsky's critique works very well to give us an alternative to the 'end of history' story. However, he does not engage with the event on the level of images as such and subsequently, he does not necessarily provide spaces in which we can gain our own critical understanding of the event. As a counterpoint, image critique – as means to creating thought-images – is intended to provide the grounds for a reflexive critique, in which differing perspectives are put on view all at once, out of which there can arise new critical awareness.

The philosopher Martin Heidegger argued, 'a world picture...does not mean a picture of the world but the world conceived and grasped as a picture' (1977: 130), a process he considered to be distinctive of the modern era. Nicholas Mirzoeff (1998) takes this idea to underlie a significant facet of 'the new visual culture', not just of modern but also postmodern culture, in which there is 'visualisation of things that are not in themselves visual' (6). His concern – whilst not intending to exclude other senses and ways of meaning – is to explore why there appears to be 'such a premium on rendering experiences in visual form' (6). In part, this trend can be understood as being technologically determined. The rise in instant history is certainly, in part, the result of developments in information and broadcast technologies of the late twentieth century. Yet, there seems to be a deeper connection between our way of thinking about the world and the way in which it is apparently visually coherent and meaningful. On the advent of the fall of the Berlin Wall, Margaret Thatcher, in her initial comments to the press, clearly was drawn to underline this fact: 'I watched the scenes on television last night and again this morning, because I felt one not only should hear about them, but see them, because you see the joy on people's faces and you see what freedom means...' (emphasis added). It would be too precarious a task to suggest there is some visual truth able to represent an abstract concept such as freedom, but, nonetheless, Thatcher's comments are clearly symptomatic of a tendency to think or believe things to be true as we see them and for this phenomenon to feed upon itself as a means to making sense of what it is we witness. In the way, then, Kracauer (1995: 86) suggests we might need to go *through* the mass ornament, I consider we need to take on the very logic of picturing the world in order to critique those televisual pictures which appear to us with events such as the fall of the Wall. What needs unpacking is a 'regime of seeing' distinct to the case history of the Berlin Wall, which I frame here in terms of a Berlin Imaginary. Historically this manifests as an underlying presence, informing at a deep level the euphoria of the final end of the Wall even *before* it was to fall.

In remaining mindful of Chomksy's warning about the potentially misleading nature (and power) of a 'conventional picture', what is at stake in 'picturing the world' is more than simply an account of events. In fact, an event such as the fall of the Berlin Wall can usefully be understood in terms of what Jean-François Lyotard (1989a: 393) describes as a 'sign of history' – with key examples for him having been Auschwitz, Budapest 1956, and the riots of 1968 in Paris and elsewhere. What is distinct about these 'signs', he argues, is that they tend to 'place modern historical or political commentary in abeyance'. Thus, with Auschwitz (undoubtedly the most potent example) the philosophical genre of 'Hegelian speculative discourse' is said to be undermined, 'because the name "Auschwitz" invalidates the presupposition of that genre, namely that all that is real is rational, and that all that is rational is real'. Or, again, in the case of the 'revolution' of 1968, the genre of democratic liberal discourse is apparently disrupted, for what is invalidated is the idea that all concerns of a political community 'can be said within the rules of the game of parliamentary representation'. In similar terms, we could argue that what is immediately invalidated with the fall of the Berlin Wall is 'actually existing socialism'. However, more than that, it is the 'genre' or grand narrative of the Cold War that actually folds in on itself. The point is not simply that liberal democracy and capitalism were seen to win over a communist world-view; rather it is that the very basis of ideological struggle and debate is thought to have dissipated. In other words, the fundaments of either side's world-view were each lost, with *all* sides having potentially lost impetus in their own grounding definitions and spiritedness (Bauman 1992; Buck-Morss 2000; Baudrillard 1994: 28–33). However, paradoxically, what is then all too tempting with the collapse of a grand narrative, such as the Cold War, is in fact 'to lend credence to the great narrative of the decline of great narratives' (Lyotard 1989b: 318). And in this case, the 'end of history', intimately bound up with the fall of the Berlin Wall, stakes out a very *grand* decline of the grand narrative. Whether we like it or not, this 'end of history' becomes the overarching and overwhelming narrative of our times.

Thus, it could be argued 'the fall of the Berlin Wall' operates something like what Lyotard (1988) terms a *differend* of contemporary politics and culture. That is, an event which gets 'stuck' in the discourse of history. Or, alternatively, the fall of the Berlin Wall is a 'stopgap' in the same sense Slavoj Žižek (2002: 3) suggests that the notion of 'totalitarianism', as an effective theoretical concept, is a kind of stopgap: 'instead of enabling us to think, forcing us to acquire new insight into the historical reality it describes, it relieves us of the duty to think, or even actively *prevents* us from thinking'. However, it would appear these signs of history bear in themselves the resource for their own critique. For, the silence imposed upon knowledge does not impose a silence on forgetting, rather 'it imposes a feeling [...] The silence that surrounds the phrase, *Auschwitz was the extermination camp* is not a state of mind, it is the sign that something remains to be phrased which is not, something which is not determined' (Lyotard 1988: 55–7). This 'feeling' goes beyond an empirical understanding making Auschwitz more than a single event, but in fact a continual historical presence and problematic. Although certainly relating to far less tragic circumstance, it is in a similar vein that, in chapter one, I sought to describe the notion of Instant History. In order to think on from the 'event' (to articulate that which has not be determined, or which is suppressed), it is an engagement with the event *itself* (with respect to its ongoing historical presence) that must transform our thinking. In chapter five, I will come to some examples of attempts at 're-staging' and so potentially transforming and/or transposing the event of the fall of the Wall. The point here, however, is first to examine in more detail the historical make-up of this *differend* or stopgap – to get in amongst the breccia of recent history, beyond the surface patterning of the binding that gives the design of a certain narrative as being a dominant one.

As a mere figure of speech the 'fall of the Berlin Wall' undoubtedly stitches together a number of significant associations. First and foremost, it is a physical or architectural metaphor for the breach (and later removal) of the entire German East/West border, as well as the eventual reunification of the two Germanies. Yet, furthermore, the Wall (having always made the otherwise imaginary 'Iron Curtain' a tangible reality) was also the chief signifier of the broader 'collapse of communism' (another oft-used figure of speech). Thus, even this relatively simple phrase of the 'fall of the Berlin Wall' embeds multiple meanings and associations. It is a figure of speech that draws upon a multifarious and powerful domain of images, symbols and myths that relate to the troubled period of the Cold War. And most importantly, if there is something which does indeed get 'stuck' (in the way that Lyotard and Žižek might suggest), it is surely felt by the way in which we never seem to move on from the initial descriptor or 'image' of the fall of the Wall (for example, those night-time scenes of people clambering upon the Wall). Indeed, it is as if we are perpetually at the beginning of this narrative of finale. The key binding forces in this case relate to two dominant and inter-related dynamics: firstly, what Zygmunt Bauman (1992) tersely describes as a 'theme of celebration', which, secondly, combines with the euphoric announcement of the 'end of history' as promulgated by Francis Fukuyama's (1989) prescient analysis of the world affairs in the year the Wall fell. Together they secure an all prevailing interpretation of events that privileges the West and suppresses any alternative political and economic reality. Before turning specifically (in the next chapter) to the political dilemmas of what can be described as 'living without an alternative', I concentrate here on looking at the so-called 'theme of celebration' and the 'end of history' thesis, as well as examining more broadly 'pictures' of Berlin and the Wall as they reflect, pre-empt and embed the significance of these two interpretations.

The Theme of Celebration

A certain generation of people will no doubt remember something about where they were or what they were doing when they heard the news that the Berlin Wall had 'fallen'. The overriding message sent around the world was undoubtedly one of hope, optimism and joy. Bauman (1992: 175) describes it in the following way: 'The official opinion…of the affluent West greeted the news, arguably the least expected news of the century, with self-congratulating glee'. And, with a certain sardonic tone, he goes on to explain:

> The theme of celebration is well known: "our form of life" has once and for all proved both its viability and its superiority over any other real or imaginable form, our mixture of individual freedom and consumer market has emerged as the necessary and sufficient, truly universal principle of social organisation, there will be no more traumatic turns of history, indeed no history to speak of. For "our way of life" the world has become a safe place. The century remarkable for fighting its choices on the battlefield is over…[f]rom now on, there will be just more of the good things that are. (175)

As briefly relayed in the opening 'story' of this chapter, the celebratory mood of the night of the fall of the Berlin Wall was indeed palpable and, as Bauman suggests here, 'well known'. Arguably, so well known that it invariably goes without saying. And, as I will come to discuss, it is this theme of celebration that neatly leads on to the idea of an end of history. Thus, putting aside the fact that there was indeed very genuine joy and optimism in the wake of the fall of the Wall, it is worth considering how a *theme* of celebration has been fashioned. In part this can be traced through the reporting of the event. The occasion was in certain key respects an ideal news item. Not only was it part of an already ongoing news agenda of the changes taking place in Eastern Europe, but – somewhat paradoxically perhaps – it came as much as a huge surprise, making it a headline-grabbing event. Ostensibly, it also lent itself well to pictorial presentation, for it was a 'live', moving phenomenon, making it particularly suited to lens-based media. However, in being both an element of ongoing news and also a rupture within that discourse, the fall of the Wall presents something of a lacuna, out of which the theme of celebration is able to fully propagate.

The theme of celebration is certainly evident from only a cursory survey of the front-page headlines in the British press. On the morning after the initial border crossings, the story is unquestionably one of surprise, euphoria and triumph for 'the people' and for democracy. In *The Times*, it announced: 'The Iron Curtain Torn Open' (10/11); 'Hammering Down the Wall' and 'Stampede Across the Berlin Wall' (11/11); and included leaders such as 'Victory for Democracy' (11/11). In *The Daily Telegraph* a similar story: 'The Iron Curtain is Swept Aside', 'The Wall Comes Tumbling Down', and 'Making History' (10/11); as well as '100,000 Take a Walk into the West' (11/11). In *The Observer*: 'A Nation Floods West' (12/11); whilst in *The Guardian*: 'Communists Open Berlin Wall…East Germans Sweep Aside Iron Curtain' (10/11). And in *The Independent*: 'Berlin Wall Breaks Open' (10/11), 'Bulldozers Move in to Breach the Wall' (11/11), as well as the somewhat poetic 'Berlin's Heart Beats Again' (13/11). As one might expect the language throughout presents an event of great magnitude. The image of the Iron Curtain being 'torn' down, or the Wall 'tumbling' or being 'hammered' down is certainly striking enough, but the sensation of a 'stampede', or 'flood' of people across to the West adds to the drama. The immediate tone of the tabloid newspaper coverage appears little different to that of the broadsheets, though characteristically the analysis is more superficial. As one would expect the headlines are bold and ludic. *The Daily Mail* ran with 'Champagne Charlie'

(10/11) and 'We Belong Together' (11/11); *The Mirror*: 'Oh Freedom! Joy as the Berlin Wall opens up...and Iron Curtain lifts' (10/11) and 'Together At Last' (11/11); whilst *The Sun* read boldly as: 'End of the Berlin Wall!' (10/11), along with punning headlines: 'Red and Buried!' (11/11) and 'Hans Across the Border – It's Wall over'. Finally, *The Evening Standard* taking Margaret Thatcher's comment as their own perhaps: 'A Great Day for Freedom' (10/11).

One of the main techniques of the papers in bringing the colour and drama of the event to its readers is to personalize the stories. The human interest story is an obvious framing device for the tabloids; news told through the eyes of witnesses is thought perhaps more palatable for the average reader, especially where the subject matter relates to events overseas. As *The Evening Standard* suggests in one report: 'The Real Story of the Berlin Wall, *the human story*...began with a young East German soldier called Conrad Schumann...' (p. 7, 10/11, emphasis added). And by 13th Monday the same paper presented on its front page the sort of story ubiquitous with coverage of the new millennium, the headline of the paper reading: 'A Baby Born to be Free' (13/11). The sense of a new beginning and/or turning point in both a private and a public history is overtly narrated by such a story, as it is echoed throughout the press coverage as a whole. However, overriding these individual stories of so-called ordinary citizens, reports were most frequently personalized either with reference to the actions and reactions of notable political figures (particularly western leaders and politicians, including, of course, West Germany's Chancellor Kohl who campaigned overtly for reunification), or otherwise the personalization of stories by way of named reporters.

Very often in the case of reactions from well-known public figures, the individuals concerned are not always as aware of the situation as the reporting might otherwise suggest. In fact, a journalists' need for personal reactions from politicians (and other figures of authority) often lead these individuals to make statements at an all too early stage, before they are really aware of even the most immediate consequences. On this occasion, then, many statements were, to say the least, unremarkable, or even patently misjudged. The day after the event, for example, the American President George Bush (Senior) said warily to camera: 'I don't think any single event is the end of what you might call the Iron Curtain, but clearly this is a long way from the harsh days of the harshest days of the Iron Curtain.'[6] Alternatively, the foregrounding of the journalists themselves, as named authors of reports, can weigh significantly on the interpretation of events. Typically on television an 'on-the-spot' journalists will usually end their report with their name and their location, whilst in the press a legend will run under the headline, or indeed the journalist's name itself will be included as part of the heading or sub-heading.[7] Of course, it is not necessary for newspaper articles to be authored in this way (many articles run without attribution), but the naming of the journalist makes for an assertion of authenticity, the journalist having 'been there' and so acting as the advocate of 'what happened'. Yet, equally this can be an assertion of *authority*, with the journalist claiming their status as a worthy commentator of events. In the case of the fall of the Wall, with reporting going on across a fragmented cityscape and amidst a mass of anonymous people, the journalist was both to become a participant and observer, thus providing a unique opportunity to communicate the 'dramatic reality' of the celebrations with real gravitas. *The Daily Mail*, for example, in its Saturday edition, claimed that its journalist *in situ*, 'for this historic 24 hours *became* an East Berliner to share their hopes and fears' (10/11, emphasis added). Despite the revelry of 'the people' clearly in

Evening Standard

LONDON, FRIDAY, 10 NOVEMBER, 1989

A GREAT DAY OR FREEDOM

Wire picture: A

...ands for East Germans climbing the Berlin Wall. Popping champagne corks, singing and dancing, 50,000 citizens of East Berlin flocked to ...st night after the GDR lifted all travel restrictions. Mrs Thatcher, declaring today "a great day for freedom", promptly offered British help ...ith the flood of emigrants.
Reports: Pages 2,3 and 5. Comment and Feature: Page 7

evidence, the *theme* of celebration was potentially more the expression of a community of journalists than the ordinary citizens around them (a point I shall return to below).

It is not only through the reporting of the news that a theme of celebration was to pervade. Indeed, it quickly permeated a much wider discourse, being represented in all areas of the media and popular culture, not least advertising. In less than two days of the occurrence of the event the beer manufacturer Heineken ran a humorous advertisement in *The Sun* newspaper. This showed a cartoon of the fall of the Wall, along with a play on the company's usual advertising slogan, with the caption reading: 'Not even Heineken can do this!' A day later, in *The Sunday Telegraph*, the manufacturer of the children's construction toy Lego illustrated (rather more elaborately) a similar scene. In this advertisement, smiling Lego figures pour out of a Lego constructed Brandenburg Gate, the caption reading: 'The Perfect Christmas Gift'. It is the reflection of public euphoria in this advertisement which no doubt allows a seemingly opportunistic marketing ploy to equally pass off as a message of goodwill and solidarity.[8] Advertisements of this kind can be said to pre-empt, or at least look forward to the capitalist transformation of the East, not only in material, economic terms, but also at a culturally symbolic level too.

It is important to note that the overall interpretation of the events changed rapidly, with the theme of celebration becoming intimately bound up with the so-called 'rush for reunification', the euphoria of the former providing the grounds for the latter. Hence, following the initial excitement on the night of the border opening, the main 'story' (and reporting framework) soon shifted emphasis. By the Saturday (i.e. in less than 48 hours) reports were orientated around questions of German unity, nationalism and reunification, largely in response to the pronouncements coming from West Germany. In turn, this had the effect of extending the interpretation of celebration. *The Guardian* on the Saturday ran the front-page headline: 'Kohl: "We Are One Nation"' (11/11). Kohl's pronouncement had been scripted very pointedly to resonate with the slogans of the protestors, who over the preceding months had been heard chanting, 'we are the people'. Kohl's phrase was soon adopted by "the people", with the slogan modified to 'we are ONE people'. The emphasis upon a notion of 'the people' is, of course, related to the fact that this was a news event all about ordinary citizens gaining legitimate access to the West. Inevitably, then, the press, as a whole, presented a story of the people's revolution and victory, perhaps best summed up by the headline in *Der Spiegel*, 'Das Volk Siegt' ['The People Win'] (13/11/89, vol. 43, no. 46). Yet, it is not necessarily the 'real' voice of 'the people' (if such a thing can be said to exist) that is able to come through, nor is it always clear exactly for who and for what reason this is in fact a victory at all.

The press and broadcast media certainly play an important role in helping us to situate ourselves in relation to events (especially those beyond the immediacy of our daily lives) and to make sense of broader historical and political concerns. However, this can often mean we are only exposed to a narrow gauge of interpretations. With the fall of the Berlin Wall it is clear, even looking beyond the immediate headlines, that the description of this event as it unfolded in the press (and on television) was premised upon a fairly homogeneous array of personal reaction and witness, international political commentary and historical contextualizing. The similarities in the coverage across all the British news media can be understood structurally as a result of what Pierre Bourdieu (1998: 71) has termed the 'journalistic field', which is subject to an ongoing 'trial by market, whether directly, through advertisers, or indirectly, through audience ratings'. He

The perfect Christmas gift.

argues this is a form of competition that breeds anxiety amongst the profession; a fear, for example, in missing a 'scoop', or running with the most important (or popular) issues. Overall, with such practical and professional constraints, combined with a culture of 'permanent surveillance' between rivals, the result is that 'rather than automatically generating originality and diversity, competition tends to favour uniformity' (Bourdieu 1998: 72).

A significant practical pressure for the British press in reporting the fall of the Wall was the very short period of time available to get the story printed. The initial announcement, given by Günter Schabowski in his now infamous press conference, was made a little before 7pm, whilst the first border crossing did not occur until around 9.30pm. This was just about the time the London newspapers would have been going to press, so giving editors very little time in which to re-write their front pages. And a particular difficulty was that only a limited range of pictures were available; in fact, a number of the papers used the exact same photograph (from a French news agency) of people on top of the Wall. It also meant, especially for the broadsheets needing to fill more space, greater reliance upon library pictures of the Wall (*The Independent* used, for example, an old image of the Wall heavily under guard) and also various iconic archival material relating to the Cold War in general. Both *The Independent* and *The Times*, for instance, used the same picture of President Kennedy looking over the Wall from a viewing platform.

It was not only pictures of the past that dominated, even whole passages from historic speeches were included in the papers. *The Independent*, for example, printed a number of paragraphs from famous speeches by the Russian leader Nikita Khrushchev (from 1961) and President Kennedy (from 1963). Thus, despite the fall of the Wall being a novel event which took every one by surprise, it was actually former, well-worn narratives and motifs of old that framed much of the reporting. So, whilst on one level the event was contextualized by the ongoing changes in Eastern Europe, it was also frequently referenced back to post-war history. In fact, in a bid perhaps to maintain maximum dramatic effect (and/or to stick to what is already familiar), rather than having opened up a new discourse, almost the opposite is evident: 'a return to Cold War rhetoric in public discourse at the very moment that the Cold War ostensibly ended' (Sieg 1993: 37). In this respect alone the reporting can be said to have been 'overdetermined...making a disordered world orderly and merging the chaotic events of history into a meaningful pattern of experience' (Cormack 1992: 49).[9] Hence, as with the 'story' I told at the beginning of this chapter, the press generally resorted to presenting the fall of the Wall in combination with remembering its very beginnings in 1961 when it was first built, or even in some cases earlier with Winston Churchill's 'Iron Curtain' speech of 1946.

It soon becomes clear there is something paradoxical about the news reporting of the fall of the Wall. Despite this fixity of the Cold War narrative as an interpretative framework, there is equally the explicit reporting of a widespread sense of surprise and of a rupture more associated with revolution. Potentially, this undermines the value of an adequate historical context from within which to report on events. We are supposedly exposed to a watershed moment, as we move into uncharted waters of dissolved ideological tension. *The Times*, for example, speaks of a 'rapid and bewildering sequence of events', which are 'no longer part of any disciplined or coherent design' (10/11/89 p. 17). And *The Independent* comments: 'As East German borders open, the world ponders a future in which the Wall has lost its meaning' (10/11/89 p. 8). Nevertheless – and again mainly as a result of the aforementioned 'habits' of news discourse – this sense of bewilderment is not long left open to interpretation. How could it be, for what then would fill the unforgiving column inches of a newspaper layout? Into the void enters the dominant views and opinions based largely on Cold War rhetoric as noted above. It is as if – just as the openness and uniqueness of *perestroika* was never really able to fulfil its full radical potential – we are unable to think about 'lost meaning' or that which sits beyond 'any disciplined or coherent design'.

The inevitability of 'papering' over this bewilderment and loss is due in part to the particular way in which 'ordinary' Berliners' own accounts of the event – despite being vital to the news story – must always remain anonymous to us (even where names are given they are in effect meaningless to the reader/viewer of the news, who will never be in a position to know who they are); this, of course, in contrast with the authoritative statements and opinions attributable to the well-known faces of the politicians, critics and experts of the day. So, whilst the numerous statements made by Berliners themselves do pepper the reports of the fall of the Wall (both with television and print news formats), seeming to offer important detail and a variety of perspectives, these quotations are nearly always anonymous and certainly ephemeral, even inconsequential. There are the ubiquitous eye-witness accounts, 'a student said that...' and 'a middle-aged woman told of her...' or – as in one specific example – 'A group of East German workers still in their blue overalls...' (*The Guardian*, 11.11.89, p. 1). Even a border guard can be reduced to a nobody, with one described, 'in his huge greatcoat', as having been suddenly 'transformed from a creature of totalitarian nightmare into an affable East German bloke' (*Daily Mail* 10.11.89, p. 1). What really compounds the celebratory mood is that the comments from these people on the streets are all limited to expressions of emotion and/or immediate intention. The following are typical:

> "I'm just going over to have a look," one excited man said. Another added: "My wife is at home crying her eyes out because she has to look after the kids and can't come".
>
> (*The Guardian*, 10.11.89, p. 1)

> "I cannot BELIEVE this!" sobs Wiebke. "Here I am, Wiebke Reed, driving freely across Checkpoint Charlie. All our lives we have dreamed of this and suddenly now, at last, it is happening. Next month maybe we will just be another nice, boring little democracy, but today I think we are the most extraordinary country in the world."
>
> (*Daily Mail*, 11.11.89, p. 3)

The sense of emotion is such that many of those speaking to reporters are all but speechless, offering only faltering and banal comments, such as 'I can't describe it...' or, 'Wonderful! Wonderful, I can't say anything' (Channel Four News, 10.11.89, 7pm). As is always the dilemma with using 'vox pop' reports, a clutch of quotations from people, who in the middle of a slightly unbelievable situation, can all too easily be taken as representative of the wider population. Overall, like the anonymity of movie extras, the 'people' – 'We the People' in this story – give the scene its undoubted verisimilitude, precisely because in many respects they are never really questioned properly, or given a chance for their voices to be heard (above the exclamations). Instead, remaining more effectively in our peripheral vision, they are part of the fabric upholding the enormity and drama of the scenes of a burgeoning history – just as, for example, the thousands of extras in Eisenstein's films fashion the breathtaking scale of his filmed events. The difference, of course, is that, unlike Eisenstein's epic panoramas which work to maintain a specific ideological message, the scenes of the fall of the Berlin Wall *unravel* ideological contest, for they portray the brand new beginning of an alleged historic end: the end of history as we know it, the end of ideological struggle itself. Fixing doggedly to the Cold War paradigm certainly does not make us, in Chomsky's (1997: 1) words, 'well-situated to comprehend what lies ahead'. Yet, with seemingly little room for the 'world' to genuinely consider (as *The Independent* put it) 'a future in which the Wall has lost its meaning', all that does make sense are the endless scenes of celebration, for and in themselves – and that is all we really have left to go on with...

An End of History?

Francis Fukuyama's (1989) thesis was originally published in article form as 'The End of History?', in the neo-conservative journal the *National Interest* in the summer of 1989. Its argument can be thought to resonate with former end of ideology debates of the late 1950s (Waxman 1968), as well as the more general intellectual notion of *posthistoire* (Niethammer 1992).[10] However, the 'end of history' that Fukuyama announces is not pitched a return to an 'end of ideology' as a convergence between capitalism and socialism as suggested by the earlier debates, but instead as the 'unabashed victory of economic and political liberalism' (Fukuyama 1989: 3). Thus, crucially, where previous debates had generally held to a pessimistic outlook of an overly bureaucratic and compartmentalized society (as espoused by the likes of Marx, Weber, Marcuse etc.) and concurrently demonstrated a longing for a 'new ideology' (Waxman 1968: 7) or utopian ideology capable of changing society (Mannheim 1968), the 'end of history' heralded by Fukuyama and his supporters is supposedly the 'Good News' of ideological *resolution*. In this respect, it marks an ending not in terms of loss, but in terms of a goal achieved; 'the end point of mankind's ideological evolution and the universalization of Western liberal democracy as the final form of human government' (Fukuyama 1989: 4).

With its explicit advocacy of (American-inspired) liberal democracy and free market economy, it is not difficult to see why Fukuyama's essay won favour with its immediate readership of the (Right of centre) *National Interest* (as well as presumably members of the State Department in which Fukuyama had worked). What is surprising, however, is that this 'end of history' thesis duly 'sped around the media of the globe' (Anderson 1992: 281), arguably becoming the most *timely* interpretation of the collapse of communism. So, whilst the article had actually gone to press prior to proceedings leading to the demise of the GDR, it had clearly been alert to the events taking place across the Eastern bloc over that year, making an association with the fall of the Berlin Wall straightforward. In fact, the celebratory mood following the opening of the Wall and the international enthusiasm for a new era is precisely what the thesis allows for in its predication of the 'end of history'. Rather than simply suggest American ideals (or even more broadly liberal democratic principles) are 'winning' the battle of ideologies, Fukuyama's claim is that the unravelling of the Cold War (evidenced by the implosion of communism and the disarray of the Soviet Union) reflects a process of a much higher order: an *ideal* resolution of ideology. It is perhaps convenient that Fukuyama finds himself firmly on the side of the victors in this resolution of History, but nonetheless the 'enlightenment' achieved is meant to be understood as having come *through* the empiricism of historical events, not as a result of them.

Fukuyama, very openly, takes his bearings from a Hegelian idealist conception of history. This is a notion of history as a linear, teleological progression or evolution, with the belief that history, though never repeating itself, holds meaning and significance, allowing in the 'realm of ideas or consciousness' for an end point (Fukuyama 1989: 4).[11] Thus, Fukuyama considers history to culminate 'in an absolute moment – a moment in which a final, rational form of society and state become victorious' (Fukuyama 1989: 4). And, since he argues this occurs 'primarily' in the realm of ideas or consciousness, it does not necessarily need to map onto the real or material world (at least not straight away). Following this formulation, then, the notion of an end of history is not meant by Fukuyama as an end to our *experience* of history – that is, the end of a passing of time with its 'occurrence of events' (though this did not stop many critics from jumping to such conclusions[12]). Thus, the proper argument for the 'end of history' is that there are now certain *structural* limits (of ideology) within which events will unfold. Understood this way, Fukuyama's reading of history seemingly offers a very credible (if unsettling) critique of the period that sees the wholesale demise of communist rule across Eastern Europe. The significance of this demise, as I will discuss further in chapter four, is that it actually describes a scenario in which it is very difficult for any adequate alternative political/critical response to be made.

Concurrent with the theme of celebration previously outlined, the end of history thesis was widely disseminated, attracting serious academic attention as well as more playful popular commentary. In part it is perhaps due to the eloquent and somewhat evangelical nature of Fukuyama's rhetoric that the notion of an 'end of history' quickly became so well known, though equally, there are many who mis-read its argument, as well as others who did not even (fully) read it, yet felt familiar enough with its title to enter into debate. Like a runaway brand label the 'end of history' would appear to speak for itself, indeed only of *itself*, coming before anything else can be said, so again forming all too neatly the sort of 'conventional picture' that Chomsky warns against. Of course, the end of history should not be thought synonymous with the fall of the Wall, but it is worth noting the importance of their association. As Perry Anderson (1992) remarks, regardless of the broader global trends of liberal economics that Fukuyama incorporates in making his argument, the prescient force behind his thesis is undoubtedly the collapse of the Soviet Union and 'its *glacis* in Eastern Europe' (Anderson 1992: 351) – all of which is symbolized by the removal of the Berlin Wall. Further to this, it can be stressed that in the context of the closing stages of the Cold War, it is the 'mood' for an end of history – the end of an evolution of mankind's ideological development – that becomes twinned with the fall of the Berlin Wall; the latter being an event which 'releases' the realization of an end point to a global spectatorship. Overall, the result is that both these phrases – the fall of the Berlin Wall and the end of history – are frequently used as shorthand for a description of 'our times', flexible enough to be used in a wide variety of contexts, across professions and regardless of political affiliations.

In chapter one, I referred to Rageh Omaar's report of the toppling of Saddam Hussein's statue as one example of the kind of editorial use yielded from the 'fall of the Berlin Wall' (and its inferred 'end of history' or ideological resolution). In this case the images of the fall of the Wall helped anchor the meaning of the event in Iraq as a significant, revolutionary achievement for 'the people' of Iraq. Here I offer a few more examples to help illustrate the ease with which this trope of *the fall of the Berlin Wall as putting end to history* has been employed. These examples are not necessarily the most important ones, but they are revealing, if only because (as is the case with at least one example here) the use of the 'fall of the Berlin Wall' can seem misplaced or surprising. My first example is the subject of a section in Noam Chomsky's *World Orders, Old and New* (1997), which draws attention to journalistic usage. Under the title 'The Berlin Wall falls again' (1997: 243–257), Chomsky examines the reporting of the ups and downs of the negotiations between Israel and the PLO. When the Oslo Agreement is made public, the *New York Times* reported the 'historic deal' as 'the 'Middle East equivalent of the fall of the Berlin Wall' (cited in Chomsky 1997: 248). As Chomsky suggests, it is 'a reasonable metaphor, given that the "historical deal" represents Palestinian capitulation' (248). But, this is again an example of the sense of resolution of a situation, indeed a sense of an end of an era, that prompts the reporter to use this trope. Thus, as Chomsky points out, it is used in an overly simplistic way to represent the 'triumph of realism over fanaticism and political courage over political cowardice' (cited in Chomsky 1997: 248).

Another quite different example (in this case taken from academic discourse) can be found from reading Esther Leslie's observation of a consensus forming in the early 1990s over the purported 'failures' of Walter Benjamin. Benjamin is perhaps one of the more unlikely names to be linked to the fall of the Berlin Wall, if only because of his very different historical context. However, when his status as a thinker on the Left is thrown into doubt at a conference held to mark his hundredth birthday (in July 1992), Leslie is prompted to remark: 'An anti-Benjamin crackdown follows on from the fall of the Berlin Wall and the self-cleansing in parts of the academy following the slow, then sudden death of Stalinism or "actually existing socialism"' (Leslie 2000: 225). It is a strange formulation. Given Benjamin's ambiguous relationship towards the political ideals of socialism (let alone any 'actually existing' form), it is not clear why this link should be made in the first place. It is also surprising to find a cultural theorist such as Leslie drawn into describing the events of 1989 in such a one-dimensional manner; especially given the fact that her book itself, being an exposition of Benjamin's philosophy, seeks to illuminate the importance of his complex and layered approach to cultural criticism. What appears to happen here is that Leslie turns her critical attention away from the complexity of the events leading to the fall of the Wall in order to dramatize a momentary shift in academic opinions. It is, in other words, simply a narrative device that requires saying what would not otherwise normally be thought credible, or at least not scholarly.

My third example is again an instance of the Wall being used as a form of shorthand, and in this case includes a direct reference to Fukuyama. In this case, it is an account of what the authors refer to as the 'present situation', prefacing a series of conference debates regarding the fate of Marxism in the face of a global collapse of communism.[13] The opening remarks in the published volume of conference papers (and repeated in the preface to Derrida's *Specters of Marx* (1994), which formed the keynote address) reads as follows:

In the wake of the orgy of self-congratulations which followed the 1989 crumbling of the Berlin Wall, the subsequent dissolution of the Soviet Union, and a series of confrontations perhaps forever to be captured best in Tiananmen Square in the image of a single individual blocking the path of an onrushing military tank, a wave of optimism engulfed the Western democratic States. This contagious optimism was best exemplified by the confidence and popularity of Francis Fukuyama's claim that the end of history was at hand, that the future – if that word could still be said to have the same meaning – was to become the global triumph of free market economies.

(Magnus and Cullenberg 1995: vii)

The conference for which these preliminary words were written was convened to explore possibilities of critique in the wake of events in 1989. It is then disappointing, especially given the assembled delegates – many of whom would place their work within a deconstructive post-structuralist and postcolonial framework – that such a crude account of history (and of Fukuyama's thesis) is so blithely drawn. There was no 'crumbling' of the Wall, and equally, in Tiananmen Square, no 'onrushing' tank (in fact, in 'reality' – or at least when viewing the video footage – the process in both cases is far slower and more ambiguous). But of course, as with the previous two examples, this is not what really concerns the authors when employing its imagery. Instead, they wish to press on (regardless) to questions which must follow from the event and the 'time' of a new era it ushers in. My objection is that in establishing this account of the fall of the Wall/end of history as the debate's *starting* point seems only to underscore the fact that what is scrutinised is always what must come *after* the Wall – forcing us, as it were, to accept our 'post-Wall' condition. Indeed, the problem put in place by the trope of the 'fall of the Berlin Wall' (with its implied sense of celebration and 'end of history') is that we are always beginning with the end – we become hostage to a perpetual post-Wall paradigm, within which we find ourselves 'living without an alternative' (Bauman 1992). Clearly the impact of Fukayama's 'end of history' can not simply be explained by the eloquence of his writing or its polemic, nor indeed its timeliness. In fact, it is probably better to acknowledge that it need not necessarily be conscious reference to Fukuyama's account that marks the ubiquity of its problematic. To take its idealist principle, Fukuyama's call for the end of history can be thought to resonate with a much deeper, embedded significance of the Wall and as associated with a more deeply inscribed sense of a coming victory for western liberalism and humanitarian 'freedoms' – as part of which the 'theme of celebration' can be thought to have been simply waiting in the wings (like one huge surprise party!). To understand more about how this coming victory manifests itself, it is pertinent to look into the history of the Wall and the city of Berlin itself in a little more detail.

A Berlin Imaginary

Due to its very unique location – an 'island' of the West landlocked by the communist East – Berlin was where the ideological stand-off of the Cold War was most *visibly* staged; exhibiting as it did a fierce ideological divide between western capitalism on one side and communist totalitarianism on the other. In particular, the Berlin Wall was the most significant site/sight of this ideological tension, making its final demise the event which really galvanized the interpretation of an 'end of history'. Yet, equally, it is evident that an end of history (and its celebration) is *pre-figured* in a series of prevailing myths and configurations of western moral dominance. In each case these configurations present a sense of the West's prior 'ownership' of the Wall, as well as an inscribed inevitability of it coming down. The latter is located both in terms of political rhetoric and more literally with respect to the physical structure of the Wall itself. Throughout its history, Berlin has always been a restless site of political, social and cultural transformation. In the post-war period, with its future determined by the international community, the city was inevitably brought under immense pressure and scrutiny. Like a pressure cooker at the heart of the Cold War theatre, with all eyes trained upon it, Berlin became a world stage for 'picturing' ideologies. Indeed, it is a city not only steeped in ideological archaeology (Ladd 1997; Balfour 1990, 1995), but also arguably a place ripe for fashioning new imagery (Manghani 2003c; Ward 2004).

The dramatic (and traumatic) changing fortunes of the city, which over the twentieth century played host to five distinct political regimes,[14] have undeniably given rise to a panoply of myths, symbols and images. In Weimar Germany of the 1920s and 1930s, for example, Berlin's public space 'was dominated by a discourse of slogans and symbols, and images, artefacts of an incessant propaganda activity', a legacy that in the city's 750th anniversary exhibition was given the heading 'Kampf der Symbole' (Ward 1996: 14–15). What emerges out of this volatile period is the amply documented aestheticization of politics associated with the Nazi regime, which employed stark iconography and monumental architectural projects to make bold national and cultural statements. The heinous nature of this regime subsequently has left a legacy of in/visible horror and trauma (Zelizer 2001). Following this period (and including, of course, the massive upheaval resulting from the Second World War), the Cold War duel between East and West Berlin is as much played out in visual terms, as it is in political discourse and rhetoric. Thus, today this historically layered and rich visual culture is what really *remains* of Berlin's past, for as the 'pieces' of its history continue to circulate (whether as architectural remnants or as elements of a collective memory) there is a perpetual process of renewal and reflection, often giving shape to new images and possibilities.[15] Perhaps, then, not so dissimilar to the 'cut and paste' of contemporary digital culture, which enables various elements to be easily combined, manipulated or disposed of, there remains available, what I would term a *Berlin Imaginary*, serving up all manner of concerns whether of past or future, East or West, local or global.

By this 'imaginary' I mean to invoke something of Lacan's (1977: 1–7) meaning of the term, which from his essay on the mirror stage we know relates to his notion of a decentred subject (to suggest a sense of loss or misrecognition in identity formation). The process that begins with the mirror stage is that we imagine on the basis of an external image of ourselves (which we then internalize) that we are unified in our body and as subject. Yet, this imaginary identity is a fiction we construct for ourselves from images outside of ourselves. We live by an *otherness* in order to uphold a sense of our self as unified; it is a fiction we come to live by. In raising the idea of a *Berlin Imaginary*, I am hardly wishing to describe some straightforward, benign force of meaning-making; although, I am not suggesting a wilful, malevolent force either. Instead, it is meant to describe a complex, accumulative process whereby an internalized political and cultural discourse of East/West relations develops as the result of an external exchange of images and myths. The process is richly fuelled by the symbolic and real division of Berlin, leading to a *spectacle* of Cold War Berlin, which both regulates and plies (as well as multiplies) the clash of ideologies. This is the fiction of the *Berlin Imaginary* that comes to be believed in, and lived by, even to the point that when the Wall falls, the same fiction remains a dominant force in relaying the new future(s) of Berlin and Germany as a whole.

Perhaps the most prominent (and long-standing) political metaphor of the Cold War period is the imaginary, though nonetheless imposing dividing line of the 'Iron Curtain'. This curious

imagery quickly became synonymous with ideological conflict following Winston Churchill's bleak, but memorable assessment of world affairs (of 1946), in which he proclaimed: 'From Stettin on the Baltic to Trieste on the Adriatic, an iron curtain has descended over the continent' (cited in Grant 1998: 14). Whilst he was not the first to use the phrase, it was on this occasion that it rang out as an overt *public* statement articulating what many were thinking only in private; his choice of metaphor capturing the imagination (and anxiety) of many in the West.[16] The 'descent' Churchill warned of was that of the territorial advance of communist totalitarianism, which by late 1947 reached as far as Hungary, Romania and Bulgaria; and by early 1948 into the former Czechoslovakia. Thus, the metaphor did soon develop a physical reality, with a 'curtain' of barbed wire, minefields and watchtowers running along the borders of these countries, along with the heavily fortified borderline that ran the whole of the 900 miles between East and West Germany. The Berlin Wall, of course, was not built until August 1961 – over a decade later. Unsurprisingly, however, this particular fortification, with its high 'visibility' as a globally recognized 'monument' of formidable design, soon became known as *the* primary site (indeed synonym) of the Iron Curtain.

Taken literally, an iron curtain would obviously be imposing, immovable and certainly impregnable (as was to be the case with the Berlin Wall). Thus, Churchill's description of an iron curtain having 'descended' over Europe immediately suggests an impasse, a closing off of two sides and with it a withdrawal from any further collaboration or negotiation. Yet it is not necessarily an image of passivity (or of a stand-off). Rather, like a safety curtain that comes down at the theatre, Churchill himself brings this curtain down (with the force of his own rhetoric) as a shield to prevent impending disaster, or at least to help define the 'enemy abroad'. As a figure of speech, which initially does not refer to a 'real' topographic division, but instead designates an imaginary one, Churchill's use of the phrase can be taken as much a threat as it is an image of one. And whilst the reality of the situation will always be more complicated than any such polarized picture suggests, in the Berlin imaginary, this image was (and remains mythologically) a deeply engrained, foreboding shadow. It was a regulatory image, keeping present the sense of threat and maintaining the need for counter-threat. Furthermore, it was a threat guarded and reared by the Wall itself (as the visual incarnation of the Iron Curtain), which equally meant it was only to be undone by the Wall itself. In other words, with the fate of the 'Iron Curtain' tied to the fate of the Wall, it is of little surprise that when the Wall was reported to have 'fallen', down with it came the Iron Curtain too.

Another important image, or mythology of Berlin during the Cold War, which again comes prior to the building of the Wall (but which has a direct impact on the perceived necessity for it), is the Berlin Blockade of 1948. This episode, as the historian Alexandra Richie notes, 'marked a profound shift in virtually every aspect of the post-war world' (1998: 673). It was a crisis prompting the absolute divide between East and West Berlin, again pushing the city into prominence as a potent symbol of the Cold War. Throughout this period, the fact that Berlin was always situated many miles east of the 'Iron Curtain', with tightly controlled access routes to the West, meant the city was always a liability for the Western Allies. Aware of this vulnerability and in a bid to force the Western Allies to change economic policies in the region (or, indeed, more fundamentally to remove them entirely from the city), the Soviet Union forced a complete blockade. This dramatic act presented a severe threat to the inhabitants of West Berlin; for not only was their security in jeopardy, but even basic amenities were suddenly

removed. The response, and resolve of the Western powers proved, however, to be firm and united; 'We are going to stay, period' was President Truman's personal response to the situation, who perceived the stark ideological divide to have reached such proportions that a climb down would mean defeat not simply for Berlin, but for 'democracy' in general.[17] It is an episode which was to seal the fate of Berlin as a barometer of (world) democracy.

America's solution to the blockade (which had shut off road and rail access to the city) was the airlift of all vital supplies into Berlin. It was thought the operation would only need to last for a few weeks before something could be negotiated with the Soviets. It actually lasted almost a year (ending in May 1949), with the threat of hostilities remaining throughout. The success of this air campaign went far beyond anyone's expectations.[18] In fact, not only did it prevent a humanitarian disaster and economic collapse, but production in the city actually managed to grow. The result was to turn the blockade around from being a severe threat by the Soviets to a sweeping propaganda campaign and victory for the Western powers. In retrospect, what is most significant about the blockade is the *economic* victory of the Western powers, the legacy of which resonates with Fukuyama's belief of political freedom standing hand in hand with (or at least stemming from) economic freedom.[19]

The immediate after-effect of the blockade was ever more entrenched economic and political East-West division; though it was a whole decade before the city would finally split 'concretely' in two. There are generally two main reasons why the Berlin Wall was eventually built. The first (actually bringing about the need for a physical barrier) was the empirical fact that each year tens of thousands of East Germans were fleeing to the West via Berlin, made possible, of course, by the fact that Berlin was an unrestricted zone nestled in the Eastern bloc.[20] The second reason (lessening any official resistance to the Wall's creation) was the fear of nuclear warfare. The Western airlift operation had undeniably marked a point at which the Cold War threatened to turn 'hot'. In the years leading up to the building of the Wall, the city became known as the 'Flashpoint of the World', from where, at any time, it was feared war – nuclear war no less – would erupt. In this context the Wall's inception can be thought of as a 'stop valve', not simply in holding back those escaping to the West, but also holding back the unthinkable. Thus, it was never simply a wall securing the East, but, indeed, a wall keeping apart two 'hotly' contested sides.

The heightened significance of the Wall (along with the very uniqueness of its inhumanity), meant it quickly entered western political rhetoric, with several distinct phases in its use, as a political symbol. This process begins with the Wall as being 'a sign of the failure of the West', with many key political and diplomatic figures placing 'blame on the United States, the Federal Republic of Germany, and the NATO allies for their inactivity' (Bruner 1989: 321). For John F. Kennedy – then newly elected as US President – the building of the Wall was initially accepted as a necessary evil, alleviating the growing tensions which, as noted, might otherwise have escalated into the nightmare of nuclear confrontation. Nevertheless, it still remained something of a political embarrassment and most definitely a sensitive diplomatic issue between the Western powers and those actually living and working in West Berlin. However, the real *symbolic* weight of the Wall (for the West) only properly came to prominence following Kennedy's visit to Berlin in June 1963; a visit he had been persuaded to make in order specifically to offer a gesture of solidarity to West Berliners (who were effectively living under occupation, albeit a benign one) and to the Western allies more generally.

Prior to making his address, Kennedy was taken to the see the Wall and he climbed one of the viewing platforms to look out to the East (this incident making for the iconic image of the President, which, as mentioned previously, appeared in the press on the day after the fall of the Wall). It is not difficult to see how with the passage of time many might think it was from here that Kennedy actually gave his historic speech. In fact, his rousing address (presented before a crowd of a quarter of a million) was made some distance away from the Wall in a square (now bearing his name) in the heart of the Schönberg district. His remarks were brief, less than seven hundred words, yet his text became one of the most defining and in many respects prophetic statements of the Cold War. He drew a sharp distinction between the 'free world' and the 'communist world', with Berlin itself, placed right at the front line of the Cold War, praised for its resilience and fighting spirit. What was most significant about the speech was Kennedy's marriage of 'freedom' and 'Berlin'. The city thus became *the* site of solidarity, where divisions between Berlin, Germany, Europe and the world could be traced. Repeated throughout was the refrain 'let them come to Berlin', suggesting the 'world' come to the city to understand the significance of freedom and solidarity, but also prescribing a global affinity and identity with Berliners; Kennedy ending on the resounding (and much cited) note '*Ich bin ein Berliner*' – only the grammatical mistake (he should have said '*Ich bin Berliner*') giving away his differences with those of West Berlin itself. As one commentator suggests, 'the speech was reminiscent of John Donne's line: "No man is an island...", a most appropriate metaphor for West Berlin, an island-city surrounded by the German Democratic Republic' (Bruner 1989: 323): but which also encapsulated Kennedy's primary principle: 'Freedom is indivisible, and when one man is enslaved, all are not free' (cited in Issacs and Downing 1998: 183). From the blockade through to Kennedy's speech, Berlin had clearly arrived as the front-line 'trench' for the West – a strategic stronghold both territorially and ideologically. It was now a key symbol or beacon to freedom (its significance never really diminishing right up until the fall of the Wall).

In 1987 – just two years before the fall – President Reagan gave an address in Berlin, the sense of occasion certainly echoing Kennedy's speech. This time, however, there was not merely emphasis upon solidarity of the West, but equally a categorical challenge spelt out to the Soviet Union. Unlike Kennedy, Reagan did in actual fact stand before the Wall to deliver his speech, the Brandenburg Gate providing the dramatic visual backdrop. Speaking from a temporary platform erected in front of the Gate, Reagan delivered his famous challenge: 'If you seek peace, if you seek prosperity for the Soviet Union and Eastern Europe, if you seek liberalization...Mr. Gorbachev, tear down this wall' (cited in Isaacs and Downing 1998: 367). The remark was consistent with the fact that above all else the Wall functioned for Reagan 'as a sign of the spiritual victory of the West' (Bruner 1989: 325). In closing his address, Reagan made a direct comparison between the spiritual values of East and West, remarking to the audience of West Berliners, 'what keeps you in Berlin is love – love both profound and abiding', whilst over in the East, he suggested, '[t]he totalitarian world produces backwardness because it does such violence to the spirit, thwarting the human impulse to create, to enjoy, to worship' (cited in Bruner 1989: 325). Then, in turning to the Wall itself (and with reference to the graffiti upon it) he concluded: 'This Wall will fall. Beliefs become reality...this wall will fall. For it cannot withstand faith. It cannot withstand truth. It cannot withstand freedom'.

There is perhaps an inconsistency of sorts between appealing to the Soviet leader to 'tear down' the Wall *and* pronouncing that the Wall will *fall* to freedom. Yet, '[t]he inconsistency is

surmounted by the implicit argument that even the Soviets [were] coming to realise the necessity of freedom' (Bruner 1989: 325). Nevertheless, in taking such a perspective, it forces *glasnost* to be interpreted not as a source of pride, but a recognition on behalf of the Soviets of both 'a spiritual truth and an admission of failure' (Bruner 1989: 325).[21] Later, this same 'heroic' representation of the West was neatly packaged by an 'official' video of German reunification, *Ode to Joy and Freedom: the Fall of the Wall*. The video inter-cuts Kennedy's 'Ich bin ein Berliner' speech of 1961 with Reagan's 1988 challenge to Gorbachev 'in an MTV-style montage sporting a zappy rap-rhythm' which, strategically placed towards the end of the documentary, works to reaffirm 'Germany's place within Western alliances, [and] downplays the FRG's agency in reunification, and diverts attention from its vested interest in it' (Sieg 1993: 38). What I have tried to describe here as a *Berlin Imaginary* is not meant as a 'mechanism' for perpetuating mythologies of a divided Berlin as if at the behest of a specific controlling elite. Instead it refers to a much more pervasive, 'collective unconscious' that out of a whole range of historical artefacts, images and events, develops for itself a regulatory fiction of ideological divisions. As a (misrecognized) unified body of social knowledge this then informs at a deep level the responses to the fall of the Berlin Wall as I described with the 'theme of celebration' and narrative of an 'end of history'. Further to this, however, the pre-figuring of this western bias and 'ownership' can even be found to exist in the very physicality of the Wall itself. To go a little 'deeper' still, then, we might usefully turn to what the Wall itself can tell us, to the pieces of the Wall and the Wall in pieces.

The Writings on the Wall (or Inscriptions of Prior Ownership)

Regardless of however much rhetoric was hurled at the Wall, its function of keeping those in the East out of the West was extremely effective,[22] to the point that both sides of the city gradually developed their own pace and cultural life. Nevertheless, certain 'products' of modern living were always able to pass freely over the Wall, including both air pollution (mostly coming from the East) and broadcast signals (from the West). The latter evince a pre- (if only partial) unification of both East and West Germany long before the Wall ever came down. Indeed, as discussed in more detail in chapter one, many commentators suggest that television played a vital role in helping to bring about a new East German consciousness.

Western cultural values permeated the Wall in other ways too. Over shorter distances the amplified sound of rock concerts being performed near the Reichstag meant that East German music fans could indulge, for free, in the latest sounds of American and British rock music; regularly East German youths gathered behind the Wall 'to hear the stars they were unable to see' (Ladd 1997: 19). And even static architectural structures were able to make an impact. In the West, the dramatic *Kulturforum* took shape in the early 1960s. Its flamboyant design could be seen in the East since it was situated in the 'periphery' of the city centre, close to the Wall at Potsdamer Platz. Another significant structure was an electric neon display board erected by the Springer Press providing rolling news from the West over the Wall into the East. Thus, the presence of the West in the East could never be fully eradicated, whilst the East (due largely to its isolationist principles) had much less impact on the West. If anything, the East was only really of interest to those in the West as an *object* of study. Federal government sponsorship, for example, encouraged people to visit Berlin and learn about the division, and school groups were required to study the Wall as part of the curriculum (Feversham and Schmidt 1999: 120).[23]

From on top of the various viewing platforms constructed along the Wall, it was possible to look over and 'down' upon the East, almost as if it were, in the unfortunate words of one visiting scholar, the 'world's largest zoo' (Gleye 1991). In addition, westerners were able to walk through the Wall and spend a day in East Berlin, able to capture a glimpse of the structure from its 'other' side. Arguably, then, whilst there are undoubtedly *other* perspectives to be found, the inevitability of western values winning over those of the East was prefigured in the unequal relation between the two sides.

However, it was equally the Wall *itself*, in bare material terms, which helped determine political perspectives upon it. This is epitomized by the fact that the pieces of the Wall chipped away by the midnight revellers and the professional 'wall-peckers' quickly become commodity items. Indeed, these chunks of the Wall fetched large sums of money, and complete sections quickly became prestigious monuments.[24] Pieces could be bought from street traders (it was even possible to rent a hammer to get a piece directly from the Wall), and 'other entrepreneurs, more ambitious and better capitalised, filled crates and trucks with this formerly East German State property, ready to supply genuine Wall fragments to American department stores in time for the Christmas shopping season' (Ladd 1997: 8-9). In the initial period the level of trade in Wall pieces was extremely high. The Wall was, of course, in demand precisely because it was disappearing. All of a sudden, these fragments gained a special aura, 'they were treated as holy relics that bespoke our deliverance from the Cold War' (Ladd 1997: 8). All in all, the Wall, the symbolic dividing line between communism and capitalism, came down firmly on one side as a capitalist commodity – 'a thing which transcends sensuousness' (Marx 1990: 163). And, in fact, this (commodity) fetishism can be seen to have always been present in the Wall when it stood, with its graffiti-covered façade acting as a kind of mirror reflecting the West back to itself.

In pure material terms the fragments having been sold over a decade and more must now far outweigh the original mass of the Wall when it had actually been standing. The Berlin Wall was a crude architectural construct, made up of cheap and poor quality materials. Yet, what really made this sub-standard building matter so identifiable and collectable were the layers of bright spray paint upon it, in other words the graffiti which had adorned the Western face of the Wall. It is pertinent to note, then, what makes the Wall so commercial and relevant to people is directly related to that which had been imposed upon it by the West itself. The graffiti had been the West's signature on the Wall, the first writings on the Wall, laying claim to a communal monument. This 'writing' was a vital ingredient in making the Wall *visible*, making sure it was never possible to ignore it or disown it. Yet, a problem which arises from this condition, indeed from the very nature of graffiti in itself, is that despite much of it having underscored official denunciation of the Wall's existence, there was equally a blurring (and internalizing) of messages, which, as I want to suggest here, again contributes to a one-sided view of events as befits Fukuyama's 'end of history' thesis and the general 'theme of celebration'.

It is often forgotten that the Wall stood solely on GDR territory, thus, technically, it was possible for border guards to police any unlawful writing on it. However, by the 1980s 'the omnipresence of graffiti and Wall art rendered such attempts futile', and besides it hardly seemed necessary since little of the work was actually in protest of the Wall itself or even the GDR (Feversham and Schmidt 1999: 154). In fact, in addition to spray-canned slogans of dissent and dissatisfaction, the Wall was filled with fantastic murals, with political messages often superseded by a

preoccupation with art itself.[25] Nevertheless, some of this 'art' continued to call attention to the injustice of the Wall and, rather than being considered a deviant social activity, the graffiti grew in credibility. After the fall of the Wall, the former mayor of West Berlin, Walter Momper, lamented its inevitable disappearance, remarking: 'We have no regrets for the Wall but we will miss Wall Art...It is important for the Wall to be remembered for being a concrete proof of political failure as well as for the way people got used to it and integrated it into everyday life by painting it. Art challenged concrete and art won' (cited in Mayer 1996: 227).

At its height the graffiti quickly spread along the vast expanse of the Wall, giving rise to all manner of images to jostle with the facing cityscape. Motifs included, for example, jumping figures, ladders, holes and even zips;[26] many of the most well-known sections employed *trompe l'oeil* effects to depict actual openings in the Wall. Sometimes these showed idyllic scenes beyond, other times only a mundane reality of the other side of the city. It goes without saying, the graffiti was never actually able to connect with those in the East. In this respect there was always something blank (besides the Wall's verso) about their message. Arguably, the graffiti actually 'assisted the border Wall's function as a screen which hid the GDR' since like a mirror the graffiti reflected back the western world, 'rendering the Wall invisible' (Feversham and Schmidt 1999: 154). It is a point echoed by Sigrid Mayer (1996: 215), who argues that 'the responses [of graffiti] made to the Wall by its Western addressees are reflected back from the Wall...the echo of the Western response to the Wall's own message'. The overall result was that the Wall (as art) became 'less ugly, less obscene, less criminal', and significantly almost solely a representation of the West, rather than of the plight of the East. Thus, this 'kaleidoscopic Western side of the Wall became either a showcase of Western freedom or embarrassing evidence of Western decadence' (Ladd 1997: 27) – the same 'freedom', of course, that underpins the 'celebration' of the 'Great Day for Freedom' marked by the demise of the Wall.

The dominant language of the verbal graffiti on the Wall was English, arguably denoting 'western directedness'; or, in other words, that the Wall writings were 'not so much an expression by Germans against a Wall built by Germans as [...] an answer by the people of the West to the concrete "stone-walling" of the East' (Mayer 1996: 218). In this sense, the Wall can be thought of as a 'message board' for the West, an internationalization fitting of John F. Kennedy's view of Berlin as a capital city of the 'free' and the 'democratic' West. So, for example, alongside elaborate works of 'art' covering the Wall there were also the crudely daubed names of visitors and tourists to the site, all wishing to leave their mark, making up a diverse community and dialogue. Wall graffiti was duly a form of art for and of 'the people', its presence epitomizing mass ownership of the Wall. Yet what kind of dialogue and community was this? Like all graffiti, the Wall art was a constantly updating form of expression. Ostensibly, its multiple layers encapsulated a diverse history of the times, harbouring, as it were, 'the vox populi in visual form' (Waldenburg 1990: 13). Potentially, this is what is powerful about graffiti; it ignores the 'borders between producers and recipients' (Mayer 1996: 218). What this means is that graffiti effectively eludes reproduction; it only really makes sense in its entirety, as an accumulation. The graffiti on the Wall is only approachable through that which binds it together, in other words by means of interacting with the Wall itself: '[w]e can not postulate a systematic structure unless the Wall itself is included somehow in the message', which in turn, of course, means that 'the only term in this system whose change would permanently change all the others

is the Wall' (Mayer 1996: 218). In this way, the Wall might be thought of as the conduit for a universal 'dialogue'.

Yet, of course, taken at face value – which by default it has to be – this conglomeration of markings was hardly likely to bear any immediate comprehension. As Iain Sinclair (2003: 1–2) eloquently argues, the 'public autograph' of graffiti is as much 'an announcement of nothingness, abdication, the swift erasure of the envelope of identity'. This, he goes on to describe, is like 'Salvador Dali in his twilight years putting his mark on hundreds of blank sheets of paper, authenticating chaos'. The continual layering of names, slogans and art upon the Berlin Wall (like its broken pieces traded in the tourist shops) is arguably no different then to the hundreds of Dali 'originals' which flooded the market in his late career. All worthless, yet priceless.

The epitome of the 'new' currency of post-Wall graffiti is the *East Side Gallery*. Along Mühlenstrasse, well *inside* the boundary of former East Berlin, there is a stretch of wall remaining of the former GDR's 'civic' inner wall which would have stood some way back from the Berlin Wall itself. In the early 90s this section was to host a new gallery of murals, some of which were copies of graffiti art previously seen on the real Berlin Wall before its demise. Over 100 artists from around the world contributed to 106 paintings running along the entire wall next to the busy dual-carriage of Mühlenstrasse. In 1993 this open-air 'gallery' gained formal recognition, its preservation officially decreed, which, in turn, prompted some confusion, for word soon spread that this was a key site to experience the *historic* Wall; despite the fact that there was very little (if anything) at this site that was authentic. The fact that Wall graffiti would never have appeared in the East only highlights this is a phenomenon imported from the West. This fact, however, has certainly not deterred the tourists from dodging the traffic to take photographs of the painted wall sections, nor from buying the postcards, T-shirts and other manufactured memorabilia at the battered old kiosk nearby (Ladd 1997: 35–36). Thus, even after the Wall has long gone, those same forces of consumerism that helped remove it, go to affect its substitute and memorial.

The question remaining is what – if anything – of the *real* East side of the Wall? In answering this, what is significant is generally what is missing; again, compounding the sense of a perceived 'takeover' of the Wall by the West. As already noted, on the actual East side of the Wall there was certainly no graffiti to speak of, chiefly because the Wall in the East was set well beyond a patrolled no-man's-land, which itself lay behind another more 'ordinary' urban wall. It was illegal for ordinary citizens in East Germany to photograph or document the Wall in any way, in fact even to think about the Wall was frowned upon; 'to evince even a passing interest in the border fortifications was regarded by the GDR authorities as being highly suspicious' (Feversham and Schmidt 1999: 120). Officially the Wall did not even exist, only a fortified 'anti-fascist protective rampart' for the people's own security.[27] Any representations of the Wall, or what lay beyond it in West Berlin, were simply removed; maps, for example, blanked out the very existence of the West. This 'Orwellian denial of reality', being 'symptomatic of attempts to normalise a bizarre situation through the suppression of any kind of comparison' (Feversham and Schmidt, 1999 120).

Looking at old photographs of the Wall (or on the East side, the absence of the Wall), comparison between the two sides of Berlin is hard to make out. In the West, the Wall was a raw, and in places vibrant, landmark zigzagging through an otherwise 'normal' cityscape. It is

only really in the West that its 'modern', brutal intervention is fully realized. Like an art installation, it stood as an object 'on view', always inciting a response (for even to ignore the Wall in the West was to respond to it, to choose to live with it). On the East side, however, the Wall was nowhere to be found, besides perhaps the odd forbidden glimpse. Instead, the Wall was really nothing more than a discrete change in the lie of the land, around which life went on as 'normal'. One illustrated city guide, published in the GDR in the 1960s, shows the usual bustle of people and cars associated with any normal capital city, despite close proximity to the Wall, its checkpoints and even the Brandenburg Gate (at this time a gateway to nowhere).

Not only was the existence of the Wall generally not discussed by the GDR authorities (referred to only as the 'Anti-Fascist Protective Rampart'), there was no mention of 'East Berlin' either. Instead, the city was referred to simply as 'Berlin', the capital of the GDR, while 'a remote and infrequently mentioned "Westberlin", appeared as a blank space on the GDR's city maps' (Ladd 1997: 28). Alan Balfour, from a close study of a specific plot of land in the centre of Berlin, offers a useful comparison of tourist maps from the mid-80s published by the two sides of the city. The map published by the East Berlin authorities leaves a large blank expanse beyond the East perimeter and unsurprisingly there is no specific 'Wall' marked out on the map. Instead a 'dotted line marks not the actual physical line of the Wall but the territory officially under Eastern control' (Balfour 1990: 184). The marking out of the West, according to this map, appears only as some large park beyond the city walls (just as it had been, in fact, in the seventeenth century). Interestingly, for those over in the West, the official West Berlin city map equally fails to acknowledge the Wall, albeit in a different way. In this case *both* sides of the city are depicted in equivalent detail, which is as much a fiction as the East German erasure of the West, since the map only records the buildings and layout as they had been *before* the Second World War (prior, that is, to the massive devastation brought about by aerial bombardment).

These cartographic descriptions/inscriptions of the two Berlins and the Wall (or lack of the Wall), taken together with the graffiti upon its Western side can again be thought of as primary writings on the Wall. Writing here means both literally forms of inscription and delineation, but also metaphorically a sign of a coming end that had *always* been foreseen or determined. It is as if the writing had always been *on the wall*, with all these markings drawing the same patterns of its ownership and/or denial. So, whilst the GDR categorically denied any official existence of the Wall they themselves had constructed (keeping it well out of sight and out of mind), the West equally erased what lay *behind* the Wall. The mirroring effect of the Wall graffiti set into motion another kind of blanking out of what lay beyond. And almost as if the official map of East Berlin were inversed, this blank reference to what lay in the East was later reinforced (or, indeed, realized) by the celebrations that took place with the demise of the Wall. Thus, whilst the fall of the Wall might be thought to have brought about (or at least forced) a renewed interest in the East, this too can be understood as the West looking back at itself. As Slavoj Žižek claims, what fascinates the western gaze is the '*re-invention of democracy*', so suggesting in Eastern Europe, 'the West looks for its own lost origins' (1990: 50). This 'gaze' enforces a particular regime of writing, seeing and interpreting from which emerges a predisposition or pattern of ownership over the Wall, the effect of which is to close down representation of East Germany and broader social debates for the future.

* * *

East Germans at the Brandenburg Gate, East Berlin, 1968.

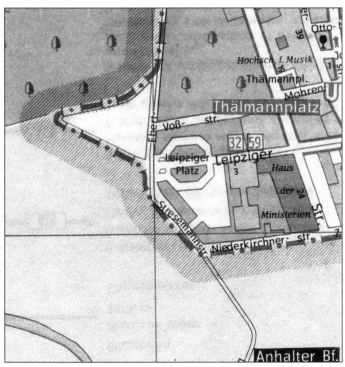

Official Tourist map of East Berlin, 1984.

Tourists at the Brandenburg Gate, West Berlin.

Official map of West Berlin, 1984.

The various accounts given here relating to the historical context of the Wall and the symbolic weighting that comes to bear within the *imaginary* of Berlin can only really be expected to have scratched at the surface of a much richer problematic. Hopefully, however, it is evident that when the Wall eventually (or inevitably) fell, it was an event for the West to 'explain' and savour. The Wall was really only ever an 'object' of interest (and concern) to the West – for at least West Berliners could physically interact with the Wall, indeed, they were the ones who could 'approach it, touch it and write, paint or spray graffiti on the increasingly canvass-like surface' (Feversham and Schmidt 1999: 120). In the East, it was instead a harsh administrative fact of life, a pathetic deceit, for either it was not meant to exist at all, or it was heralded as an instrument to protect 'the people'. Either way it was not approachable or, perhaps, even imaginable. Crucially, this one-sided nature of the Wall has meant that with its fall the Wall has seemingly given rise only to a dramatic (though, nonetheless, ubiquitous) sense of 'end', finale and political closure, an 'end' made particularly explicit by the timeliness of Fukuyama's thesis of an 'end of history'. In other words, with the removal of the Wall there is no prompt for two separate sides to face each other once again, but rather for the 'natural' rejoining of only one divided 'self'.

It was not only commentators on the Right who have been willing to adopt this frame of perspective, since the 'end of history' as a figure of thought runs across political persuasions and pervades journalism and scholarly enquiry alike. It is an end perpetually marking the beginning of the end – an ending which, as I discuss in the next chapter, would seem only to repeat again and again. Like a bookend, the 'fall of the Wall' becomes a hidden prop for all that comes to stand after it. 'The fall of the Berlin Wall', 'the collapse of communism', 'the cutting of the Iron Curtain' are each ways of poetically spiriting away the past, each a turn of phrase which blots out the complexity of what led to the events and dilemmas that were to come afterwards; of there being actually *two* 'really existing' sides. The 'fall of the Berlin Wall' all too simply allows for a story to begin anew, again and again, as a resolution in and of itself. Lacking in any critical reflection, it becomes a mere shorthand of history that can be put to work as an introduction, a chapter heading and explanatory footnote. And always as an ending – a happy ending – from which we can confidently begin again. Yet, like the graffiti that was sprayed only on one side of the Wall, this is only a partial telling of a fuller story; presenting, as it were, only one half of an ending – no better, surely, than a pump that has lost its handle.

Notes

1. Hagen Koch, following the collapse of the GDR regime, went on to found the *Berliner Mauer-Archiv*, which maintains a vast collection of unpublished documentation, including a wealth of classified material from the former GDR. Held at the Bernauer Strasse Museum, amidst ongoing financial insecurities, this archive has yet to be properly collated and catalogued. See http: //www.berliner-mauer-dokumentationszentrum.de/.

2. The structure of the Wall was constantly improved and strengthened. By the end of the first decade of its existence, the original structure had been completely upgraded by 'a concrete wall 4.9-metres tall. Behind it was a 91-metre-wide "death-strip", floodlit at night, patrolled by dogs, and overlooked by watchtowers. An electrified fence at the East Berlin Edge of the strip completed this formidable barrier' (Grant 1998: 29).

3. Whilst an exit visa (to leave the GDR permanently) was, at least in theory, obtainable at any police station on presentation of an identity card, a short-stay visa required a passport which most East Germans did not possess.

4. Cited from 'Berlin Night: The End of the Wall' *BBC Knowledge*, BBC Bristol, 2001.

5. Inevitably the account presented here, which relates to a history spanning some 40 years, cannot hope to be anything other than a collection of brief sketches. For the interested reader, some of the more accessible English-language accounts, from which I have drawn, include: On Berlin and the Wall: Richie (1998); Large (2001); Hilton (2001). On the GDR and German reunification: Childs (2001) and Fulbrook (2000). And on the Cold War: Young (1996) and Isaacs and Downing (1998). The latter is an excellent source book that accompanied an acclaimed twelve-part television series, which brought together for the first time a huge range of documents, references and interviews.

6. Quote taken from 'Berlin Night: The End of the Wall' *BBC Knowledge*, BBC Bristol, 2001.

7. Take, for example, 'Martin Woollacott and Anna Tomforde in Dresden on opposing visions of socialism...' (*The Guardian*, 6.11.89, p. 8), or 'Timothy Garton Ash celebrates the end of East Germans' humiliation' (*The Independent*, 11.11.89, p. 32).

8. In another example, again of a print-based advertisement, though in this case published nine days *before* the fall of the Wall, the mobile phone manufactures Nokia-Mobira wittily appropriated an image of Mikhail Gorbachev speaking on a portable phone. Supposedly – to cite the slogan of another well-known telephone company – their message is that in the era of *glasnost* (initiated by Gorbachev himself) 'it's good to talk'.

9. It is, of course, a habit of news discourse to filter discursive alternatives, indeed 'to censor out the unrealised discursive potential of events' (Fiske 1989: 178), which is a form of censorship not so much intended to mislead or misinform its audience, but rather more to ensure the news-worthiness of the 'story' – again an effect of the professional ideology of journalism itself, rather than an overt political ideology. In turn, the problem with a journalistic contextualizing of history is not that it necessarily makes for a false argument, but more subtly, that it presents historical 'opinion' in relatively neutral terms (Cormack 1992: 52). News commentaries by default close down alternative interpretations and are not subject to complex forms of interrogation. As a result 'other' historical aspects are left unsaid and, in general, the ambiguities and greater complexity of the situation left unexamined.

10. Niethammer's (1992) concept of *posthistoire* refers to a 'structure of feeling' collectively expressed by a diverse (even contrasting) group of twentieth-century thinkers, including the likes of Henri de Man, Arnold Gehlen, Carl Schmitt, Alexandre Kojève, Ernst Jünger, Henri Lefebvre, Walter Benjamin and Theodor Adorno. The sentiment expressed – in various ways – revolves around a feeling that history has somehow reached an end point, as if the world is both exhausted from the burden of bureaucracy and commercialism, as well as without limits. As Nitehammer puts it, in the post-historical society 'the rulers have ceased to rule, but the slaves remain slaves' (1992: 156).

11. In contrast to Kant's philosophy of a perpetual human condition, Hegel accepts the human condition as open to change from one historical moment to the next. It can be argued that Hegel (as is also the case with Marx) considers an end point to the overall progression of change, yet this is as much a *reading* of their work than gleaned from any overt statement on the subject. Of course, it is not difficult to see how Hegel can be considered to have formally announced an end. In the *Lectures on the History of Philosophy* (1956), for example, he clearly states that a new epoch has arisen: 'the

standpoint of the present, and the series of spiritual forms is therewith for the moment concluded' (cited in Anderson 1992: 286). Nevertheless, whilst the sense of closure is a recurring idea, it is never actually developed emphatically – this, however, is precisely how Kojève (1969) formulates the concept of history in his influential introductory lectures on Hegel's *Phenomenology of Spirit* (1977), and, as Fukuyama acknowledges, it is from this reading specifically that he takes his bearings.

12. All too frequently, Fukuyama is faced with a facile demand to explain just 'what happened', considering that time obviously did not stop. As he later acknowledges, 'people pointed to the fall of the Berlin Wall, the Chinese communist crackdown in Tiananmen Square, and the Iraqi invasion of Kuwait as evidence that "history was continuing"' (1992: xi-xii). In one response, for example, the author reads Fukuyama's thesis as an overtly postmodern argument, remarking: 'If you think about it, this idea that nothing new can happen is really scary. It starts to seem like a repetition compulsion: the harder we try for the "shock of the new,"...the more we get a mere recycled micro-event, whose stimulation-value is immediately debased by the recognition that it is, in fact, mere simulacrum' (Stoekl 1997: 29). More recently, following the events of September 11th, Fukuyama (2002) has published an article entitled 'Has History Started Again?' which in part provides yet further response to such critics.

13. The event referred to was a major, 'multinational, multidisciplinary conference' held in 1993, entitled *Whither Marxism? Global Crises in International Perspective*. It attracted (from within the humanities) 'distinguished thinkers and participants from China, Russia, Armenia, Poland, Romania, Mexico, Germany, France, the United States and elsewhere' (Magnus and Cullenberg 1995: ix).

14. Following the unification of Germany in 1871 and the establishment of an imperial power that continued until the disarray at the end of the First World War, the city was to witness the inauguration of the Weimar Republic, the fascist totalitarian state of Nazi Germany and communist rule of the German Democratic Republic (GDR), before embodying the democratic federalism of today's 'United Germany'.

15. The literature on monuments, museums and public space in Germany gives some evidence of this active and often contentious process of reflection and renewal of Berlin's image reservoir, see Balfour (1990); Feversham and Schmidt (1999); Huyssen (1997); Ladd (1997); Leach (1999); Ludes (1994); Pejiç and Elliot (1999); Young (1992); Zelizer (2001).

16. Stalin had become much more explicit about a triumphant Soviet system of government that he believed would give rise to a communist cause capable of overthrowing capitalism. It was an outlook that greatly alarmed the American administration. One policy adviser to the government described it a 'delayed declaration of war against the United States' (cited in Isaacs and Downing 1998: 29); and in a key diplomatic report the prediction was 'nothing less than a lengthy, life-and-death struggle between democracy and communism' (Isaacs and Downing 1998: 30).

17. A stark question had arisen as to whether or not the Americans would consider the use of the new atomic weapons. In fact, despite deeply felt anxieties about the utter destructive nature of such weaponry, a fleet of US Bombers carrying atomic weapons were flown over to stations in Britain amidst great publicity. The planes were never actually equipped with atomic warheads, but this was a much guarded secret. As Isaacs and Downing (198: 75) note, '[t]heir arrival was mainly a signal to Moscow that the West meant business over Berlin, and Washington took advantage of the crisis to get congressional approval for permanent overseas military bases'.

18. At its peak, during the winter of 1949, the Berlin airlift was a highly impressive logistical operation, with planes landing every ninety seconds and turning around within six minutes, sometimes managing to deliver up to 6,000 tons of supplies in a single day.

19. The change of fortune for West Berlin (following the airlift operation) is subsequently mirrored in West Germany as a whole. The so-called *Wirtschaftswunder*, or 'Economic Miracle', experienced in West Germany during the 1950s was excellent 'propaganda' for a free market economy. Furthermore, the episode of the Berlin blockade can be recognized as pivotal in the subsequent development and legitimation of both a divided Berlin *and* a divided Germany. On the 23rd May 1949, virtually simultaneous to the Soviet's lifting of the blockade, a Federal German Basic Law, or constitution, was issued by the Western Allies. This gave West Germany full sovereignty, bringing into existence the second German democracy of the twentieth century, the same democracy that, forty years later, would orchestrate the return of its communist counterpart, the GDR into a fully (re)unified Germany.

20. Despite being far 'inland' in East Germany, away from the fortifications of division, Berlin offered unrestricted escape, since before the Wall was erected movement between the four military zones was unlimited. Anyone from East Germany could simply slip into East Berlin, move over to the west side of the city and settle or, of course, take leave of the city altogether and head for the 'West' through the various American and British access corridors. Huge reception centres existed in the Western sectors to receive 'refugees' from the East. Here they would be 'processed', fed, sheltered and then flown out to West Germany, all at the expense of the West German state. By 1957, the GDR authorities declared *Republikflucht* (fleeing the country) a criminal offence, punishable – if caught – by prison sentence. Nevertheless, from the inception of the GDR in 1949 to the year of the building of the Berlin Wall, almost three million Germans left for the West and the 'good life' they associated with it. And what made matters worse was that over thirty thousand of these had been students, who having completed their studies at the expense of the East German government, then left for the opportunities that a booming West German economy offered.

21. It can, of course, be noted following on from his radical pronouncements of *Perestroika* and *glasnost*, marking a period of unprecedented openness and a commitment to reconstruct the Soviet economy and political system that Gorbachev had taken the initiative in a series of high-profile peace summits to achieve arms reduction. In February 1987 (prior to Reagan's visit to Berlin) Gorbachev made an agreement with the US, with no strings attached, to dispose of all intermediate-range nuclear forces in Europe. The signing of the treaty took place in the White House at the end of the year, carried live on US and Soviet television. For Reagan, the fact that no concessions had been required on his behalf was a clear sign of Soviet weakness, boosting US confidence at an international level.

22. Soon after the building of the Wall, there were many attempts by individuals and small groups from East Berlin to get through to the West, but the risks were great and many lost their lives. The most infamous incident occurred in August 1962 when 18-year-old Peter Fechter became the first person to be shot by border guards as he attempted to climb the wall. He was left to bleed to death at the foot of the Wall. In all, 86 people are known to have died trying to cross the Wall (Grant 1998: 28).

23. Prior to the fall of the Wall there was a whole discipline devoted to the study of the GDR and East Europe as a whole. As Bauman remarks, 'thousands of university departments and research institutes, world-wide networks of congresses, conferences, publishing houses and journals [were] all dedicated to "Soviet and East European Studies"' (1992: 176).

24. The Museum of Modern Art in New York, the Vatican, the Imperial War Museum in London and various private and public collections all over the world all own Wall segments (Feversham and Schmidt 1999: 154).

25. The first real associations of Wall graffiti do, in fact, date back to the student protests of 1968; although, as Hermann Waldenburg remembers, the 'scriptural struggle of the '68 generation took place more in the city itself, at the university, in and on public buildings' (1990: 11). And whilst the same political impetus for the graffiti seen in France (with slogans such as 'structures don't take to the streets') was equally evident in Germany, the specific context of a divided Berlin meant that most of the writings on the Wall were slogans directed against American military presence. The Wall at this time was still relatively simple in its construction and its rough, uneven surfaces were not conducive to elaborate works of graffiti art synonymous with the Wall today. It was not until the late 70s and the 'fourth generation' of the Wall, with its smooth and seemingly endless surfaces, that it could finally offer an 'irresistible canvas for the outpourings of an unfettered democratic society' (Feversham and Schmidt 1999: 154). However, it is not really until the early 80s that the graffiti work most associated with the Wall really emerges. This work reflected the new emerging graffiti aesthetic (and culture) of the period, which, far from being socially committed, was influenced by the 'democratic' principles of the up-and-coming commercial artists such as Joseph Beuys (who, as Ladd (1997: 27), notes, 'confounded official opinion when he declared that it would be best to increase the Wall's height by five centimetres to give it more aesthetically pleasing proportions') and Andy Warhol, as well as heavily indebted to the 'New York subway style,' popularized, for example, by books such as Subway Art (Cooper and Chalfant 1984). It is, perhaps, also worth pointing out that whilst the East had early on made attempts to keep the West side of the Wall clear of graffiti, it remained more of a concern for the West – indeed, 'it was the Western authorities who hurriedly obliterated anti-American and anti-Reagan slogans before the president's visit to the Brandenburg Gate' (Ladd 1997: 28).

26. The zip was a metaphor used by East Berlin writer Lutz Rathenow to illustrate the idea that even whilst divided (unzipped as it were), both East and West Germany were still held together (ready to be zipped back up again). The underlying point being that both East and West were intractably intertwined, whether for good or bad (Rathenow and Hauswald 1987: 154).

27. The East German authorities justified the building of the Wall as a necessary defence against the atavistic forces of the West. According to this view, 'the proletariat was defending itself against lingering influences of the bourgeoisie', and specifically the forces of fascism, thought to threaten the progress of socialism. Thus, 'Marxists usually defined fascism as a degenerate form of late bourgeois capitalism. The "antifascism protective rampart" shielded the triumphant proletariat from the remnants of pre-1945 German fascism' (Ladd 1997: 23; see also Ward 1996).

CHAPTER FOUR

LIVING WITHOUT AN ALTERNATIVE

Having previously worked through the dominant interpretation of the fall of the Berlin Wall, as being all about celebration and the victory of capitalist, liberal democracy (neatly captured and promulgated by Francis Fukuyama's (1989) thesis of an 'end of history'), this chapter examines what it might mean to present the 'other' side of the story. One needs to ask: what is the difficulty in bringing to light an equivalent opposite to the aforementioned dominant interpretation? East Germany as it had existed quickly devolved to become part of the West, to become constituted within a united federal democratic state of Germany. Arguably, then, there has been a distinct lack of an alternative in both practical terms (i.e. with the GDR ceasing to exist rather than being reformed in some way) and more philosophically, with the collapse of any confident discourse of socialism and Left politics. Any potential 'other' story seemingly remains unknown (even perhaps unknowable). What is apparent is a one-sided perspective; a 'greying' out of the East as either a mere object of the past or place of the mundane, with the effect of always placing the East aside as some 'perpetual abroad'.

* * *

It would be imprudent to want to consider the removal of the Berlin Wall in anything other than a positive light. Architecturally it had been a loathsome sight and a brutal, inhuman division. As a political symbol it marked the ideological dead end and nihilism of the Cold War. Equally, it would be erroneous to suggest the spontaneous celebrations that erupted with the demise of the Wall somehow masked a *hidden* reality or agenda. And today – setting aside a short-lived and ideologically vacuous resurgence in ultra-right groups in the early 90s[1] – few perhaps would contest (at least at root) that 'the Federal Republic looks in remarkably good shape' (Childs 2001: 157), or disagree when suggested 'that for all its difficulties, the process of German unification has started "to take"' (Maier 1997: xix).[2]

Nevertheless, even with the fifteen-year anniversary of the fall of the Wall in 2004, the so-called 'syndrome' of the *Mauer im Kopf* (literally, the wall in the head)[3] was still apparent for many Germans. The Berlin listings magazine, *Zitty*, marked the anniversary by issuing a twin edition: one for sale in the former West, with the cover '1,000 good reasons to live in the East', and, for those in the East, '1,000 good reasons to live in the West'. The lists were certainly light-hearted and tongue-in-cheek ('The kebabs are better in the West', 'When you have sex the Stasi don't know about it'), but nonetheless they perhaps reflect a deeper truth still current at this time. Arguably, the anniversary was only a further uncomfortable reminder that the 'flowering landscapes', promised at the time of reunification by Chancellor Helmut Kohl,[4] had in many instances 'bloomed' only into mass unemployment, biting austerity measures and the sporadic return of communist and neo-Nazi parties. In fact, despite an estimated 1.5 trillion euros of support through grants, subsidies and taxation from the West to the East, unemployment in the former East in 2004 stood at 20 per cent, and nearly one in seventeen inhabitants had moved to the West. Furthermore, the situation was not necessarily so much better in the West, which faced 8 per cent unemployment and the continued levy of a 5.5 per cent *Solidaritätszuschlag* (solidarity tax).[5] When combined at the time with Chancellor Schröder's 'Agenda 2010' plans to cut pensions and welfare rights, it is perhaps of little surprise that the residents of the West (and East) became less enamoured with the results of reunification. So, whilst the scenes of jubilation – whether on the night the Wall was first breached or, indeed, later with official reunification – marked an irrefutably happy occasion, there is an argument to be made for complicating the story of the fall of the Wall. There is a need, in pulling out of the singularly euphoric and one-sided interpretation, for a more critical awareness of the nature and process of social and political change. More specifically, it is not so much the practicalities of the event of the fall of the Wall, nor necessarily the 'end of history' as mere economic reality which might concern us the most, but rather an accumulative, underlying political and philosophical effect that comes – to use Zygmunt Bauman's (1992) phrase – of 'living without an alternative'.

It is generally assumed that the collapse of the communist system dealt a fatal blow not only to 'devotees of the communist faith', but equally to 'any cause, however loosely related to the "left" tradition of disaffection, critique and dissent, of value-questioning, of alternative visions' (Bauman 1992: 177). As Jan-Werner Müller (2000) argues, for example, the defensive reactions towards reunification from a 'sceptical generation' of West German intellectuals (including the likes of Günter Grass and Jürgen Habermas) betrayed a sense of crisis for the political Left. The idea, for example, that socialism might be what was to come *after* capitalism was clearly put into doubt by the 1989 'revolutions' (Lash 1990). And Bauman (1992: 177) argues, more significantly still, that the overt discrediting of communism portrayed by the dramatic changes across Eastern Europe removed a so-called Other 'of *our form of life*, as the *negative* totality which injects meaning into *our positivity*'. The result was to disqualify in advance, 'any doubts about the unchallengeable superiority of the really existing regime of freedom and the consumer market'. Put simply, the outright removal of the 'negative' of communism left the liberal, capitalist form of life permanently switched on as 'positive'; hence, enabling the prevailing 'Good News' of Fukuyama's alleged end of history.

The argument, then, is that where before the political landscape had been made up of alternative and opposing ideologies, the notion of ideological resolution eliminates all alternatives, leaving us with 'unprecedented freedom' in which the western form of life can enjoy 'construing "the other" of itself and, by the same token, in defining its own identity' (Bauman 1992: 183). Yet, the result is that any so-called current western form of life 'has neither effective enemies inside nor barbarians knocking at the gates, only adulators and imitators. It has practically (and apparently irrevocably) de-legitimized all alternatives to itself' (183). Such circumstance leads Lash (1990: 146), for example, to suggest that the notion of 'capitalism' in itself 'is no longer very useful in understanding social change'. His point is that it is perhaps no longer tenable to achieve social change by describing capitalism as a *historical* stage, as if we are 'somehow en route from feudalism to socialism'. In this case, the 'post' prefix (of post-industrialism, post-Fordism, postmodernism) is no doubt useful in describing how contemporary society is 'systematically no longer what it once *was*', yet equally is unsatisfactory in telling us little of 'any sufficient degree [about] what comes *after* what was'. The result is that we are potentially engulfed by an open-ended, but seemingly singular economic/political paradigm of liberal democracy.

Jean Baudrillard (1994), in describing the collapse of communism as the 'thawing of the East', warns of the prospects of what he calls a 'depressurised' form of liberty:

> *Perhaps defrosted liberty is not so attractive as all that. And what if it turned out to be intent on just one thing: bartering itself off in a binge of cars and electrical goods, not to mention mind-bending drugs and pornography...it may be that the thawing of human rights is the socialist equivalent of the 'depressurising of the West': a mere discharge into the Western void of the energies trapped for half a century in the East (1994: 29).*

As two polar opposites (of the Cold War discourse) slide into one another, or rather as one gushes forth into the *other*, the ability to take up a critical stance is undercut. An analysis of the fall of the Wall becomes as much about an analysis of what does not fall, i.e. the West; with the problem being that the "depressurising" of the West does not present any obvious critical agenda or site. The real concern, then, is not so much the collapse of an opposing order, but rather the sudden leakage or 'freedom' of the other, of 'our' own nemesis or mirror. Viewed this way, one can argue for the same, if not greater, need of critical engagement with 'the really existing regime of free consumers and free markets' (Bauman 1992: 177).

Fukuyama's original pronouncement of the 'end of history' was met with almost universal rejection; for once 'most of the Right, Centre and Left were united in their reaction' (Anderson 1992: 284). Nevertheless, the degree to which it was felt there was required some kind of critical response highlights a greater collective anxiety that Fukuyama's thesis has come to represent: an anxiety of precisely *what* might successfully take its place. As Perry Anderson (1992: 336) puts it, the end of history 'is not the arrival of a perfect system, but the elimination of any better alternatives to this one'. In other words, rather than *adding* something discrete to the political spectrum, the 'end of history' refers to a political landscape in which all that previously existed (and that is not desirable) is eliminated or levelled out. Any significant reply to the circumstance Fukuyama describes must go beyond merely pointing out problems that remain within the world he predicts. Instead, a properly 'effective critique must be able to show that there are powerful systematic alternatives he has discounted' (Anderson 1992: 336), which predictably has proved difficult. Thus, in promoting a thesis espousing potential ideological resolution, the issue is not about whether or not Fukuyama was correct to take as his starting point the collapse of communism. The problem is rather that in 'the din of celebration', as Bauman put it, 'the few voices of doubt are barely audible. Some doubts do not dare to be voiced. Some inarticulate worries have not even congealed into doubts fit to be put into words. One can only guess what they are' (Bauman 1992: 175). This, then, is the critical 'problem' that arises from the images of the fall of the Wall: there are seemingly no alternative pictures of the event adequate for its robust critique.

One very significant question that barely gets asked is just why it need follow that, with an 'end of history', socialism can not remain an alternative to capitalism. Why is it the case that if the end of history really has arrived, 'it is essentially because the socialist experience is over' (Anderson 1992: 351–352)? Fundamentally, the predicament is not so much that Fukuyama is right but that his argument is symptomatic of the cul-de-sac that 'living without an alternative' places us in. In fact, it is a problem that Fukuyama himself bleakly acknowledges: 'The end of history will be a very sad time...the willingness to risk one's life for a purely abstract goal, the worldwide struggle that called forth daring, courage, imagination, and idealism, will be replaced by economic calculation, the endless solving of technical problems' (Fukuyama 1989: 18). It is easy to forget that the title of Fukyuama's article ends in a question mark, 'The End of History?' This to be meant not to doubt the overall thesis, but rather as rhetorical punctuation which adds greater stress to the title, as if to say: 'the end of history – is this all we get?' Such emphasis only becomes clear in the closing paragraph of the article, as in the lines cited above, or when, for example, he writes: 'In the post-historical period there will be neither art nor philosophy, just the perpetual caretaking of the museum of human history...Perhaps this very prospect of centuries of boredom at the end of history will serve to get history started once again? (Fukuyama 1989: 18). At this point (though with no further elaboration), Fukuyama's argument would appear to come full circle, with a stolen glance towards the next evolution in mankind's ideological development. In fact, the neo-liberal 'ideology' he describes can be argued to centre around the view that moral standards (and a 'common cause') can best be maintained through the creation of an overarching mythology of the nation. Understood in this way, Fukuyama's concerns neatly dovetail with the former ideology debates of the 1950s and 1960s. Chaim Waxman, for example, suggests in this earlier period 'what we desperately need is a new ideology, not of the fanatical, closed-system character...but most certainly a broad, plastic ideology (corresponding somewhat with what Mannheim defines as "Utopia") which will enable us to transcend our current situation' (Waxman 1968: 7). The distinguishing problem we face in more recent times is the very *success* of the 'end of history' combined with the dominant meaning of the fall of the Berlin Wall, which take away the need to hold a critical debate regarding adherence to a new ideology, whether plastic or otherwise.

Susan Buck-Morss (2000) laments our circumstance of an 'end of history' as being a time in which we can now no longer pursue 'collective dreams'. In her sociocultural re-evaluation of the Cold War period, she argues that the disintegration of Soviet socialism actually marks the abandonment of the idea of mass utopia on *both* sides of the ideological divide. She shows how throughout the twentieth century it was both capitalist and socialist ideologies that drove the incessant process of industrial modernization. And the result was that both enabled the 'construction of mass utopia...an immense material power that transformed the natural world, investing industrially produced objects and built environments with collective, political desire' (ix). Whilst she quickly acknowledges that the flip side of such visionary practice was, in so many cases, simply catastrophic. Yet, her argument is that ideologies nonetheless provided an inherent ability to dream; an ability, she urges, that should not be allowed to pass away. It is the 'collective dream' she suggests which 'dared to imagine a social world' (ix):

> As the century closes, the dream is being left behind...the mass-democratic myth of industrial modernity – the belief that the industrial reshaping of the world is capable of bringing about the good society by providing material happiness for the masses – has been profoundly challenged by the disintegration of European socialism, the demands of capitalist restructuring, and the most fundamental ecological constraints.
>
> (Buck-Morss 2000: ix–x)

In the wake of this supposedly daring and collective imagination, the 'end of history' privatizes the ability to dream. A distinctive feature of liberal democracy (and arguably the reason it becomes our only, albeit abundant, alternative) is a process inherent to its system that Bauman (1992) describes as the 'privatisation of dissent', whereby political action is paired down to single-issue campaigns and where any appetite for 'change' is refashioned as a search for improvement. Crucially, whilst there may well be strong grounds for opposing the legitimacy of 'our' current, liberal form of life just as one might once have opposed the legitimacy of communist rule, it is unlikely that such dissent can be put to practical test. Indeed, 'western civilization seems to have found the philosopher's stone all other civilizations sought in vain, and with it the warranty of its own immortality: it has succeeded in re-forging its discontents into the factors of its own reproduction' (Bauman 1992: 182). Thus, what might be described in another system as potential crisis and breakdown, in 'our' case is seen only to add to its overall strength and standing. Jean-François Lyotard (1993: 263) explains, for example, that with critique itself being 'needed by the system for improving its efficiency in the direction of emancipation' the critic's role is subsumed into the process, their job being 'to detect and denounce all the cases in which the system fails to improve the process toward emancipation'. His point being that emancipation, far from being about the potential for any radical change, is merely a process of litigation.

Ironically, then, though the fall of the Wall was undoubtedly a collective act, it leads us towards only private ends of history. Lyotard (1993: 264) argues this pointedly with an anecdote following his visits to East Germany just before and then after the fall of the Wall. He notes the concern held by East German intellectuals to 'save, maintain, or elaborate a view enabling all of us to criticize both Eastern totalitarianism and Western liberalism'. Yet, equally, he makes clear his own scepticism for maintaining such a critique, asking: 'How could the demand for radical criticism, as formulated by the East German colleagues be satisfied if criticizing, questioning, and imagining [...] actually require the openness that only an open system provides?' (265). His complaint is, of course, not with the East Germans with whom he meets (and who for the first time are 'open' to assert their opinion), but rather the system of liberal democracy itself; the fact that the ideal of critical reflection and emancipation are simply operations subsumed into the liberal system as one goal among many.

Parallel to the argument of the preceding chapter, regarding the imposition of a western view (and/or ownership) of the Wall, there is genuine difficulty in bringing to the fore the rights and voices of those from the former East. Needless to say, in pursuing alternative interpretations and responses to the fall of the Wall, it can not be so simple as to state alternative histories and articulate 'other' voices; instead there is the need to allow elements of the past to speak for themselves, to come to the surface and puncture the dominant hegemonic discourse. Below, I consider some of these difficulties in more detail, looking first at the events in Berlin in the autumn of 1989, followed by some final remarks on the perpetuating of the East as an 'abroad', as an unobtainable location, which in turn thwarts any consideration of a potential *other* side of the wall/representation.

A Peaceful Revolution, or "We are the People"

There remains ambiguity as to the status of 'change' that took place in East Germany, with the question often raised as to whether or not the fall of the Berlin Wall did genuinely mark a revolution. In popular discourse the event is frequently referred to in terms of revolution, so suggesting a determined change of direction *from within*, with one ideology overturning another. And certainly at the time many held out hope for just such change: 'the fragile coalition of opposition groups in the GDR, for a brief period, offered the chance for radical social change'; not merely in terms of goals and agendas, 'such as a commitment to *Basisdemokratie*, civil rights, ecological principles, alternative life-styles, and socialist ideals, but also in terms of political structures, favouring the round table, minimal consensus, and collective reflection' (Sieg 1993: 40). Yet, 'change' envisioned in this way never really came to fruition. Instead, due to the process characterized above as 'depressurization', the result was not so much a revolution, but a kind of *resolution* that comes with the levelling out of so-called ideological evolution.

As discussed previously, the initial newspaper coverage presented a story of unequivocal victory for 'the people'. And the rhetoric of revolution was in the early stages certainly backed up by a collective body taking to the streets. In the early autumn, East Germany was already witnessing regular street demonstrations, most prominently in Leipzig and Dresden (for a thorough account, see Maier 1997: 108–167). Later, Berlin became the focal point, particularly when, on what was to be the last weekend before the fall of the Wall, the city was overwhelmed by a rally held in the main square, Alexanderplatz. The event, organized by the various opposition groups, proved to be particularly galvanizing, with an estimated one million people (from all over the country) in attendance. The demonstration was broadcast on western television, but more significantly was also carried live by East German television; this being a new, and daring, move by the GDR regime, especially since many in the Politburo feared demonstrators would attempt to breach the Wall (a rite that would have to wait only a few more days). Banners bore many slogans urging new freedom, equality and sincerity, but the most popular motto was the most simple: 'We are the People'. And even if this were considered as mere performance or rhetoric, the message was undoubtedly to resound powerfully throughout the period from the collapse of the GDR to the creation of a reunified Germany. In an address to the massive crowds, for example, the famed East German writer Christa Wolf ended with the remark: 'let our rulers parade past our people' – her phrase powerfully resonating with the sentiments of 'the people' gathered before her, who on an annual basis would have witnessed the military and civic processions on state anniversaries marching past the political leaders.[6]

However, despite the obvious and profound collapse in the legitimacy of communist rule, there are some who believe the interpretation of revolution is somewhat misleading. As Katrin Sieg (1993: 36) points out, 'the term "revolution" underwent a conspicuous change of meaning. Whereas it first appeared in connection with the mass demonstrations its referent was

replaced with the November events following the opening of the Wall'. Thus, a confusion arises as to the most significant aspect of the 'fall of the Wall' – was it about the demonstrations in the weeks leading up to the fall of the Wall, or those in the weeks and months that followed its removal (*after*, that is, the ruling GDR regime had been as good as unseated)? Or, indeed – as it is mostly remembered and referenced – was it simply the crowds climbing upon and hammering at the Wall on the night the borders first opened? This latter, resonant image is, of course, what leads to the kind of prevalent remarks that somehow the whole system of the Cold War rather more *dissolved* than changed. As Buck-Morss (1994: 11) puts it, for example, the system is described as having 'imploded...[w]ithout war, without revolution, without cultural renaissance, it simply came to an end'.

More generally, the dramatic events of 1989 taking place across Eastern European are frequently referred to as the 'velvet revolution' (Ash 1999). The term is intended to describe the non-violent nature of political change, relating especially to (the former) Czechoslovakia's relatively smooth change from communism to western-style democracy. The phrase is obviously to be read in a positive light, yet, nonetheless, equally betrays certain doubts regarding the true depth and means of change. Dirk Philipsen (1993: 5–6), for example, is of the opinion – specific to the case of the collapse of the GDR – that the common descriptive phrase of 'a peaceful revolution from below' was inaccurate. He notes how, by the early months of 1990, a new term, *Wende* (meaning simply 'turn' or 'turnabout'), began to appear. In his view this gave the sound of something much more 'sober and cautious', a change in terminology symptomatic of the fact that perhaps 'the vast openness, the perceived 1989 world of immense opportunity, had become something much narrower...something far less invested with hope'. In line with this argument, both Hungary and Poland, for example, have been described as going through a process of 'refolution' rather than revolution; meaning 'a mixture of reform and revolution' (Ash 1994: 344).

In the GDR doubts over the nature of its revolution were always evident,[7] particularly as any expression of opposition had previously only ever been achieved by 'exit', often at the behest of the regime itself, which sought to expel its more controversial citizens rather than risk their notoriety. Thus, as the historian Timothy Garton Ash (1994: 345) remarks, 'The old quip that "emigration is the German form of revolution" was actually a bitter one, implying as it did that Germans were not really capable of revolution'. Further compounding such an idea, Jürgen Habermas puts forward the view that the 'revolution' was much more an *imposition* of western interpretation:

> It's a dead giveaway that the population of the former GDR talks about a 'turn' when they describe the fall of the SED[8] regime. Our fellow citizens in the East don't seem to have the feeling that they made a revolution – or even that they were present at one. The revolution interpretation was something we Westerners pressed on them – perhaps to cover the need for remedial work, for making up for lost time...
>
> (Habermas 1994: 39)

His point echoes the discourse and 'imaginary' of the Wall examined in the preceding chapter, which evinces a western ownership of the Wall and its fall (or at least the interpretation of its fall), and being symptomatic even of the 're-invention' of democracy that, as Slavoj Žižek (1990: 50) suggests, comes with an internalized western gaze.

None of the above is to deny that in the weeks leading up to the fall of the Wall, the mass exodus of East Germans 'escaping' to the West across the Hungarian border (and camping out in the West German embassy in Czechoslovakia) prompted a crisis in the stability of the GDR regime. Indeed, in only a matter of a few days of the Hungarian decision to remove the barbed-wire fencing which sealed off its border with Austria – being the first conspicuous opening of the 'Iron Curtain' – some 13,000 East Germans fled to the West, taking the rate of population drain back to its levels just prior to the building of the Wall. The problem, however, is that again the 'fall of the Wall', remembered in terms of the all too pervasive 'theme of celebration', tends to overshadow the significance of the genuine organized political opposition that arose within the country. Moreover, this opposition, *after* the fall of the Wall, subsequently failed to impact upon the political developments of the GDR. In the swift process of reunification, any specifically East German political perspectives were obscured in favour of a more plainly defined nationalism of a united Germany.

There were – contrary to opinion – a number of important opposition groups based in the GDR that came to prominence in the period leading up to the collapse of the state, perhaps the most well known of which was *Neue Forum*. The main appeal made by this group was for renewed links between the state and society, their concerns ranging over issues of justice, democracy, peace and the environment.[9] According to their rhetoric, the group had little or no intention of bringing the government down, or dismantling the GDR in anyway. Instead it sought reform, to bring all members of society back together. As events ran their course, however, the organization was perceived by many to be more outspoken and oppositional than perhaps it really was. Arguably, the Politburo might have retained more control by actually granting legal status to *Neue Forum*, undercutting its potentially radical nature by *permitting* it to operate as a dissident group within the mainstream. By not taking this course of action, the group could be said to have developed a much greater following than it might have done otherwise (Childs 2001: 77).

Another prominent alliance that formed during this time was *Demokratie Jetzt* (a group based on a pamphlet publication of the same name). The alliance brought together members of the Church (who were significant figures for a 'legitimate' opposition) and 'critical Marxists', in a bid to think about the 'future, about a society based on solidarity' (cited in Childs 2001: 77). The group advocated an end to a command economy and the privatization of some sectors of the economy. However, despite making strong criticisms of their own contemporary political and economic situation, the group was equally critical of West German capitalism (Childs 2001: 78). Similarly, another 'underground' movement, the *Sozialdemokratische Partei*, also held strong reservations about the West, despite actually receiving assistance from organizations in the West. The group appealed for a properly democratic GDR, with one of its key figures noting: 'We do not want to be simply integrated into the other German state...We want something like Socialism...a second functioning capitalist German state at the side of the Federal Republic would be senseless' (cited in Childs 2001: 79). Their concerns would prove to be well founded, since without any achievable socialist alternative, the GDR was inevitably limited to becoming a set of new *Länder* (or states) within a single, unified federal Germany.

Another group worth noting (though it is significant that they generally receive little attention) was the women's association *Unabhängiger Frauenverein* (UFV).[10] This group (like those mentioned above) belonged to the Round Table Committee established in the interim period after the fall of the Wall which eventually helped steer towards reunification. Initially, however, all members of this committee generally looked towards a 'Third Way' or democratic socialism for the GDR.[11] The favoured prospect was to 'leave the GDR intact as a political entity...and negotiate the relationship between East and West Germany under conditions that would grant some degree of autonomy to the East' (Sieg 1993: 40). A central concern for the UFV, in particular, regarded the rights to abortion, an issue that highlighted significant difference of status for women in East and West Germany at the time.[12] What this particular debate indicated (along with other issues such as child-care and employment rights) was that 'from a feminist point of view the balance sheet of real existing socialism was not so easily subsumed under the West-East schema of right and wrong, victory and defeat' (40).

What is common between the opposition groups is that they each initially held out for a *reformed* GDR rather than its complete overthrow. And in this respect, prior to the fall of the Wall, they proved to be influential in galvanising public protest against an ailing state. Yet, once the Wall had been removed they each largely failed to succeed with any of their longer term objectives. So, for example, in the case of the UFV, 'calls for a historical inventory sensitive to gender issues remained unheard, and their warnings against German reunification occurring at the expense of women were rendered inaudible' (Sieg 1993: 40). As it transpired, the opposition groups were out of step, or at least lagged behind the critical mass of public opinion as it developed – or rather as it changed – following the jubilant scenes of people mounting the Wall and shopping in the West. What encapsulates this shift in opinion is a modification to the original slogan of 'We are the People', whereby in adopting the sentiments of the conservative politicians' call for a single, unified nation, the new declaration was to become: *'Wir sind EIN Volk'*, or 'We are ONE People'.

The use of the definite article had originally invoked 'the people as the addressee of the constitution and supreme political agent in the socialist state' (Sieg 1993: 36). The strength of this principle was to articulate a relatively differentiated body of voices, making for a more inclusive and open forum. In this way, regardless of motivations and allegiances for being amongst the opposition, 'We are the People' became the overarching rallying call, foregrounding 'the discrepancy between the SED as the ruling party and those it claimed to represent' (36n). Charles S. Maier (1997: xiv), for example, without wanting to imply a 'coherent collective actor' (noting that 'Michelet's *peuple* remain too romantic a construction to be [his] kind of *Volk*'), is certainly of the opinion that it was the East Germans' collective action (in this formation of 'We are the People') that gave appetite for change. Thus, rather than subscribe to the simplistic view that the GDR somehow imploded, 'as if some worn-out machine finally just broke down', Maier draws attention to the extent of agency (though not necessarily heroism) involved in the collapse of the GDR, arguing that 'by repeatedly managing to claim a public space against the will of their regime, East German protestors provoked a crisis of government and set in motion the greater powers around them'.

Yet, following the relative success of 'the people' in bringing down its government and despite most opposition rhetoric having had called for GDR reform, it was soon clear popular opinion veered towards German reunification. For Maier (1997: xx), the critical point is not that we might have been at fault for having failed to predict the upheaval of 1989, but rather that we had not foreseen how profound and persistent 'the economic and spiritual difficulties of exiting from communism would be'. In the immediate months following the fall of the Wall, migration and absenteeism continued unabated, which of course meant the economy grew ever weaker (in turn prompting yet more to leave for the West). Understandably, perhaps, many looked towards unification as some kind of solution to the problem, especially as more and more were led to believe this would bring the wealth and prosperity of the West *into* the East. Yet, in some cases 'joy at being able at last to travel soon turned to anger', when many found that 'the prosperity in the West was even greater than they had gleaned from watching Western television' (Childs 2001: 89). In one ethnographic study of consumption in Eastern Germany following the fall of the Wall, there is a striking account of a young East German man having entered a large West German department store: 'I stood there, in front of the rack where the toasters were displayed, I really felt sick, and I left the shop. I just couldn't stand looking at it. This big rack, filled with different kinds of toasters...we were happy when we got four toasters a month' (cited in Veenis 1997: 157). Nevertheless, the more well-known scenes of throngs of East Germans shopping for the first time over in the West, when combined with the rapid procession towards reunification, would seem only to vindicate Fukuyama's (1989: 8) basic view that economic liberalism leads to political liberalism. As he puts it, the very 'spectacular abundance of liberal economies and the infinitely diverse consumer culture made possible by them seem both to foster and preserve liberalism in the political sphere'. He summarizes his position on the relationship between the political and the economic with a somewhat blunt statement, suggesting ideological resolution manifests as 'liberal democracy in the political sphere combined with easy access to VCRs and Stereos in the economic'.

Of course, presumably as an idealist, Fukuyama seeks to avoid material determinism (i.e. the claim that liberal economics inevitably produces liberal politics), his more lofty belief being that 'both economics and politics presuppose an autonomous prior state of consciousness that makes them possible' (Fukuyama 1989: 8). In the case of the reunification of Germany it was certainly more than a matter of economics at stake, indeed, a whole series of unresolved historical, political and cultural concerns (relating to Germany's Nazi legacy and post-war division) were greatly pronounced by the events of the fall of the Wall. And, significantly, what appears to happen is a shift in the collective *spirit* or consciousness to exhibit a distinct desire for German-German unity.[13] This, in fact, occurs very quickly after the opening of the Wall, made evident by the aforementioned change to the indefinite article in the rallying slogan of 'the people'. By making this single, though very significant change to 'We are One People', a 'return' to German identity is signalled as being 'racially, culturally, and ethnically homogenous – and unified' (Sieg 1993: 36). And it is specifically against such sentiment that the opposition groups were unable to maintain their original position, unable to seize what they had previously held as a unique opportunity to forge a renewed collective 'dream' of a *reformed* political and social order. In fact, many of the organisations themselves gradually came round to the idea of German unity. The East German *Christlich Demokratische Union*, for example, which previously had backed democratic socialism, began calling for 'early economic, currency and energy union with West Germany and a German confederation in united Europe' (Childs 2001: 108). As a general trend, 'the aim became, in the long unsung words of East Germany's own national anthem, "Germany, united fatherland."' Thus, whatever had previously been meant by *die Wende* now become 'what German historians have called "the turn within the turn"' (Ash 1994: 345).

Were the situation of the dissenting citizens of East Germany to be put into terms of Hegel's master-slave dialect, whereby the slave 'turns out to have the key to independence in what apparently encumbers him' (Connell 2002: 40), we might suppose that the fall of the Berlin Wall had the potential for a similarly liberating effect – it was for the East Germans an equivalent moment in which 'everything solid and stable has been shaken to its foundations', unveiling 'the simple, essential nature of self-consciousness, absolute negativity, pure being-for-self' (Hegel 1977: 117). Yet, like the unfolding events *after* the French Revolution, the rush for German reunification (although no Reign of Terror) was hardly an achievement of universal freedom. Instead, the abstract freedom of German Unity lacked the social means to manifest a new 'East German' order. The result is that all critical and political agendas moved 'westward', any critical moment becoming lost to the scenes of partying and 'revolution' before the last remains of the redundant Wall. All we are really left with are the pictures that *show* this very scene – and not just once, with the *actual* fall of the Wall, but at least three times, with the scenes of celebration replicated on the opening of the Brandenburg Gate and, later, on the 3rd October 1990, following the official declaration of reunification – a date which is now marked as a national public holiday.[14]

The momentum for reunification was such that it was little over a month following the fall of the Wall before the two Germanies had entered negotiations for a 'treaty of community'. And only a matter of days into these talks both the West German leader, Chancellor Kohl, and the East German head of the new coalition government, Hans Modrow, were seen standing side by side before the Brandenburg Gate as it was ceremonially opened for the first time in 28 years. The Gate, having already functioned as a key symbol throughout the history of the Berlin Wall and a prominent site for the witnessing of its demise, was yet again the photogenic backdrop to a key historic political change.[15] Once more huge crowds from both East and West Berlin gathered before the Gate – 'Champagne, Sekt, beer were drunk. Souvenir photographs were taken. Those East German border guards not called upon to have their photographs taken...looked on in amazement, still dazed by the dream-like quality of the event' (Childs 2001: 110). The crude idea of the 'end of history' to mean the end of historical time as such, might have seemed (if only for an evening) to have been valid that night. Indeed, like a record getting stuck, these images – that we associate with the 'theme of celebration' – emitting from the site of the once formidable Wall seem to repeat themselves here and again for the official reunification of Germany the following year (as well as on various national holidays, notably, for example, the seeing in of the new millennium in the year 2000). In each and every case, there is the same potential effect of remembering an event of 'the people', or more appropriately 'One People', since these celebrations seemingly forget the *two* sides of the story, they forget the social and political complexities. Sieg (1993: 36n) sums this up well when she describes a video produced by the West German weekly *Der Spiegel*:

> [It] begins its account of the "German Revolution" with a slow-motion sequence of GDR-citizens breaking through a Berlin check-point, reinterpreting the impetus of a diverse and diffuse uprising against the SED regime [the ruling Socialist Unity Party of German] within the East-West dichotomy, and ascribing to it a single direction – westward, ho!

It is not my intention, however, to engage in debating the rights and wrongs of reunification. My point of concern is not so much of the history and politics of this period as such, nor specifically Germany's social, cultural and economic make-up. Instead, my overarching interest relates to the *images* of the fall of the Wall, those images we remember *at the time* of the event (being in many respect *the* event) as well as being images which continue to circulate *now*, impacting on how we think critically about past and future political debate. On the one hand these images play a part in asserting a dominant interpretation, but equally they might be thought available as a form of critique in themselves. The point I wish to make – and pertinent to any practice of image critique – is that we should not underestimate or undermine the importance and authenticity of the scenes of jubilation at the site of the fall of the Wall. Instead, we would do better to accept these images for what they are (without the need to unmask any 'hidden' meaning), to acknowledge that any critical approach needs in fact engage *more* with these images. As cited previously, a critical approach might suitably orient around Kracauer's (1995: 86) motto that it lead 'directly through the centre of the mass ornament, not away from it'. My argument, then, is that only by going through (or along with) the images of the fall of the Wall can the (missing) political aspirations outlined in this chapter find a way to rise above the noise of the dominant, euphoric narrative of an end of ideological history.

The *Other* Side of the Wall

An important underlying concern is that throughout the many accounts relating to the event of the fall of the Wall there persists a figure of the 'East' that fundamentally maintains East Germany as a perpetual abroad; its 'people' either being spoken for, or left to, an unobtainable *other* place. The difficulty, if not impossibility, is to find adequate means to write and comment upon the events in former East Germany without imposing an interpretative framework that erases the voice of the East. In an extensive literature review, the historian Mary Fulbrook (2000) characterizes the development of post-unification studies in terms of three overlapping phases. Initially, during the early 1990s, there was a 'highly politicised phase...of what might be termed "heroes, victims and villains" literature' (4). These writings are made up of eye-witness accounts, interviews, memoirs and journalism, as well as archived ephemera of the 1989 revolution.[16] Following this output, a second more empirical and scientific phase develops relating to various archives that became available with the demise of the GDR, in particular, the notorious *Stasi* files.[17] Finally, in a third (and arguably now waning) phase of scholarly interest, broader social and cultural studies of Eastern Germany have been developed.[18] What is surprising, however, and despite a flurry of GDR studies, is that there was very little scholarly interest in the 'fall' of the Berlin Wall itself.[19]

Nevertheless, popular interest in the Wall evidently remains, with various publications having continued to surface from the late 1990s onwards. Notable examples include: Oliver August's (1999) *Along the Wall and Watchtowers: A Journey Down Germany's Divide*; Anna Funder's (2003) *Stasiland*; Christopher Hilton's (2001) *The Wall: The People's Story*; and *Unchained Eagle: Germany After the Wall* (2000) by the Reuter's reporter Tom Heneghan. Amongst others, these are typical of a journalistic, and/or travelogue genre and, so, in a sense, brings Fulbrook's suggested three phases full circle, back to a dominant mode and interest in the victims, villains and heroes. Inevitably, whilst these accounts certainly bring to life various interesting episodes and demonstrate the daily, often mundane impact the Wall had on many people's lives, they tend to construct overly simplistic, stereotypical portraits of East Germans and East Germany. So, for example, based on relatively limited (and not always verifiable) eye-witness accounts and memoirs, the stories and gossip collected in these books about the 'East' tend to blend one with the other. Furthermore, the very idea of dividing up citizens as 'heroes, victims and villains' places emphasis upon a heroic fall of the Wall and the victory of 'freedom' over communism.

The philosopher Jacques Derrida (1993) confronts this problematic of representing the 'East' when attempting to recount a visit to Moscow – a trip he made just after the collapse of communism. Before putting pen to paper, he is aware of the full predicament of writing about his travels and the people he has met, aware of the fact that he is potentially signing away the authority of that place and of those people speaking for themselves. This predicament is not about any one single diary that he or anyone else might write, as such, but more a concern with the structural relationship between a literary genre and political history, principally, the genre or mode of the 'travelogue'. Specific to his particular journey to Russia (and back), Derrida refers to this 'tradition' of literature as a collection *back from the USSRs*.[20] As a parallel to which, I suggest the literatures, discussion, commentary and rhetorics of the fall of the Wall taken together can be said to form an equivalent trope, *back from the Wall*. On being 'back from', suggests a certain beyond, which in the first case, Derrida notes, relates to 'pilgrimage narratives, of every poem in the direction of a "paradise lost" or a "promised land," of all utopias' (1993: 199). Yet, by contrast, at the close of the century, with the case of the fall of the Wall and more broadly the collapse of communism, these utopias are inverted; any *back from the Wall* is framed as a fleeing from dsytopia (leading the way *back*, according to Fukuyama and others, to the 'promised lands' of liberal democracy). Fundamentally, the assertion of being 'back from' – whether it is found in travelogues or political commentary – reveals the *privilege* of being able to travel (and think) freely, as well as to remind of the fact that the place of return is the centre (to an *other* periphery). It goes without saying, East Germans were never allowed to visit the West, never able to create their own representation of the other side, whilst those living in the West were privy to a *whole* other view of their neighbours. The result of which is that (and as part of a general discourse of the 'East') the eastern 'edge' of Europe can be considered (even to this day) to bear symptoms of an *Other* Europe.

This state of affairs can in part be described in terms of orientalism (Said 1978). Karen Franz (1996) makes a convincing case for the use of this framework in her content analysis of local US news coverage of the event of the fall of the Wall. Echoing what I term the 'theme of celebration', Franz notes how through a continuation of Cold War rhetoric and the use of specific visual images of the East that construct a certain 'imaginative geography...of the life *behind* and *in front* of the Wall', the reporting of the event reinforces simplistic dichotomies, ultimately making the coverage of the Berlin Wall open to 'imperial enterprise'. As she notes, this makes for something of a paradox, 'since the initial motive for covering the event as a prominent international news story was the perception that the Wall as a barrier between different ideological state systems had been successfully taken down'. Yet, we find this division – if in a different form – only persists. Overall, Franz shows how the local television news of the event of the fall of the Wall constructs a cultural group, of East Germans, as 'Other'.

To develop Franz's argument further, the particular and quite prevalent phenomenon commonly termed *ostalgia* (meaning nostalgia for the East, or *Ost*) is an example of a somewhat *inverted* form of orientalism. The inversion occurs in that, whilst there is a trend to dominate this East, both in terms of political and economic conquest, any quest for 'oriental' mystery and sexuality is either reversed as being located in the West[21] or is in fact substituted by a quest for greyness and impotency. The writer and critic Lesley Chamberlain neatly captures this sentiment in her autobiographical reflections on traveling across Eastern Europe in the early 80s, where she describes herself as, 'a discontented Westerner, *dazzled by austerity*' (Chamberlain 1990: 23, emphasis added). I read this travelogue almost a decade *after* the fall of the Wall, at a time when I was living in a very small undistinguished town in former East Germany; a town still finding its feet in the new social and economic climate of reunification. On my return home to the United Kingdom (on being '*back from...*' and being surrounded again by the full range of mod cons and rich temptations of consumer life), I felt I knew exactly what was meant by being 'dazzled by austerity' having just come from 'a way of life not super, not prepackaged, not alienated' (Chamberlain 1990: 23). This feeling was, of course, as much to do with the fact that I had been a tourist of this lifestyle, *indulging* in the severity of a so-called *ostalgia*.

This nostalgia for the products and ways of the former GDR has been a genuine feature of popular culture in both East and West Germany following the collapse of the GDR regime. For East Germans it has been a potentially significant tactic in reasserting an identity specific to the former East Germany. Yet, it has equally been a fetish of the western viewer, characteristic of the orientalist vision, a vision of which the desire is *not* to know. In other words, an espoused 'knowledge' of East German culture is based not on accuracy and utility but on the degree to which it enhances the self-esteem of the viewer. This is achieved, 'by making fiction more real, more aesthetically pleasing than truth'; the result being that such orientalism is 'a constructed ignorance, a deliberate self-deception, which is eventually projected on the Orient' (Sardar 1999: 4).

Dominic Boyer (2001: 11 – 12) provides a revealing case study on the 'Branding of the East' in the populist magazine *Super Illu*. As he explains, the magazine is a product of the (western) Bavarian publishing house Burda-Verlag, but which circulates in the Eastern German print media market. The magazine 'cultivates a hybridized East German cultural and consumer subjectivity within the context of a broader national process of assimilating post-socialist citizens into western German society'. It redefines the GDR social experience as 'cultural heritage', and generally considers itself 'an emancipatory force in eastern German life by helping East Germans to celebrate their heritage'. The argument, however, is that the dominant process of political and economic union (or assimilation) in Germany is worked through by 'transfiguring societal difference as cultural difference and by defining cultural difference, as a matter of consumer preference'. A significant observation Boyer makes is that the publisher's own rhetoric of 'success' for this publication as a 'sign of eastern "cultural authenticity"' is directly related to the 'marketing strategy for the magazine in *western* Germany', with the publishers using the *Super Illu* brand to secure advertisements from western firms. Thus, it offers, as it were, 'an ethnographic portal into the cultural values and behaviors of an East German minority population'. More worrying still, however, is the idea that '*Super Illu*'s public resonance is not entirely imaginary', that in fact it plays a part in 'a decisive if subtle and differential effect upon the formation of social identity in eastern Germany'.

The seeds of such a new cultural/consumer consciousness might well date back to the Cold War period, and certainly becomes evident in all the 'excitement' of the fall of the Berlin Wall. Take, for example, the well-regarded historian and commentator Timothy Garton Ash. In his account of Berlin in 1989, which he was *privileged* to witness first-hand, it is evident the voice or presence of East Germans (as the main protagonists) is written up in a curiously diminished fashion, if not erased. In a passage in which he consciously tries to put the *other* side (of the story) to the pictures of the joyful celebrations of the fall of the Wall, Ash (1999) describes the apparently muted attitude of the East Germans. Yet, on closer examination, it would seem to bear all the same traits of the imposition of an attitude that comes from a privileged 'western' perspective in/of East Berlin. I quote here a passage at length to give the full flavor of the description:

> Most of the estimated two million East Germans who flooded into West Berlin over the weekend simply walked the streets in quiet family groups, often with toddlers in pushchairs. They queued up at a bank to collect the 100 Deutschmarks 'greeting money' (about thirty-five pounds) offered to visiting East Germans by the West German government, and then they went, very cautiously, shopping. Generally they bought one or two small items, perhaps some fresh fruit, a western newspaper and toys for the children. Then, clasping their carrier-bags, they walked quietly back through the Wall, through the grey, deserted streets of East Berlin, home.
>
> (Ash 1999: 62)

In similar fashion to the way I described (in chapter three) the status of East Germans in news reports as the 'extras' on a film set, these quiet, cautious citizens, 'clasping their carrier-bags' are evidently portrayed as being rather passive, almost insignificant, despite it being 'their' day to remember. And what is more, the return to the 'grey, deserted streets' would seem only to invoke an 'abroad' in relation to the West. The East is never really allowed to be a proper home; or, at least we are never given anything specific about this interior. It is left as only a perpetual abroad, awaiting its return, if not its inclusion back 'home' (in West or United Germany). Again, like the out-of-date city maps referred to in the previous chapter, there is no sense in which land is opened up to the east of the Wall. There is no *beyond* the Wall (not simply territorially, but politically and culturally too).

Ash was a direct witness to the events and his journalistic styled account is purposely written as if out of immediacy, so legitimately lacking the 'long view' that hindsight may bring. Thus, whilst Ash is pertaining to be sensitive to issues of whose voice is being heard, he is inevitably caught up by the conditions and constraints of the situation (including his decision to write in diaristic mode), as well as indeed by the ease with which (due to his western status) he can move about both a real and a fictional terrain. The latter, he himself acknowledges: 'Travelling to and fro between the two halves of the divided continent, I have sometimes thought that the real divide is between those (in the West) who have Europe and those (in the East) who believe in it' (Ash 1999: 153–154). Such a supposition is no doubt meant as polemic. Yet, as I have stressed with respect to ownership and literature of the Wall, it is something that gets continually reinforced (including by Ash himself). So, again, what is inscribed, or rather prefigured, in this *other* side of the Wall is the evident lack of an alternative. Or, where there is supposedly an alternative it comes via a western perspective – whether as in this case the 'grey, deserted streets of East Berlin' or the cultural/consumer consciousness of an *ostalgic* citizen of a United Germany.

In the face of this western bias, the point of an image critique is undoubtedly to undo the one-sided accounts of the Wall and of East Germany. In part, it might well seek to give some life and colour back to this grey, other place of East Germany. The films I discuss in the next chapter certainly attempt to do something of this kind. They indulge fully in an *ostalgia*, but done so in an ironic fashion, revealing their own narrative construction and appropriation of icons and identity. In this vein, the films re-stage the event of the fall of the Wall for new critical examination, breaking out of the mono-perspectivism of the dominant narratives of the Wall. As an underlying principle, we do not necessarily need consider the images of the fall of the Wall

to *require* a critique as such (as if somehow in itself that would solve matters), but rather to consider what value they hold in enabling critique. Thus, instead of allowing the images of the fall of the Wall to lure us down a 'one-way street', in which we only seem to bring out a privileged perspective that does little to hear alternative voices, the point of an image critique is to draw out of the images themselves some kind of critical engagement; to re-awaken ourselves to the event they portray and which we may have been caught up in. In doing so, the images can inform and *make* for us a (re)newed critical space, allowing multiple perspectives to co-exist, broadening and enriching our understanding of the event of the fall of the Wall from 'both' or all sides.

In the previous chapter, I began by telling a simple story of the Berlin Wall – a story bringing together two ends of history; the first end being the building of the Wall (and all that it entailed in dividing a nation), the second, the eventual 'fall' of the Wall and the subsequent collapse of communism. Following which I sought to unpack a number of aspects relating to what Victor Burgin (1996a: 184) terms the 'imbricated time of our global lived space': an attempt to get in amongst the cracks of history as it were and hopefully along the way to have enlivened, for critical purposes, aspects of the past by bringing these into new configurations. The history of Berlin and the play of its symbols, images and myths have become embedded in our ways of thinking in the present. They have become the forces which guide both our use and understanding of history and the writing up of history itself. Arguably, in picking my way through the 'wreckage and debris' of recent accounts, I have tried to hold to what is a difficult line of argument, that the fall of the Berlin Wall was not necessarily the joyous event we tend otherwise to remember. By the same measure, I hardly wish to suggest the Wall should somehow have remained standing. My argument has not been so much about the politics of the fall of the Wall, but rather about what an event such as this does to our ability to engage politically and critically. Of course, I might well have to accept my place amongst the so-called 'prattling classes', which Slavoj Žižek wonderfully describes as follows:

> academics and journalists with no solid professional education, usually working in humanities with some vague French postmodern leanings, specialists in everything, prone to verbal radicalism, in love with paradoxical formulations that flatly contradict the obvious. When faced with the fundamental liberal-democratic tenets, they display a breathtaking talent to unearth hidden traps of domination. When faced with an attack on these tenets, they display a no less breathtaking ability to discover emancipatory potential in it.
>
> (*The Guardian*, 19.2.05, p. 23)

I am attuned to the fact that in proposing a so-called image critique I must be wary of 'verbal radicalism', and clearly in attempting to critique the events of the fall of the Berlin Wall I may well be prone to displaying the fanciful 'talent to unearth hidden traps'. Žižek wrote the above remarks in the context, post-9/11, when 'the prospect of a new global crisis is looming'. It is a time, he notes, that breaks Fukuyama's 'dream of the "end of history."' Today, new battle lines have been drawn up, with the ruling ideology having 'appropriated the September 11 tragedy', using it to impose the stark message that 'it is time to stop playing around, you have to take sides'. The key point he makes, however, can be related to both scenarios, either after the Wall, or amidst the contemporary so-called 'War on Terror'. His advice is that it is precisely in those times when the choices seem overtly clear (when which 'side' you should be on goes without question) that there is a great deal of critical work to be done. He concludes his argument with a joke to illustrate this point:

> Recall the old story about a worker suspected of stealing. Every evening, when he was leaving the factory, the wheelbarrow he was rolling in front of him was carefully inspected, but it was always empty – till, finally, the guards got the point: what the worker was stealing were the wheel-barrows themselves. This is the trick that those who claim today "But the world is none the less better off without Saddam!" try to pull on us: they forget to include in the account the effects of the very military intervention against Saddam. Yes, the world is better without Saddam – but it is not better with the military occupation of Iraq...
>
> (The Guardian, 19.2.05, p. 23)

Something similar can be said of the fall of the Berlin Wall. Of course, the world is a better place now that the Wall is no longer standing and Germany is once again a united country. However, what has consistently been left out of the picture have been the voices of the East and the evident failure of an alternative socialism to take root, despite the optimism and opportunity for its new beginning. We are better off for ridding of the inhumanity of the Berlin Wall, but that does not mean we are necessarily better off with respect to the current breadth and depth of social and political debate and organization. Living without an alternative can lead us to forget why or at least for what we are all living for!

Notes

1. For those living and working in East Germany, the socio-economic impact of the speed of transition from planned to market economy was enormous. The relatively unprotected process of change, including currency union on the politically advantageous but economically disastrous one-to-one basis, led very quickly to massive unemployment and growing insecurity for those still in work. In turn, this 'gave rise to a range of individual psychological ills; and social tensions often also led, for some, to political extremism and racial hostility' (Fulbrook 2000: 86). In fact, in the first two years following reunification, violent attacks on ethnic minorities increased, with new waves of anti-Semitism and neo-fascism widely reported. For more detailed studies relating to the process of integration of the five new Länder into the Federal Republic of Germany, see Gerber and Woods (1993;1994); and for a comprehensive overview of extreme right-wing parties in the context of European Union, see Fieschi et al., (1996).

2. Following reunification, Germany maintained its leading role in European affairs and regenerated many towns of the former GDR, along with Berlin itself, which is now home to the German governmental and diplomatic community, as well as being a primary site for key business sectors. On a domestic level, reunification meant for Germany major political and economic change and, also, led to a re-mapping of its international context. Germany quickly occupied an even more central, commanding position in the ensuing process of European integration, and almost immediately following reunification was faced with re-defining its political and military role for the wider international community.

3. The phrase 'Mauer im Kopf' (or Wall in the head) was coined by Peter Schneider in his much acclaimed Der Mauerspringer (1982) [The Wall Jumper, 1983], a collection of surreal tales centring around the lives of those living with the Wall. The phrase, which has since been widely and popularly cited, refers to the cultural and psychological condition of division between Easterners and Westerners that the book's narrator suggests will remain long after the Wall itself. Somewhat

prophetically, it is stated: 'It will take us longer to tear down the Wall in our heads than any wrecking company will need for the Wall we can see' (119). In his post-Wall follow-up, *German Comedy: Scenes of Life after the Wall* (1991), Schneider reflects again upon the dilemmas of (healing) division. The book, written in a similarly polemic and comical style, notes at one point: 'it was the Wall alone that preserved the illusion that the Wall was the only thing separating the Germans' (13).

4. For a transcript of Helmut Kohl's speech to the *Bundestag* in which he details his 'Ten-Point Plan' leading to German reunification, see: James and Stone (1992: 33–41).

5. Figures cited from *The Statistical Yearbook 2004 for the Federal Republic of Germany* (SFG Servicecenter Fachverlage, Reutlingen, Germany).

6. For a complete transcript of Christa Wolf's speech, see James and Stone (1992: 127–129).

7. For documentation and critical commentary concerning the role (and for many the perceived failure) of intellectuals with respect to the demise of the GDR and the process leading to German unification, see Huyssen (1991); von Oppen (2000); James and Stone, eds. (1992); as well as a special issue on German unification in *New German Critique*, no. 52, Winter 1991. For a consideration specifically of the western perspective, see, also, Müller (2000).

8. *Sozialistische Einheitspartie Deutschlands* [Socialist Unity Party of Germany] – the ruling communist party in the GDR from 1946 to 1989.

9. The state and future of the environment was a key concern for many of the opposition groups, which, later, following the dissolution of the communist government, would prompt the inauguration of an official 'Green Party'.

10. As Stephen Brockmann observes, 'the vast majority of the intellectuals expostulating on German unification were conspicuously men' (1991: 28). Even where parties such as Linke Liste/PDS and the Greens established links with feminist groups in order to attract women voters, neither side sought to enforce quotas to help women get elected. Indeed, the Green Party 'who had formed a coalition with the UFV, cheated their partner out of mandates in the Volkskammer, the East German Parliament' (Sieg 1993: 40). Katrin Sieg speaks of a 'feminization of the GDR as princess-bride' (39), taken over by the West and a 'masculinist, homosocial structure and naturalising language' of its ensuing process. Citing the critic Sabine Wilke, for examples, Sieg notes that the feminist political agenda was systematically marginalized, not only in terms of high politics and across party lines, but within 'the revolutionary process of the fragile opposition movements, through the streamlining of politics towards professionalization and efficiency, due to the pressure of events' (Wilke cited in Sieg 1993: 40).

11. The Round Table committee was set up specifically to include a broad spectrum of interest groups and met on sixteen occasions between December 1989 and March 1990. The emphasis – on all sides – had been upon reforming (and indeed saving) the GDR, with work progressing towards a new constitution. However, regardless of such attempts for inclusive debate, the committee was rather swept aside by a groundswell of support for early German reunification.

12. For a more in-depth enquiry into this debate (and other matters related to the status and role of women in the two Germanies), see Sharp and Flinspach (1995).

13. The extensive debates and the anxieties raised over German nationalism and the country's troubled past are collectively referred to as the 'German Question' – namely concerns over German national identity, German unity (including a consideration of reunification as a 'natural' course of action), the place and role of Germany in international and more specifically European affairs, as well as the seemingly ceaseless angst over German power. For an excellent, detailed account of these concerns, see Verheyen (1999).

14. It is perhaps worth noting, the German authorities preferred to promote celebrations of reunification rather than the fall of the Wall. In fact, it is the 3rd October – the date of formal reunification in 1990 between the Federal Republic (the West) and the GDR (the East) – that is a public holiday, and not the 9th November when the fall of the Wall took place. Of course, it must also be pointed out that the anniversary of the fall of the Wall somewhat awkwardly shares its date with *Kristallnacht* in 1938 (during Berlin's Nazi period), which was a night that saw vicious attacks on Jews, the burning of synagogues and Jewish-owned businesses.

15. The Brandenburg Gate was the most famous landmark along the course of the Wall, but it never functioned as a crossing point, including on the night of its 'fall'. However, this did not stop East and West Germans breaking through into the area. In front of the Brandenburg Gate, the Wall was at its widest, making it possible to climb up and stand on top of the Wall itself. Lines of people formed along its brow, while beneath many more were drinking Sekt, dancing and singing. And not far from this site, at the Wall's other most famous location, Checkpoint Charlie, lines of cars were beginning to form. As these vehicles crossed over to the West – the majority of which were the GDR's infamous Trabant cars – they were greeted by crowds cheering from either side of the road, like the jubilant spectators flanking at the end of a marathon race. It was from both these sites that the key television pictures were filmed, as the news journalists took up positions to file their live reports.

16. The majority of these publications take an anthropological and/or journalistic approach. See, for example, Ash (1999); Borneman (1991, 1992, 1998); Darnton (1991); Gleye (1991); Heins (1994); Stokes (1993); and Philipsen (1993).

17. For examples of this more empirical phase of research, see McAdams (2001); Grix (2000); Opp et al. (1995); and specific to the *Stasi* files: Fulbrook (1995); Childs and Popplewell (1996); Glees (2004); Dennis (2003); Koehler (2000); Miller (2004).

18. In this third phase, research interests have ranged widely over, for example, the role of German intellectuals (see Bialas 1996; von Oppen 2000), problems of cultural integration (see Gerber and Woods (eds.) 1993, 1994) and cultural identity (see Gerber and Woods (eds.) 1996; Borneman 1998; Viehoff and Segers (eds) 1999). In addition, the study of material culture has been of particular interest, with, for example, research into the symbolic significance of pop music in the GDR (Wicke 1996) and patterns and styles of consumption following reunification (Veenis 1997, 1999; Bertsch et al. 1994).

19. Besides architectural interest (see Ladd, 1997: 7–39; Feversham and Schmidt 1999; Leach 1999; Balfour 1990, 1995), the only specific academic publication on the Wall after its 'fall' has been Schürer et al., *The Berlin Wall: Representations and Perspectives*, (1996). This book, aimed at a relatively narrow, specialist Germanist and literary audience (seemingly doomed from the outset to hardback obscurity) brings together a collection of articles each tending to concentrate on specific literary texts to offer politicized accounts, predictably bringing into focus issues of under-representation of East Germans and East German culture.

20. The phrase 'Back from the USSRs' purposely echoes a song title of the Beatles, 'Back from the USSR'. In this song the lyrics ironically tell of someone returning to from the West to the East, so as apparently to give voice to the East.

21. The consumerism of West Berlin during the Cold War is frequently listed as a determining factor to the gradual relaxation of GDR state policies. For some useful studies on this subject, see Borneman (1991, 1992, 1998); Darnton (1991); Heins (1994); Stein (1993, 1996: 333–346); and Veenis (1997, 1999).

[Newsflash:] "...our Comrade Erich Honecker, in a typically generous humanitarian gesture, granted political asylum in the GDR to West Germans seeking refuge in our Prague and Budapest embassies. Honecker sees this as a historic shift in East-West relations and promised everyone entering the GDR 200 Marks 'welcome money.' Unemployment, bleak prospects, and the increasing success of the neo-Nazi parties in West Germany have caused many worried West Germans to turn away from capitalism in recent months...."

– from Goodbye Lenin! (2002)

CHAPTER FIVE

PUBLIC SCREENING: CRITICAL PICTURES OF THE WALL

An image critique as a critical strategy need not achieve resolution or conclusion in its 'analysis' (nor even a stable interpretation), but instead seeks to maintain 'polyperspectival' critical reflection. The point is to 'thicken' the picture, to afford ourselves 'situations of writing' (or picturing) in which to keep open certain questions and to make sense not only of events themselves, but also our own place within them. An image critique, then is to provide the means to re-stage events with the prospect that images (as images) get to look back at us, not the other way round. It lets *their* 'wonder' be a means to intrigue us again, to give recourse to (re-)think things through. In this chapter, I consider more concretely what an image critique of the fall of the Berlin Wall might actually *look* like, for which I draw upon the example of two popular artworks. Both happen to be film comedies set around the time of the fall of the Wall. The first is Thomas Brussig's (1995) *Helden wie wir* [*Heroes Like Us*], which was originally published as a novel and later made into a feature film in 1999. The second is Wolfgang Becker's acclaimed film *Goodbye Lenin!* (2002).[1] These works have both been highly popular (particularly with German audiences). Both, I want to suggest, present us with 'metapictures' of the media event of the fall of the Wall. Here I refer to Mitchell's (1994: 35–82) notion of metapictures, which he describes as 'pictures that refer to themselves or to other pictures, pictures that are used to show what a picture is'. The effects of the metapicture can be seen with the two films in one quite obvious sense, since they both incorporate *real* news/documentary footage into newly constructed narrative contexts, a technique in common, for example, with films such as *JFK* (1991) and *Forrest Gump* (1994). In this fashion, the 'real' event of the fall of the Wall is re-enacted (or, perhaps, more literally re-inscribed) for new and frequently comic effect. At the same time, however, to take the concept of the metapicture in a less literal sense, both films construct a layered, loaded narrative that work towards something like a polyperspectival re-visioning of the fall of the Wall.

Whilst the two films discussed here do exhibit important aspects and principles of an image critique, neither film should be taken as synonymous with the notion of an image critique. In fact, commentary on them (relating only to very specific scenes) is embedded in a broader theoretical discussion in which I consider both how an image critique might be shaped and designed, as well as how it is to be seen *publicly*. The latter issue raises questions about the place and purchase of images in the public sphere (as well as questions about how we might consider such a sphere to be visual and visualized). Following, then, an introductory overview of the two films, I develop a more theoretical account by examining concepts of public deliberation. I argue against the privileging of verbal reasoning and denigration of the media common in theories about the public sphere and, in doing so, consider illustrations from the films as they disrupt the usual interpretations of the fall of the Wall.

A key underlying concern is the importance of the visual in our ways of thinking and acting politically and philosophically, with the potential that the image – as a form of critique – might actually help maintain the ideal of an open, multivalent public sphere better than verbal reasoning. It is a prospect I develop with respect to what Kevin DeLuca and Jennifer Peeples (2002) term the 'public screen'. Their concept takes on the very logic of media technologies and accepts the contemporary conditions and prevalence of multiple media 'screens' through which all public debate must flow. A key tenet of their argument is that debate and critique is communicated more by means of dissemination than dialogue. Whilst acknowledging something of this premise (indeed, dissemination can be said to explain the *play* of the Berlin imaginary described in chapter three), I look to image critique as a means to maintain greater complexity and reflexivity over ideas and images. The point is not simply to enter into what Kevin DeLuca (1999) refers to as 'imagefare' – whereby one set of images appears only to overturn another. This phenomenon is aptly demonstrated when 'image-events' as a form of activism are staged specifically for high media impact in order not only to gain wide public dissemination, but also to re-direct public opinion in the process. As I will consider below, DeLuca's argument is certainly compelling and I readily accept the idea that an image-based critique can be effective in this manner. Furthermore, his slogan for an image politics, '[c]ritique through spectacle, not critique versus spectacle', would seem equally apt for what I describe here as an image critique. Nonetheless, I argue that there is always something incomplete about this largely antagonist process of responding to, or upstaging, one image with another. Hence, I draw upon the aforementioned idea of the metapicture to describe the potential of an image critique's greater reflexivity over the notion of 'critique through spectacle'.

Thus, instead of simply adding to the exchanges of a public screen, a more complex play of images could provide a point of concentration whereby a public can 'screen' or 'filter through' multiple aspects of what can be seen. In broad terms, what I describe here is a shift from the concept of the public sphere to the public screen and then to a notion of public *screening*. In the closing commentary which follows this chapter, I describe the 'shape' of this process in terms of a crystalline structure, which refracts and reflects an array of different visual meanings; the overall effects of which I refer to as the broaching of what Susan Sontag (1979: 180) once eloquently termed an 'ecology of images'. As part of which, I suggest, *practical* engagement with images is appropriate to contemporary visual culture. Of course, it is still frequently the case that much media and visual analysis remains 'guided by a hermeneutics of suspicion' (Hariman and Lucaites 2003: 35). Nicholas Mirzoeff (2005: 3), for example, describes an all too prevalent ritual performance of 'exposing' images, unmasking their bias or declaring their lack of reality. Subsequently, visual *practice* is all too often overlooked for its critical import, or, at least, it is rarely considered 'equal or superior to discursive media for enacting public reason or democratic deliberation' (Hariman and Lucaites 2003: 35). An image critique ought to contrast with such a tendency. In the context of Instant History and a new transparency of the media (see chapter one), we surely need to turn to the practitioner of the image as much as we might rely on the theorists – or, perhaps, more appropriately, let the distinction dissolve. It is in this vein that we might best understand Mitchell's (1994: 395) comment at the close of his discussion of Spike Lee's Do the Right Thing (1989): 'What seems called for now, and what many contemporary artists wish to provide, is a critical public art that is frank about the conditions and violence encoded in its own situation, one that dares to awaken a public sphere of resistance, struggle and dialogue'. It is this kind of work, then, that an image critique should profess to do – indeed, the kind of work that hopefully can be seen to have begun with the films I consider below.

New Critical Pictures of the Fall of the Berlin Wall

Following very soon after the fall of the Wall a wave of new German films, literature, art and popular culture (including, for example, magazines, clothing, games and even a potential GDR theme park) all contributed to a process of reflecting upon the former GDR. Much of this output can be classified under the banner of ostalgie, which, as I discussed in the previous chapter, refers to a sense of nostalgia for the East (Ost). As I noted, this can be considered an important tactic in reasserting a distinctive East German identity. Equally, however, the term can be understood to describe a western fetish and even a marketing strategy for selling the 'East' back to the East. Whatever the politics, however, ostalgie lives on unabated: East German memoirs regularly appear on the best-seller lists; T-shirts bearing the GDR logo are considered fashionable by many youths; hundreds of DEFA (Deutsche Film-Aktiengesellschaft) film classics have been re-released;[2] and as recently as 2003 a new television programme, The GDR Show, began regular transmission hosted by Katherine Witt, a former Olympic athlete often dubbed 'the beautiful face of socialism'.

Interestingly, for all this cultural output very little has been concerned specifically (or even partially) with the images of the fall of the Berlin Wall. In this regard Thomas Brussig's Helden wie wir (1999) and Wolfgang Becker's Goodbye Lenin! (2002) are notable exceptions. Both play upon ostalgic themes in the double sense of being both a distinctive East German tactic as well as a means of selling the East – though not only selling back to the East, but to a broader European audience. Not only have these films been highly popular with a German audience, but their stories have also managed (in one form or another) to reach beyond the borders of German-speaking countries. Goodbye Lenin!, in particular, was well received across Europe, winning numerous European film awards and gaining wide press coverage. Helden wie wir as a film is available only in the original German, but as a novel has been translated into English,[3] reaching both British and American audiences and gaining scholarly interest along the way (see Fröhlich 1998; Amann 2003; Prager 2004).

The story of Helden wie wir is told solely through that of its adolescent protagonist, Klaus. In the novel, he tells his story to a fictional New York Times reporter, each chapter supposedly being another reel of interview tape. Whilst the film dispenses with this narrative device, the story is similarly constructed from Klaus's own rather deluded point of view. Klaus certainly has a dramatic and purportedly historic story to tell, yet, as we soon realize, it is a quite indulgent and even ridiculous story. Essentially, in opposition to all that we thought we already knew, Klaus tells the world of how he *alone* – in quite fantastical circumstances – managed to topple the Berlin Wall. In fact, despite all that we may have heard from historians and journalists, with their grand pronouncements of 'The end of divided Germany', 'The end of the Cold War', and even the 'The end of history', Klaus tells us in his characteristic frankness that the story of the Wall's end is, in fact, intimately related to the story of his penis!

The film presents a dual private/public narrative, with Klaus getting himself caught up in a larger political history. Klaus, himself, can hardly be described as a political creature, but instead exhibits a certain fickleness; a sometimes keen socialist (eager, even, to be a prominent role model for *all* East Germans), yet equally drawn by the lure of western capitalism (evident in particular with his passion for a certain lingerie catalogue). It is only ever through his hapless nature that he becomes involved in the political world to which he is born and which eventually leads to his 'heroic' act of toppling the Berlin Wall. Before which, however, the narrative winds its way through a series of burlesque follies in which we learn of Klaus's oppressive parents and his guilt-ridden attempts to understand and later realize his sexual desires. We are also told of his fumbling exploits as a Stasi officer (although for the whole duration Klaus is never quite sure if it is the real Stasi he is involved with). Before the closing scenes in which we finally get to find out just what he means when he suggests that he alone manages to breach the Wall, there is a series of the most unlikely events (including two visits to hospital and the saving of Erich Honecker's life through blood donation) that end up with Klaus's penis having miraculously grown to gigantic proportions. It is when he leaves the hospital for the second time, encumbered by his now dramatically oversized genitals that he finds himself in the thick of the crowds amassing at the site of the Berlin Wall, calling for the opening of the border. Swept up in the excitement of it all he is inspired to expose himself to the border guards. It is with this *fantastical* gesture that he claims to bring an end to the Berlin Wall, since the guards' stunned silence is taken by the crowds as the green light to pass through the barrier gates into West Berlin. Despite the ridiculousness of this occasion (and despite his own 'naked' vulnerability), Klaus is presented less a hero of the people and more a critic of what is going on around him. At one point he describes the crowds around him 'a pathetic sight':

> There they stood, thousands of them confronted by a few dozen border guards, and they didn't dare to make a move. They shouted "We are the people!," the principle slogan of recent weeks, and somehow it hit the nail on the head. They were indeed "the people." Who but "the people" would have stood there in such a docile, diffident way, shuffling from foot to foot and hoping against hope?...It wasn't tanks that deterred them, it was ten or a dozen ashen-faced, trembling border guards who did their duty by bracing themselves against the gate....the missing feature was an outburst of righteous public indignation.
>
> (Brussig 1997: 244–245)

As we are led to believe, Klaus' lurid spectacle makes for this much needed outburst of indignation, so placing him as the vital, missing link in this historical event.

The magic realism of *Helden wie wir* is underscored by farce, exaggeration and the obscene, all of which fits a tradition of grotesque-comic laughter as found in the carnivalesque. As Mikhail Bakhtin (1984) argues, the critical value of the carnival is in its abolishing of the boundaries between the public and private spheres, between participants and spectators and, crucially, in inverting a hierarchy, with fools and outsiders becoming 'kings' for the day. The carnival is a mocking challenge to authority with the potential to force popular political renewal. In the 'carnival' scenes of Klaus standing naked before the Berlin Wall, the film links the comic to sexuality and obscenity in order to create a dramatic 'turning point' that we might suggest works to parallel and, indeed, critique the turning point (die Wende) associated with the fall of the Wall. The book is certainly full of images and spectacles, not least because Klaus thinks in pictures, makes all sorts of clumsy spectacles of himself and throughout mixes up all sorts of images from the media (including, as discussed in detail further on, a satirical attack on a televised speech by the real-life and eminent East German writer Christa Wolf). The film version of Helden wie wir translates many of these images directly onto the screen, as well as offering its own visual language in complement. Perhaps one of the best examples of an episode not in the book is a classroom scene. After having shown an old film reel as part of a history lesson, the teacher (much to the delight of the class) plays the film backwards, making war-torn scenes repair themselves and whole armies retreat. As a comic image of historical re-visioning it offers a neat motif for the film in general, which uses various archive footage (including that of the GDR leader Erich Honecker and, of course, scenes of the fall of the Wall) to create new comic situations similar, for example, to the effects achieved in the film Forrest Gump (1994). In this way, the film usefully illustrates various aspects of the book, and it is really as a film that its ostalgic ambiance truly comes to life.[4]

Goodbye Lenin! echoes various aspects of Helden wie wir, particularly in that its main protagonist is also a young male adult with no real political allegiances, and, again, whilst the story revolves around personal and familial life, it similarly intersects with a more public, political history. The story centres on the character Alex, who under communism works in a state-owned television repair collective in East Berlin. The film begins with the fortieth anniversary of the founding of the German Democratic Republic (GDR), which includes the typical bombastic military displays through the streets of the city. Rather like the intersection of public and private histories we find in Helden wie wir, this event shakes the whole apartment in which Alex and his family live. It is in the weeks leading up to the fall of the Wall that Alex – despite his general apolitical outlook – gets caught up in a demonstration calling for regime change. His mother, Hanna, a faithful socialist, witnesses this scene just as Alex is arrested by the police, at which point she has a heart attack and falls into a coma.

In the period before Hanna wakes up from her coma, the Berlin Wall is opened and the GDR regime disbanded, with just enough time for capitalist market forces to take root. The crux of the film rests on the fact that the doctors tell Alex any undue excitement or shocks could lead to his mother having a more fatal heart attack. Alex decides he must shield his mother from knowledge of any of the recent changes. He brings her home from the hospital to recuperate and she remains in bed in her own room, which for the duration of the film becomes a kind of ersatz GDR oasis. In order to maintain the illusion, Alex has to embark on a ridiculous project to get hold of original East German products. He becomes obsessed, for example, with locating brands once so common in the GDR such as Mokkafix instant coffee, Globus peas and Spreewald gherkins. He also arranges for neighbours (attired in their old 'GDR' clothes) to visit for his mother's birthday, and hires children to dress up as Young Pioneers and sing socialist tunes. The film presents a certain celebration of a distinct East German cultural identity, which arguably is made palatable to a wider audience by the nature of its depoliticized plot. As Julian Kramer (2003) puts it, '[t]his film is not about failed political trajectories, but about how personal emotions and family life help preserve space for humanity away from the tightly controlled public realm.'

However, whilst playful, there is nonetheless a significant political dimension to this film. With the increasing encroachment of western consumerism even Hanna's bedroom is soon invaded by the new commercialism, made all too evident when, on the apartment buildings seen through her window, a huge banner advertisement for *Coca Cola* is seen to unfold. This spectacle prompts Alex to take matters a whole step further, enlisting the help of his new western work colleague (who happens to be a film enthusiast) to produce GDR-styled news programmes. The videos they make together are then 'broadcast' into Hanna's bedroom at precise times so as to appear like real live news programmes. In a series of such broadcasts Alex is able to bring his mother gradually up to date with the full reality of post-Wall Germany. In doing so, however, he manufactures a complete reversal of history, with westerners flocking to the GDR in search of the 'socialist dream' and the fall of the Wall being a *victory* for the East. The reports include the standing down of Erich Honecker (as he did in real life), which is followed not by the news of the interim leader, Egon Krenz, but instead the heroic Sigmund Jähn, the one-time East German cosmonaut (much celebrated in real life, but whom, in his fictional incarnation, Alex discovers working as a taxi driver).

In contrast to *Helden wie wir*, *Goodbye Lenin!* is certainly less confrontational and 'explicit' about the event of the fall of the Wall. Having to deal with the private turmoil of his mother's heart attack, the actual fall of the Wall all but passes Alex by. Thus, he does not engage, let alone intervene, in the event in any direct way as does Klaus in *Helden wie wir*. Nevertheless, through the fictitious news reports Alex creates, which effectively replay (in order to delay) the fall of the Wall, the film equally engages head-on with the legacy of the images of the fall of the Wall and re-stages the site of spectatorship (around the television set) for new critical ends. So, whilst the film is less provocative, it is rather more contemplative and emotional. Alex's mother (with whom we empathize throughout the film) eventually dies peacefully and (as we are implicitly told) in full knowledge of what has truly taken place politically. The result of which is that we become torn about which memory of Hanna to hold to, so helping us at least acknowledge the *possibility* of an alternative memory of the GDR and the fall of the Berlin Wall.

In common with many other o*stalgic* cultural phenomena, both *Helden wie wir* and *Goodbye Lenin!* are very much tongue-in-cheek in their representations of the former GDR. Comedy of this kind will no doubt raise concerns about whether we find ourselves laughing *at* instead of *with* the subject. Both films present fairly benign views of the GDR. So, for example, there is no mention of Stasi oppression (*Helden wie wir* does portray the *Stasi* but only in a comic, slapstick manner) or the infamous *Bautzen* (torture prison) for political dissidents. Nor, indeed, is there any concern expressed for the neo-Nazi movement which emerged immediately after the fall of the Wall (the only hint of this, in *Goodbye Lenin!*, is a brief glimpse of a swastika in the apartment elevator). Generally, then, both films offer an ambiguous comment on what for many former GDR citizens (especially among the older generation) was a bitter disappointment. The political status of both these films relates specifically to the fact that in each case the main protagonist is an adolescent who represents a generation of young East Germans uninterested in politics, with little or no feeling for their socialist upbringing. Nevertheless, a constituent element of the biting humour of these films is equally that, as unlikely heroes, the protagonists find themselves either (as in *Helden wie wir*) coming to the rescue of their fellow citizens, or (as in *Goodbye Lenin!*) resuscitating the lifestyle of the GDR in order to keep alive a socialist dream.

The youthful re-visioning of the GDR is crucial to how these films attempt to break away from dominant interpretations of the fall of the Wall. As discussed in the preceding chapter, the prevailing sentiment of the GDR as only grey, drab and incarcerating has arguably prevented a more complex and vital portrait of 'really existing' East German culture. By contrast, these films use comedy and colour to engage with the past in a completely different way. In an interview, the author and screenwriter of *Helden wie wir*, Thomas Brussig, makes this point clear:

> When the GDR existed its own self-perception was only ever the result of intense, deep-mined introspection. Now, since its demise, we suddenly realise it is possible to tell the story of the GDR as much through its profanities and absurdities. The GDR had an everyday life and it had an actual interior, within which are embedded a great many good and up until now neglected stories.
>
> (Brussig 1999: 255)[5]

Both *Helden wie wir* and *Goodbye Lenin!* can be understood to mine this 'actual interior' in order to produce their humorous (and at times absurd) stories about the GDR. These are by no means frivolous stories, but cleverly layered narratives that make insightful reuse of East German iconography, as well as the archive images of the Wall in order to refocus the past and reopen to the scrutiny of a public sphere a counter-commentary of the events of 1989.

In watching the films' intersecting of the public and the private, two important points come to light. The first relates to the principle of their narrative construction and the second, their relative lack of a definite political message. These points can be made clearer by drawing comparisons with Mitchell's account (1994: 371–96, 397–16) of Spike Lee's *Do the Right Thing* (1989) and Oliver Stone's *JFK* (1991). These films, Mitchell argues, 'are notable, if not for their "transparency", for a certain frankness about their rhetorical address to the spectator'. They are explicit about making (and posing as) social/political intervention. In this respect they are an overtly *public* form of art. A particular, defining feature of these films is 'a kind of crudity and naiveté in narrative construction' (Mitchell 1994: 369). *Do the Right Thing*, for example, tells a story about ethnic conflict in relation to notions of the public sphere and private property. It shows how the various tensions are relayed in terms of specific images, fetishes and symbolism. Of particular note is the way in which the film portrays various black stereotypes, for which Spike Lee has been criticized. Yet, arguably, the larger-than-life caricatures that inhabit the film are not to be thought of as realistic in any straightforward sense. Rather, they are designed to be 'highly realistic representations of the public *images* of blacks, the caricatures imposed on them and (sometimes) acted out by them' (Mitchell 1994: 390 [original emphasis]). A similar case is made for *JFK*, which it can be suggested is a film not so much about the assassination of President John F. Kennedy, as about the myth-making of this historic event (Mitchell 1994: 397–416).

Thus, both these films assimilate relevant characteristics of contemporary visual culture, incorporating its failings as much as its achievements. *Do the Right Thing*, whilst undoubtedly 'a critique of the effects of capital in a multi-ethnic American community', incorporates the use of commodity fetishism as part of its storytelling. Significantly, the meaning of these fetishes, 'is not confused with labelling them as fetishistic. They are treated critically, with irony, but without the generalised contempt and condescension generally afforded to "mere" fetishes' (Mitchell 1994: 394–95). It is in such regard, then, that both these films provide what might be described as a form of immanent critique, situating themselves within the terms of some 'original' *mise-en-scène*, combined with an overt sense of their own narrative construction. The consequence of such critique is palpably to engage us with ethical dilemmas and to remind us of the very conditions of our own spectatorship.

Helden wie wir and *Goodbye Lenin!* can be said to exhibit a similar kind of frankness about their rhetorical address. *Helden wie wir* (through the preposterous posturings of Klaus) is certainly explicit about posing as some kind of social/political intervention. And, in both cases – whether as a result of Klaus's exhibitionism or Alex's fabricated news stories – these films represent very overt public forms of art or communication. Furthermore, both films function with respect to a kind of self-conscious crudity or naiveté in their narrative construction. Indeed, even putting aside the explicit reuse of archive footage, in simple formalistic terms both films exhibit the irreality of the world they represent. In *Helden wie wir*, in scenes of Klaus as a young boy, we see through the window of the apartment strange cartoon sequences. Similarly in *Goodbye Lenin!* cartoon animation is intercut at odd moments into the live action and various sequences are shown in slow motion or with time-lapse photography (the latter particularly evident in a humorous sequence in which the mother's bedroom is converted back to its former GDR 'glory').

A further important observation to make about these films is that as a result of the ironies that arise from the comic, self-conscious constructions of their narratives, they remain relatively ambiguous in terms of any overall 'message' about the fall of the Wall. Significantly, then, whilst both film-makers undoubtedly hold their own particular political beliefs, they do not necessarily impose these upon our *experience* of watching the films. And, it is precisely because there would appear to be no final thesis on the whys and wherefores of the fall of the Wall that I want to suggest we can suitably understand these films as offering 'spaces' (or a medium) through which new critical pictures of the event can be publicly exchanged and deliberated over. These are not pictures of interpretation that somehow supplant their predecessors (if such a thing were possible anyway). Instead the films can be thought to picture a *continual picturing* of the event of the fall of the Wall. They open out and maintain a greater complexity and architecture of the event, reinvigorating and challenging public debate about the fall of the Wall. In following this line of thought, it is perhaps pertinent to think of new definitions of the public sphere, specifically with regard to how *visual* critical engagements can offer new, different possibilities to those of verbal, rational debates.

Picturing the Public Sphere

The 'public sphere' refers to a model of social space in which private citizens publicly and rationally negotiate ethical and political matters; it is a space that mediates between civil society and the state, both legitimating and keeping in check the latter's power. In 'reality' the public sphere is really only something of an ideal or even a myth of democratic society. Nonetheless, as DeLuca and Peeples (2002: 128) point out, even its fervent critics usually come round to the idea that it is a *necessary possibility* for the hopes of social and political theory. The origins of the public sphere are most commonly ascribed to Ancient Greece with its overtly strict division between public and private affairs. The distinction, however, is different from that between simply inside and outside, for the public sphere is a domain in which both subjective and worldly (or communal) experiences are brought together. Of course, the public sphere of the Greek *polis*, which excluded women, children, labourers, non-residents and slaves, hardly equates to our modern, inclusive understanding of democracy. Nevertheless, the Greek conception has remained useful for defining or imagining a place outside the realm of power and special interests, a space in which one can become *openly* public. Of particular note, the public sphere is on occasion described as a visually oriented arena, offering the ability to see and be seen. So, for example, the Ancient Greek, 'could use his or her eyes to see the complexities of life', for, in a very tangible sense, the 'temples, markets, playing fields, meeting places, walls, public statuary, and paintings of the ancient city represented the culture's values in religion, politics, and family life' (Sennett 1990: xi).

Richard Sennett (1990: xii) describes how this ability to see the 'complexity of life' is one that allowed emotional, ethical and spiritual concerns to be given representation in and as a result of the immediate surroundings. Moreover, he refers to the sense of 'openness', whereby public spaces function as sites in which people can come together publicly and citizens are able to open their eyes, 'to think about political, religious and erotic experiences'. By comparison, with its proliferation of many more *privately* experienced public spaces (such as the shopping centre, automobiles and leisure complexes), Sennett argues that our own contemporary culture has closed down such openness, thwarting our ability to see complexity in this way. Arguably, then, we have lost or at least neglect something of this ability to see. Nevertheless, following Mitchell (1999: 12), it might be argued that visual cultural phenomena might usefully be thought of as 'go-betweens' in social life, offering an important 'repertoire of screen images or templates that structure our encounters with other human beings'. The images of the fall of the Berlin Wall, for example, not only portrayed a scene of human engagement, they also provided the opportunity to strengthen these relations, bringing more people out onto the streets and gaining the attention of the world's media. In effect, these images provided a means not only to share, but also believe in something larger than the sum of its parts. A phenomenon that allowed for the display of civic 'emotions,' for a social body to 'interrupt' itself as to mark some shared occasion (Dayan and Katz 1992: viii-ix). Furthermore, the importance of these images hold an after-life, we might still think of them as providing a specific, shared visual experience through which we see, if not the 'complexity of life', the complexity of a particular political/historical occasion.

Sennett's account of the demise of the public sphere reflects a key concern of Jürgen Habermas' (1989) more definitive study of the structural transformation (and demise) of the public sphere in the modern period. Habermas too retains something of the Ancient Greek conception when referring to 'an essential part of the life world in which people interact and make sense of their lives' (Hohendahl in Habermas 1998: viii). More specifically, he considers a public sphere of private individuals, historically rooted in the bourgeois public sphere of the eighteenth and nineteenth centuries and the concomitant rise of a new sociability that marked the separation of society from its ruler (the State). Habermas' account is of an ideal typified by the culture of salons and coffee houses, along with the dramatic growth of the literary sphere with its impact on the availability of public information. His critical argument is that by the twentieth century this Enlightenment model of a literate, freethinking public has been transformed, due largely to the emergence of mass culture and 'commercial industrial publicity'. For Habermas, then, the contemporary public sphere is to be considered more as an arena for advertising than critical debate. It is a sphere in which the state, corporate actors and special interest organizations make use of what he terms 'publicity work', the aim of which is to strengthen 'the prestige of one's own position without making the matter on which a compromise is to be achieved itself a topic of public discussion' (Habermas 1989: 200). It is an argument that leads many to herald Habermas as the rightful heir to the intellectual project of the Frankfurt School, at least in the sense that it laments a fall from high to low culture, from literary culture (and verbal reasoning) to culture of new media forms (and *visual* reasoning).

Following Habermas' account the proper functioning of this sphere is predicated upon a linguistic mode of rational discourse; a mode of apparently unrivalled analytic enquiry obviating any other mode of communication, including the visual. This is a recurrent if not dominant theme in much analysis and theorization of the public sphere and its relation to the media.[6] Jon Simons (2000) brings it to attention acutely in his discussion of critical approaches following the shift from ideological- to media-dominated politics. All too frequently, he argues, images of all types come to be regarded as the *impoverishment* of politics, seen as contributing to the distortion (rather than the means) of communication. Habermas (1999: 435–439) does in fact attempt to make some distinction between media practices that resemble discursive communicative process and those that actively seek to sway opinion and influence behaviour. His argument is that mass communications *in themselves* should not to be taken as the distortion of communication. However, his general appeal to 'the fundamental norms of rational speech' as the underpinning of deliberative democracy has led commentators to overemphasize the difference between verbal reasoning (a systematic presentation of ideas/ideologies) and non-verbal reasoning, as we might find with visual and narrative representations (Simons 2000). In this way, deliberation is all too simply considered an antidote to the images and 'scenes' of political life; or to put it another way, images are not taken to actually play any part in the *act* of deliberating itself, but instead are something over which we might deliberate. Such a view would inevitably have little to say about the kind of *displays* of political deliberation evident with the autumn street protesters in East Germany and the actual 'televisual' event of the fall of the Wall itself.

Approaches in cultural studies and more recently visual cultural studies have argued for a more sophisticated measure of our consumption of an image culture, allowing the possibility, for example, of 'negotiated' and oppositional readings. Yet, here again – abiding by a linguistic turn, not a pictorial one – there is still a tempering of the image in line specifically with a linguistic (and semiotic) framework of analysis. Take, for example, Stuart Hall's (1980) much cited encoding/decoding model for understanding media messages. Breaking from a traditional view of communication as a circuit that simply moves messages on in a linear fashion, this model gives credence to *distinctive moments* in the articulation of messages. Each message form is afforded 'its own specific modality, its own forms and conditions of existence' (Hall 1980: 128), so allowing for greater complexity in understanding the 'passage of forms.'[7] Nevertheless, from Hall's account, it is apparent that each 'message form' is understood to derive from the symbolic (languaged) order. A consequence of which is that observable 'reality' is always set apart from its representation. As Hall (1980: 131) puts it, '[r]eality exists outside language, but it is constantly mediated by and through language'. Even a 'live' event such as the fall of the Berlin Wall is a product of discourse, or what Hall refers to as the 'operation of the code':

A "raw" historical event cannot, in that form, be transmitted by, say, a television newscast. Events can only be signified within the aural-visual forms of the televisual discourse. In the moment when a historical event passes under the sign of discourse, it is subject to all the complex formal "rules" by which language signifies. To put it paradoxically, the event must become a "story" before it can become a communicative event.

(Hall 1980: 129)

It certainly makes sense to say an event such as the fall of the Wall will inevitably be transformed in transmission as a television newscast, adhering to various journalistic codes and technical conventions. In order to communicate this event, it is necessary somehow to anchor meaning – to tell a 'story'.

Nevertheless, to refer to the event of the fall of the Wall only in terms of a communicative event that adheres to the 'operation' of codes would seem rather too convenient. It surely misses an important point about the resonance of these images of the fall of the Wall as *images* (as 'things' that surround us), not as a code or story. In this respect, it is useful to return to Hall's understanding of the media and, in particular, point out the critical value of his emphasis on *form*. It is an emphasis that allows us to make sense of the practical effects that ideas and concepts have in organizing social groups and making meaning. Language in Hall's view is not referential, but rather a *medium* through which meaning is made. The problem, however, would seem to be that following this logic he fails to consider the image itself as form, but merely as content in need of (verbal) critique. As Simons (2000: 96) highlights, Hall makes this conjunction explicit when describing the difference between ideology (like language) as a structure or set of rules which frame various *contents* of images and concepts. In many other respects Hall would seem to understand all too well the importance of images in political mediation, evident in his analysis of the rise of a new 'image' of Britishness, linked to the popularism of Thatcherite politics in the 1980s (see Hall 1983). Although he does not suggest any specific counter-strategy as such, he does at least make it clear there is much to be learnt from the detrimental effects on British Left politics of the negative images (such as trade union strife) that took root at this time. Significantly, in this case, his point is not to 'expose' the falseness of such images, but instead to engage in the reality of them, the sort of 'reality' of images that, as I noted, we find Spike Lee engaging with in his film *Do the Right Thing* (in this case images of Black stereotypes). Similarly, then, in relation to both *Helden wie wir* and *Goodbye Lenin!*, it is possible to consider how they operate on the level of images themselves as a means to form a critique.

When Margaret Thatcher stepped out into Downing Street to give her initial reaction to the fall of the Wall before the awaiting media, her message was to remind us of the need not only to hear about the scenes on television, but to watch them for ourselves: 'to see them because you see the joy on people's faces and you see what freedom means'. Inevitably, she used the occasion to make a political comment on the virtues of liberal democracy, but which she achieved not so much through verbal rhetoric, but more shrewdly by letting the images 'speak' for themselves; accepting and even indulging in their reality. The problem with this, however, would seem to be that for those wishing to take a more cautious or critical stance there is apparently no *other* way of watching these scenes. In other words, looking at the very same images, there is a difficulty in making use of them for alternative ends, for a Left politics, for example, and/or the all too brief optimistic new politics of the East German opposition groups.

A useful illustration of this dilemma can be made with Habermas' commentary on the event. As noted in the previous chapter, Habermas (1994: 39) was certainly very critical of 'revolutionary' interpretations of the event, arguing that these were imposed by the West, 'perhaps to cover the need for remedial work, for making up for lost time'. Yet, those very same images that Thatcher suggests show us 'what freedom means' can be of no less significance to Habermas. However, whilst he does acknowledge their importance (at least in that we can not *not* take notice of them), we still find him suggesting we somehow put them to one side:

> *Images of liberation and of capitulation telescope into one another; what's left behind is the mournful fact that, of all the data that have brashly been declared as 'historical,' hardly one of them will impress itself on the collective memory of coming generations. What happened at the beginning was purity of feeling, a moment of solidarity and joy, indeed a glimpse of the sublime for everyone who empathized with the elated celebration on the television screen; the utterly civil enthusiasm of the streams of East Germans rushing westward, reclaiming their immediate physical freedom. I'm afraid that no historically lasting memories will crystallize from this emotional beginning.*
>
> (Habermas 1994: 41)

Habermas' line of argument is quite consistent with his concerns for the decline of the public sphere. On one level, then, it is quite straightforward: the media images of the fall of the Wall distract from the more important historical and ideological shift that brings about the whole collapse of communism and, in Germany, the procession to unification. The images are potentially the distortion of this 'communicative event', against which Habermas (1994: 41) would seem to prefer to take the view that the 'mode of the unification process itself is more important', adding that the event will be interpreted 'retrospectively' with respect to the fact that the tempo of change was 'dictated' by the federal government of West Germany. This is, indeed, how numerous accounts of reunification are explained,[8] but rarely are they *remembered* in the way that the *images* of the fall of the Wall are remembered and re-cited. In this light, we might accept Habermas' comment on these images to refer not so much to a distortion of the event as to a failure. The event these images depict, he suggests, 'may well have objectively brought about a "turn," but weren't able to complete it'. He goes on to argue that, unlike the French Revolution, the revolutionary 'consciousness' that was palpably (and visually) in evidence with the event of the fall of the Wall was not in the end able to secure its future. Thus, the 'purity of feeling', the 'utterly civil enthusiasm' and sense of solidarity that the images of this event portrayed were not, in the end, able to fulfil their potential, to carve out a *new* political future for East Germany, but instead, through reunification, helped settle an existing political and economic framework. This, above all, is the apparent burden the images present for critics of the event.

Peter Uwe Hohendahl (1995: 27) makes a similar observation, explaining that whilst the events of the fall of the Wall are agreed by most to have been 'the right stuff for television', it is also the case that any subsequent debate about the meaning and implications for the future of Germany and Europe has been thought to be more appropriately conducted through the print media. Thus, he notes that the 'public demand' for more in-depth information and analysis is argued to have occurred 'precisely because the events that resulted in the unification occurred so fast that those who participated in them [...] found it difficult to get a *complete picture* of the structural transformation' (Hohendahl 1995: 27). But what would this 'complete picture' look like, if not something like what we already see with the eventful images of the fall of the Wall? The *idea* of a 'complete picture' suggests a movement *away* from the actual images of the fall of the Wall, as if somehow they were never going to be able to show us anything of the 'true' nature of the event. Such a view maintains a Platonic distinction between the images of the event and the 'reality' of the transformation behind them. Susan Sontag (1979: 179), in writing about our photographic era and the industrial rise of what she calls our 'image-world', argues how such a distinction is now 'less and less plausible'. And whilst, in part, she means this as some kind of lament, Sontag equally suggests we have to understand images to be a part of our 'real' world. She interjects a certain ethical dimension, arguing that as much as real things in the world, we need 'an ecology of images'. Her point is that we need to sift through images in order to make sense of what is truly important about them and crucially, in light of a seemingly overabundance of images, we need to find strategies to keep critically aware of them. In other words, we must not become complacent or fatigued simply because the same images seem to appear again and again (with the same story to tell). Quite the opposite, we need to find the means to remain fresh to the surprises (the affects) that images make. Above all, she would seem to suggest there is always a social (collective) responsibility in maintaining critical strategies towards the image-world we have come to make and inhabit. And, significantly, she accepts that our strategies in this case can come in the form of the images themselves, noting that the camera is both 'antidote and the disease, a means of appropriating reality and a means of making it obsolete'.

Towards *Other* Kinds of Public Deliberations

The films *Helden wie wir* and *Goodbye Lenin!* both seek to re-stage the image event of the fall of the Wall, which specifically enables a critical engagement with the *moment* of solidarity (for all its 'purity of feeling') that Habermas otherwise finds unhelpful to our understanding of the situation. Both films renew our experience of the event, whilst concurrently furnishing it with new critical opportunities. In *Goodbye Lenin!* the events of the fall of the Wall are retold as a 'what if' story: what if the Wall had fallen because *West* Germans had wanted to escape from their economic and political context? This re-visioning of history is depicted as an overt fiction, told through the series of fake news broadcasts. The sequence of these news reports almost literally takes the media event of the fall of the Wall apart piece by piece to put it back together again from an East German point of view. Arguably, this is a stereotypical, *ostalgic* perspective that is presented, but, equally, we are 'in on the act' and know these reports to be an ironic invention of the facts. We watch the 'broadcasts' not so much for what they say, but rather more for *how* they manage to negotiate the past to claim a victory for the GDR. So, for example, following a scene in which Alex's mother ventures outside and witnesses at first hand the influx of West

German consumerist culture (she literally meets a young West German man moving his 'fashionable' belongings into her apartment block), we wait to find out how Alex's manages to acknowledge this new reality in a way that is still in keeping with his mother's ideals. The news broadcast he fabricates is a report on how the GDR government, 'in a typically humanitarian gesture' have arranged to take in a growing number of political asylum seekers coming from West Germany. The *real* scenes of East Germans taking refuge in the Prague and Budapest embassies (which were genuinely aired on western television news programmes at the time leading up to the fall of the Wall) are appropriated as if to show *West* Germans fleeing their country. After watching these scenes Alex's mother immediately suggests they have room in their flat to take in refugees and it is their duty to do so! Her response inevitably only further complicates matters for Alex, prompting yet further refashioning and re-cycling of past news events. Overall, this re-negotiation of the past – placed in the context of private family emotions – makes for an intriguing 'thought-experiment' that brings to the fore various ethical, political and emotional concerns specific to East Germans going through this period of change.

Helden wie wir similarly replays to new effect the event of the fall of the Wall. Again, in part, this is achieved in the film version through the use of actual archive footage of the event. However, disrupting the main flow of events is the blundering, egocentric teenage protagonist, Klaus. As explained, his claim throughout the story is that he *alone* opens the Berlin Wall and as the narrative develops we are eventually led up to the 'real' scenes of the crowds standing before the Berlin Wall, calling to the border guards for the gates to be opened. It is into this 'original' scene that Klaus is inserted. As we know, following a freak medical accident leaving him with genitals of 'fantastic' proportions, Klaus is able to shock the border guards into opening the gates simply by exposing himself to them. Despite this being an obviously ridiculous sequence we are nonetheless presented with the scene of the fall of the Berlin Wall as we *might* otherwise have known it (complete, in fact, with a montage sequence of library images of the night of the fall of the Wall, edited to Louis Armstrong's 'What a Wonderful World').

Similar, then, to *Goodbye Lenin!*, the narrative of *Helden wie wir* incorporates 'real' representations of the event of the fall of the Wall, yet situates them within a blatant, even ridiculous fiction. As Margrit Frölich (1998: 27) contends the 'reckless' satire in *Helden wie wir* of recent German history has 'a liberating effect', for in 'exposing to laughter the stifling and asensual climate underlying the fabric of East German life...helps alleviate the weight of the past and the loss of identity resulting from the vanishing of the East German state'. Her comment might just as easily be said to describe the effect of *Goodbye Lenin!* However, although still relatively ambivalent in terms of any overt message, *Helden wie wir* does present a rather disenchanted view of the event and in particular a critique of 'the people' of East Germany. As we know, Klaus is a most unlikely, even an exaggerated and unreliable 'hero' of the story. Interposing him as the missing link in the event of the fall of the Wall makes a rather provocative statement. It is a statement perhaps best encapsulated by Klaus himself when he exclaims to the reader: 'look at the East Germans today: as passive now as they always were. How could *they* have demolished the Wall?' (Brussig 1997: 248). The overtly grotesque, satirical comedy of *Helden wie wir* would seem to turn the 'magic moment' of the civic uprising of the fall of 1989 on its head, asking us to question again its display of civic protest and change. In this sense, it can be seen to have reclaimed (for critical evaluation) the images or spectacle of the fall of the Wall as a moment of incompletion, even failure.

The point of view expressed by *Helden wie wir* would seem in many respects to parallel Habermas' critique of the event. So, just as Habermas is highly critical of interpretations of revolution, the account offered by *Helden wie wir* is rather scathing about 'the people' of East Germany, suggesting they were never actually capable of revolution. The difference in approach is that unlike Habermas, *Helden wie wir* – particularly as a film – can engage directly with the images of the fall of the Wall, considering them vital to our subsequent understanding of this period of history. This level of engagement with the image maintains our connection to the event of the fall of the Wall in the very terms by which we most remember and experienced the event. In so doing, not only does *Helden wie wir* re-stage the event in a newly critical and provocative manner, but also manages, through the very same spectacle of the fall of the Wall, to fill something of a 'blind spot', which at the very least is to 'entertain' an East German perspective and, in particular, 'the view of someone from a generation of young East Germans' (Fröhlich 1998: 28).

It may be more appropriate to suggest – contra remarks of a 'complete picture' only coming through the print media – that the picturing of the event of the fall of the Wall is only complete when we acknowledge that it exceeds any one interpretation and that it can not be fully grasped and exchanged in verbal discourse. This is evidently the case with both *Helden wie wir* and *Goodbye Lenin!*, which appeal not to the 'fundamental norms of rational speech' but rather to the nature of the spectacle and the fictional (and even, in the case of *Helden wie wir*, the bodily). Both films manage to engage directly with the images of the fall of the Wall – for all their 'purity of feeling' – yet equally put forward a view quite different to that, for example, noted by Margaret Thatcher and all those who likewise looked on the media images – *without* questioning them – as a singular celebration of an ideological end of history.

Taking account of the new critical possibilities enabled by these films and going beyond arguments asserting the merits of verbal reasoning over the distortions of the media, we can begin to consider how we think (and act) politically as well, if not better, through the use of images as we do through ideas (Simons 2000: 94). In fact, Habermas' own definition of the public sphere can alert us to the force of this argument. In parallel to Sennett's (1990: xi) remarks on a 'visually orientated arena', Habermas too tells us how 'only in the *light* of the public sphere did that which existed become revealed, did everything become *visible* to all.' (Habermas 1989: 4, [emphasis added]). Mitchell (1994: 364) emphases this link between visual representation and uncoerced discussion to describe Habermas' template for the public sphere 'as a theatrical/architectural imagetext, an openly visible place or stage in which everything may be revealed, everyone may see and be seen, and in which everyone may speak and be heard'. Historically speaking – akin to the paradox of demarcating the rules or boundaries of a democracy – the fortunes of the public sphere have largely depended upon exclusions of one sort or another, exclusions of those who are deemed not of the 'right' age, gender, class or creed etc. If, then, a contemporary public sphere is truly to be a more all encompassing forum, it must surely be able constantly to imagine and re-imagine its space or stage, to open up to new possibilities. The public sphere should not be a fixed idea, nor a static place or stage. It is in this sense that we might consider the *images* of the fall of the Wall a vital means for our understanding and critique of the event, since the images are precisely that which we have to think about, or, indeed, think *with* in order to make sense of the event. The framing through journalistic codes obviously generates specific points of view, or ways of seeing the event, but nonetheless, since these codes were and remain a nodal point in which we all share in the event of the fall of the Wall, they are a crucial resource – as drawn upon so vividly by the films *Helden wie wir* and *Goodbye Lenin!* – bringing to light a whole *other* range of interpretations and possibilities.

The Public Screen

The 'world of television news' can be argued to be much more remote than, for example, the narrative of a soap opera (or even television fiction in general), so much so that the news is often 'beyond critical judgement for many viewers' (Lewis 1991: 141–2). Yet, equally, a significant and almost paradoxical point can be made that despite the distance or incomprehension viewers experience with the news, the interpretative frameworks they fall back upon to make sense of news events actually 'come from *within* the news itself' (Lewis 1991: 141–2). The implication of which is that in order to critically engage with the news, it is important to do more than simply deal with the key issues and debates that are raised by a particular report. In fact, it is just as important to consider what aspects of a news report are pivotal to the way meaning is made and sustained, as well as how levels of incomprehension (as much as comprehension) contribute to such a process (Morley 1999). With respect to the fall of the Wall, my argument has been that the *images* of the event frame our understanding. Yet, importantly, without wanting to consider these images in an overly simplistic way as either the site/sight of a new freedom (as, for example, Thatcher remarks) or the impoverishment of a 'deeper' understanding of the event, I suggest it more appropriate to accept them as a constituent and complex kind of *visual knowledge* of the event. Such a form of knowledge helps sustain a complex and differential set of meanings, out of which various elements can be redrawn for different critical purpose – as shown, for example, with the two films' alternative representations of the fall of the Wall. It is in this respect that the aim of an image critique is to maintain – to *keep in view* – the dynamic of this complexity.

In relation to Habermas' remarks, we might well accept a potential loss of critical value as a result of the images themselves, yet, it need not then follow that the images somehow be put to one side, to look past them. On the contrary, since the images form the very framework or fabric out of which we come to make sense of the event, it is vital we engage with them directly. *Goodbye Lenin!*, in using the norms of news reporting to refashion the news of the fall of the Wall, is evidently a good illustration of this, showing exactly what it might mean to appropriate the 'logic' of these media images for new critical effect. Potentially, this use significantly alters the very basis of public debate and deliberation, prompting us perhaps to re-think the concept of the public sphere – to mark a shift towards what DeLuca and Peeples (2002) term the public *screen*; their argument being we need to accept the conditions of a mediated public arena and engage directly with images in political contexts (even create new ones) in order to play a part in contemporary public debates and opinion-making.

DeLuca and Peeples (2002: 131) take the view that as a normative ideal the public sphere holds to unrealistic notions of consensus, openness, dialogue, rationality and civility. All of these values tend to ignore the social and technological transformations of the late twentieth century, particularly the dramatic growth in new mass media technology. As something of a supplement, then, they introduce their own concept of the 'public screen', the point of which is to recognize 'that most, and the most important, public discussions take place via "screens" – television, computer, and the front page of newspapers'. They argue that we need to take communications technology seriously and to accept the work of media theorists who have suggested that 'new technologies introduce new forms of social organisation and new modes of perception'. Overall, they propose that it is only by engaging in the very terms of these new forms of organization and perception that it is possible to connect with a contemporary public; to enter an arena no longer considered a unitary whole, but rather one which is found to be in many fragments, though – like an exploded diagram – no less complex and sophisticated for it.

DeLuca and Peeples (2002: 129–131) hold to two central theoretical propositions: that the concept of *dissemination* and the *visual* describe the dominant modes in contemporary culture and politics. The public screen is first and foremost intended as a challenger to the basic premise of the public sphere as being 'a place of embodied voices, of people talking to each other, of conversation'. Instead, they suggest that in the public screen communication is more appropriately considered in terms of dissemination; that is, 'the endless proliferation and scattering of emissions without the guarantee of productive exchanges'. Arguably, it is the 'open' form of dissemination that perhaps best profits a public forum, a forum that as a result is potentially 'more democratic, open, public, equitable, receiver-oriented' . The arena of the public screen is also described as being predominantly visual. On a practical level, for example, they note how television trades in a *visual rhetoric*, 'in a discourse dominated by images not words'; and, more significantly still, that this has become so dominant 'that even newspapers can do no better than imitate TV, moving to shorter stories and colour graphics' (DeLuca and Peeples 2002: 132–133). However, rather than necessarily see this as an impoverishment of politics, DeLuca and Peeples ask us to consider this more the condition of contemporary politics. Inevitably, it is a politics in which 'there is no real public, but, rather that the public is the product of publicity, of pictures'. Images become important in the public screen not because they represent reality as such, but because they can *create* it: 'They are the place where collective social action, individual identity and symbolic imagination meet – the nexus between culture and politics' (Hartley 1992: 3). The point of engaging in the public screen is to engage in a contemporary form of citizenship, which involves a circulation of images as much as words. Releasing pictures into the world (or onto the public screen) is not simply about representing the world, but about being active in it; contributing to *being* in the world (DeLuca and Peeples 2002: 127).

Taking Walter Benjamin's (1992: 211–244) line of argument that this is a mode of perception most appropriate to the technological transformation of modern (and postmodern) culture, DeLuca and Peeples (2002) describe how the speed and images of the public screen necessitates distraction and the 'glance' as its primary forms of perception. For DeLuca (1999), the environmental pressure group Greenpeace is one useful example of a group working *through* the media, which, to put it in the words of Benjamin, gets its message heard 'much less through rapt attention than by noticing the object in incidental fashion' (Benjamin 1992: 233). In many cases Greenpeace's attempts at direct action (e.g. to stop whales being hunted, or to close down nuclear testing sites) have rarely been immediately successfully, but, instead, their activities as events *caught on film* – as image-events – have proved to be much more effective in the longer term. During the incipient years of the group's campaigning (in the 1970s), its director described these image-events each as the launching of a 'mind bomb' that then explodes 'in the public consciousness to transform the way people view their world' (Hunter cited in DeLuca 1999: 1). For DeLuca, this so-called 'mind bomb' really best describes the public screen's mode of 'deliberation', describing a *forceful* exchange of images as a means to maintaining and re-orienting public debate.

Of course, it might be argued that associating both *Helden wie wir* and *Goodbye Lenin!* with the workings and effects of a public screen is to compare quite disparate things. The images events that DeLuca and Peeples discuss might seem quite different in that the events are much more immediate and topical (being themselves events staged for the news media), whilst films play only after the event and to relatively passive audiences upon a contained cinematic/televisual screen. However, DeLuca and Peeples (2002: 146) themselves argue that *both* news broadcasts and films be considered part of a public screen. In their view the contents of the public screen is to range widely from pundits on television and electoral campaigns organized by spin doctors, to sitcoms and 'national "discussions" on race, class, feminism, and sexual identity [as they] take place on *Cosby, Roseanne, Ally McBeal,* and *Ellen*'. They also include 'films that deliver the definitive verdict for public memory on such key moments as the Holocaust (*Schindler's List*), World War II (*Saving Private Ryan*), the Kennedy assassination (*JFK*), and the 60s (*Forrest Gump*)'. To this list, then, can be added both *Helden wie wir* and *Goodbye Lenin!* However, there is a significant point of difference to note: neither *Helden wie wir* or *Goodbye Lenin!* should be thought to provide a 'definitive verdict' on the events of the fall of the Wall. Instead, just as Mitchell (1994: 414) has argued that *JFK*, as 'a genuinely "naïve" work of cinematic art', does not reach a definitive verdict, but rather combines and parodies various public narratives of Kennedy's assassination for renewed public scrutiny, both films picture a more complex set of exchanges in respect of the event of the fall of the Wall. As image constellations their separate critiques of the event of the fall of the Wall are more reflexive, incorporating a view on their own narrative construction and provoke us into a way of looking back at ourselves in our own spectatorship.

Making a Spectacle of the Public Sphere in *Helden wie wir*

In comparison, then, to the public sphere with its associations of rationality, presence of dialogue, consensus and civility, the public screen highlights dissemination, images, publicity and distraction. Importantly, the point of the public screen is not to measure contemporary discourse by the criteria of an idealized public sphere, which generally only leads to a sense of failure or nostalgia, but instead to face up to the complexity and 'reality' of a mediated world, for all its opportunities and dangers. There is a dramatic scene towards the end of the novel of *Helden wie wir* that playfully illustrates this shift from a conception of the public sphere to that of a public screen. The episode in question sets up a conflict between the rational and civil debating style of the revered East German writer Christa Wolf and the 'spectacular' behaviour of the novel's protagonist, Klaus (and by association, some would argue, the novel's author Thomas Brussig). In real life, Wolf is, of course, an acclaimed East German author and during German division was popular in *both* East and West Germany. In this scene, where as it were fact meets fiction, Klaus tries to come into direct contact with Wolf. The scene displays an antagonism that runs not only along political lines, but also generational and stylistic ones. The overall effect is to bring into direct opposition a verbal form of reasoning and authority with a visual, tactile and distracted mode of engagement.

The scene begins with Klaus arriving at the huge demonstration in Alexanderplatz (East Berlin) that took place in real life on the 4th November 1989, the weekend just prior to the fall of the Wall. The event had been organized by various intellectuals and artists in East Berlin, with Christa Wolf a prominent participant. Her speech at the rally has been considered by many to be pivotal in finally galvanizing the ongoing public demonstrations. Klaus himself remarks (despite his derision of the speech): 'it's still regarded as the point at which the autumn '89 situation crystallised' (Brussig 1997: 221). Unusual for a novel, the speech is printed practically verbatim, so bringing it into the narrative's wider play of intertexuality, which enables a re-*playing* with/of history.

The tone of Wolf's speech – like much of her writings – can be described as rich, literary and probing. She opens with a 'difficult', conceptual line: 'Every revolutionary movement also liberates language' (Wolf 1992: 127). She then proceeds to query in rather elaborate and esoteric terms various words and phrases relating to the 'revolution' and its political hopes. So, for example, Wolf notes her difficulties with the word '*Wende*' [turning point] – for which she gives this somewhat obscure analogy:

> It makes me think of a sailboat with the captain calling out "Prepare to jibe!" because the wind had turned, and the crew ducks as the boom sweeps across the deck. Is this image true? Is it still true in this situation that is moving forward with every passing day?
>
> (Wolf 1992: 128)

Wolf suggests it perhaps better to speak of 'revolutionary renewal' (as coming from below), and notes how in the weeks leading up to the event in Alexanderplatz many had come together for discussions in unprecedented ways; 'never with this passion, with so much rage and grief, and with so much hope'. Yet, strangely, she then appears to undermine this new forum: 'This is called "dialogue," we demanded it, now we can hardly bear to hear the word and yet haven't really learned what it means' (Wolf 1992: 128). Arguably, in a bid to quell any potential fragmentation of the opposition movement and even, perhaps, to forge a clear (i.e. rational) political agenda, Wolf can be said (whether consciously or not) to take on a role for herself (alongside other intellectuals) as some kind of leader figure for 'the people' (a role that is later more formally acknowledged when Wolf is commissioned by the Round Table to draft its constitutional preamble).

In general, East German intellectuals came to play quite active roles in the political process following the demise of the GDR, due largely to their privileged status and relative neutrality. However, as I have considered in more detail in the previous chapter, the process that eventually led to reunification was felt by many to be based on economic and political terms that were more than favourable to West Germany and had not been in keeping with the initial hopes and aspirations of numerous opposition groups. Subsequently, there developed a critical discourse about the perceived failure of these intellectuals (see Huyssen 1991; von Oppen 2000). All in all, this proved to be a rather fractious and introspective period, which Schneider (1991: 89) perhaps summed up all too well when he wrote at the time: 'while the East German intellectuals spend their energies keeping their backs covered, and West German intellectuals spend theirs on the attack, neither camp has come to grips with the issues posed by the failure of socialism'. It is evidently this critical discourse that weighs heavily on Brussig's account of Klaus as he strives – in all his naivety – to pitch himself against the reasoned dialogue of Wolf, an indisputable intellectual 'heavyweight'.

Klaus exhibits only irreverence towards Wolf, in fact, on approaching Alexanderplatz, he singularly mistakes Wolf for Jutta Müller, a former East German ice skating coach (another 'real' public figure about who Klaus often fantasizes during his childhood). In light of this blatantly ridiculous confusion he goes on to describe Wolf's 'grand' political speech as a 'genuine ice-skating coach's speech...Studied elegance and purple passages guaranteed to earn good marks for style, coupled with a breathless, short-term political programme in which a few botched or omitted leaps remain unnoticed by the besotted audience' (Brussig 1997: 222). Klaus is thoroughly irritated by Wolf/Müller's layered rhetoric which he suggests is at complete odds with an espoused 'liberated language'. At one point in the speech, Wolf notes a pervading sense of distrust and unease, which she then counters with what would appear to be her own utopian language: 'language is jumping out of the bureaucratese and newspaper German, in which it was wrapped, and is remembering its emotional words. One of them is "dream"; so lets us dream, with our reason wide awake' (Wolf 1992: 128–9). For Klaus, the fact that language may be breaking away from the strictures of the GDR media and officialdom is certainly not then improved by what he considers to be the pretentiousness of Wolf's high literary style. The conjunction here of 'dream' and 'reason' perhaps best capturing what he perceives to be her contradictory and overly authoritative tone. He is also critical of Wolf's plea for a reformed socialism, especially following the use of what was to become her much repeat phrase 'if demands become rights, and therefore obligations...' This, Klaus tells us scathingly, only reminds him of his mother, a figure in the novel who is a caricature of the righteous, fussing parent forever imposing an impossible sense of duty. By way of riposte, Klaus subverts Wolf/Müller's own carefully chosen words to make a plea of his own:

...before we allow Jutta Müller and her friends to signal the next round of Imagine-if-this-were-socialism let us remember, with alert common sense, that socialism is an abstract idea, and that everything worthwhile can be expressed more concretely – as long as we take care to use "emancipated language." Even today, when everything suddenly "flows freely from our lips," they speak of socialism and not of our need for unrestricted access to the world at large.

(Brussig 1997: 223).

His anger and frustration growing, Klaus pushes his way through the crowds to get to the stage where Wolf is speaking, intent on seizing the microphone for himself. He realises the quickest route is to use a subway entrance – to go underneath the crowds – and re-emerge close to the stage. It is at this point he 'expresses' himself in an all too concrete manner (with all too little 'alert' common sense). On reaching the subway steps he trips over an abandoned cardboard placard mounted on a broomstick. His fate turns out to be worse than simply falling headlong down the stairs. Instead the broom handle spears his genitals and he proceeds to 'pogo' down each and every step. As he recovers consciousness at the foot of the stairs, a woman rushes over to help and asks what had happened. He replies: 'Yes...Jutta Müller, the ice-skating coach, gave a speech. I was trying to get to the microphone...' (224). Klaus is pronounced delirious and promptly sent to hospital where we then discover the fantastical outcome of his fall, his penis having swelled to its imponderable size. Thus, due to sheer clumsiness, Klaus never gets to 'have it out' with Wolf/Müller; he never manages to have a free and frank exchange in *person* with his self-styled nemesis. Instead, we get only his slapstick spectacle that effectively overwrites Wolf's eminent speech and disrupts any importance attached to the event of the Alexanderplatz rally.

There is an important subtext to Klaus' sustained attack on Wolf, which relates to the so-called *deutsch-deutscher Literaturstreit* (German-German literary controversy) of the early 1990s. During this time Wolf was criticized severely by West German critics for retroactively positioning herself as a victim of the system that she supported (and had been supported by).[9] There are numerous reasons for the controversy, but notably Wolf's own style and mood of writing sets up particular problems. Her signature brand of 'engaged literature' stakes out a 'so-called writing of interiority', employing a 'poetics of "subjective authenticity"' (Frölich 1998: 28). As a result, running throughout her work 'like a red thread' is a certain claim to sincerity, which inevitably makes her vulnerable to questions over her own sense of authenticity and sincerity. There is also tremendous ambivalence in her writing (something Klaus is thoroughly irritated by) which has fuelled the debates about her writing and status post-1989. In *Helden wie wir*, Klaus makes direct reference to this literary controversy and as one might expect wades in with his own ideas. Having come to realize that Jutta Müller had all along been Christa Wolf, he begins to question what it is he has actually done by toppling the Wall. He can not help censuring himself for having done this *'with no definite end in view'* (Brussig 1997: 236). He feels that had Wolf clearly advocated the breaching of the Wall during her speech in Alexanderplatz then that would have made proper sense of his actions. In lieu of such a statement, however, he promptly works his way through her entire oeuvre in hope of finding any stray reference that, albeit retrospectively, can back up his undeliberated actions. As he explains sardonically: 'I would still be the person who had breached the Wall, but I would at least have acted in tacit collusion with my country's best-known literary figure' (237).

However, it is not until *after* the fall of the Wall, when Klaus comes across a 'new' short story by Wolf – supposedly based on an old, unseen manuscript (this text being the one that actually sparked off the literary controversy in the first place) – he at last thinks he has 'yielded something tangible'. He proceeds to read aloud from Wolf's own text, interjecting with his own typically sarcastic remarks:

> *She's talking about the departure hall at Friedrichstrasse station,* popularly known as "the Bunker of Tears," in which the transformation of citizens of various countries, my own included, into transients, tourists, emigrants and immigrants was accomplished in a light reflected by greenish tiled walls...Oh...*how extravagantly descriptive of light and colour!*...a light that issued from very high, narrow windows in which henchmen of the master of this city, attired as policemen or customs officers, exercised the right of restraint or release. Had its outward appearance matched its function, this building would have been a monstrosity...There...that *was what I'd been looking for all the time, an injunction to erect a monstrosity rather than demolish the Wall.*
>
> (Brussig 1997: 238)

Of course, he does not actually find any proof to justify his actions. Rather, as this quotation quickly tells us, he remains intent on ridiculing Wolf for her seeming inability to say anything straightforward and unequivocal on the subject of the Wall and the East German people in general. His rant continues, thus:

> I'm regularly afflicted by attacks of thoroughgoing anti-intellectualism at such moments. "The Wall must go!" would have said it all, but that stemmed from Ronald Reagan, the voice-test president, not from Christa Wolf. Absolute simplicity: no greenish light, tiled walls, or high narrow windows.
>
> (Brussig 1997: 238)

We can look upon the scene in Alexanderplatz, in conjunction with Klaus' subsequent rants about Wolf and the literary controversy surrounding her, as establishing a clear contrast between Wolf's intellectualism and rationalism and Klaus' bawdy, clumsy spectacle. The latter is affiliated also to his apparent 'trust' in the immediacy of publicity, suggested here, for example, by reference to the media-friendly sound bite of a certain 'voice-test president'. In effect, what is brought to our attention is a disparity (at least as Klaus would see it) between Wolf's highfalutin, but equivocal rhetoric of the events leading up to the fall of the Wall and the actual 'forceful' debates and actions of 'the people' who participated in them.

Charles Maier (1997: xiv) goes some way to acknowledge the 'agency' of 'the people', arguing that it was only after ordinary East Germans made repeated claims upon public space (against the will of their government) that there provoked 'a crisis of government and set in motion the greater powers around them'. Significantly, then, the shift in the political landscape would appear to have come from the chaotic and spontaneous groundswell of public protest and not any specific ideological or intellectual project. Understood this way, the protest demonstrations relate well to the kinds of new social organization and modes of perception that DeLuca and Peeples (2002) argue underlie contemporary social and political transformations of the public screen. Arguably, then, we might suggest East Germans brought the Wall down in a state of 'distraction' (to include – as we are told with the lurid account in *Helden wie wir* – the 'distractions' of the border guards too!); that the formidable task of bringing the Wall down makes sense less as a form of considered, political intervention and more as a form of 'tactile appropriation', as something that occurs 'less through rapt attention than by noticing the object in incidental fashion' (Benjamin 1992: 233). *Helden wie wir* certainly replays this state of distraction through Klaus' ill-planned exploits. And, rather too knowingly, perhaps (though again demonstrating a rhetorical frankness about the narrative construction), Klaus himself explains this as follows: 'My own contribution to the debate is the story of my perversions...my impotence, my abnormal masturbatory fantasies, my combination of megalomania and staggering naivety. Hardly a success story...' (Brussig 1997: 241).

We can understand Klaus to be a metaphor of 'the People'. For the majority of the story, as he is growing up, he exhibits the docility he describes of his fellows citizens in the lead up to the fall of the Wall. Thus, Klaus' constant sense of failure and lack of confidence as it manifests in his impotence throughout his early life is to be taken to reflect the impotence he tells of ordinary East Germans (those 'heroes like us'). By the end of the narrative Klaus is able to overturn this position of subservience, '[he] becomes its grotesquely exaggerated opposite – namely, an omnipotent virility capable of toppling the Berlin Wall itself' (Fröhlich 1998: 22). His behaviour at this point suggests the inexplicable and even irrational force needed to bring the Wall down.

In this context, it would seem clear the antagonism established between the representation of Christa Wolf and the character of Klaus relates well to the shift from the forum of reasoning of a (Habermasian) public sphere to the competitive, visual arena of a public screen. The public sphere as a rational forum does not appear to adequately capture the nature of the events leading up to the fall of the Wall. For example, Wolf's attempts to rationalize and articulate the emotions evident at the time, come across only as being rather clumsy, reductive and, most significantly, as lacking the kind of spontaneity that is so crucial to the effective action of 'the People'. Whereas, the public *screen* does appear to explain more accurately the nature of the event of the fall of the Berlin Wall; indeed, it is arguably an event of this screen culture. Paralleling the 'logic' of the public screen, what Brussig achieves in *Helden wie wir* is to stage his critique in a further series of spectacles. So, for example, with the sequence in Alexanderplatz, he re-stages the rally as a means to turn Wolf (along with her 'liberated language') into a spectacle all of its own, or, more accurately perhaps, to *return* it to the status of an image-event as it had been for those either attending the mass demonstration or sitting at home watching its live broadcast on television. And crucially, the point of such a critique, as DeLuca and Peeples (2002: 144) would argue, is that we too take image-events more seriously; which means, for example, understanding them as *visual* discourse and not as a mere bridge to the supposedly 'real' rhetoric of words. The public screen denotes a whole new critical approach, one which, DeLuca (1999: 22) neatly sums up in the slogan: '[c]ritique through spectacle, not critique versus spectacle', which is meant not as an iconoclastic gesture to 'smash' the public screen, or the harbouring of doubts about the impact of the media on politics and culture. Instead it is about considering appropriate (or, as with Klaus, perhaps, inappropriate) means to *appear* on the public screen.

...Through the Public Screen: Beyond 'Imagefare'

When DeLuca and Peeples (2002: 144) refer to image-events as both mind bombs and also 'visual philosophical-rhetorical fragments', a certain predicament arises. What is suggested is that the critical image is somehow both *immediate* and *contemplative*. In other words, we are told that on the one hand the image has the potential to make thoughts immediately revealing. Yet, on the other hand, it is also inferred that the image somehow generates and sustains meaning that is puzzling, complex and contemplative. In negotiating this potential contradiction, DeLuca and Peeples (2002: 144–5) make explicit reference to Benjamin's notion of the dialectical image, by which they understand 'any moment can be the moment that changes everything, the moment that redeems the past and the future. And it is all there on the surface'. In looking at their account a little closer, I want to mark an important point of difference between what I refer to as an image critique and what DeLuca and Peeples' describe as an image-event. My point is certainly not to undermine the concept of the public screen; as I have described above, it is through media screens (and the re-citing of these screens) that we might envisage an image critique to be most effectively borne. Nonetheless, I want to bring to attention a different relationship between images, as well as motivation for their use. In doing so, I draw on a different reading of Benjamin's concept of the dialectical image, which unlike DeLuca and Peeples' account is not to describe a forceful, crucial image. Instead, as I have already suggested, an image critique is more reflexive and incorporates into its own 'design' what Mitchell (1994: 35–82) refers to as a metapicture. The point of which is to think about pictures *with* pictures themselves.

DeLuca and Peeples (2002: 145) give a contemporary example of a dialectical image with the news pictures of the windows of multinational-owned stores (including those of Starbucks, Nike Town and McDonalds etc.) shattered during the 1999 World Trade Organization (WTO) protests in Seattle. These windows, they explain, were smashed by a hammer, an everyday object, suggesting in a Benjaminian sense the 'familiar made strange, the shock of recognition that the familiar is not necessarily innocuous'. The smashing of the windows is certainly a public act of violence against private property. However, it is not simply a physical act of violence but a symbolic one too. Further explanation is provided from an interview with a protestor involved in the event. At its simplest level the smashing of the windows is explained as an attempt to make the meetings of the WTO uneconomical. More significantly, however, it is argued how on a psychological level the point is to find an effective means to reconsider the kind of society we live in: 'You stare at a television', the protestor explains, 'and you see logos and you're in a daze and these symbols pop up everywhere in your life. When that is shattered, it breaks a spell and we're trying to get people to wake up before it's too late' (cited in DeLuca and Peeples 2002: 145). The emphasis – going beyond material concerns – is on staging a *spectacle* for political, rhetorical ends. Thus, the *serial* smashing of the windows of multinational-owned stores (as a response to the serial repetition of logos in everyday life) is meant to be more than a direct attack on specific businesses; it is rather the staging of an image-event, to get a 'message' into people's minds *through* the mass media.

As DeLuca and Peeples (2002: 144–145) describe the concept of the image-event, '[i]t participates in order to be aired – it is brief, visual, dramatic, and emotional. It punctures to punctuate, to interrupt the flow, to give pause'. However, understood this way, the image-event would seem to be less about a contemplative 'dense surface' and much more about its ability to 'provoke in an instant the shock of the familiar made strange'. Thus, if we are to accept the image-event with reference to a Benjaminian 'dialectical image', it would appear to fall into the same trap that James Elkins (2003: 97) argues is evident in much of the secondary readings on Benjamin. Typically, he remarks, the 'dialectical image serves as a code' of something overly simplistic, 'it denotes "crucial image," or simply "forceful image"'. When we conceive of the image-event as a so-called mind bomb, a crucial, forceful image exploding in the 'public consciousness' to transform people's view of the world, we can understand this (to use one of DeLuca's phrases) as an act of 'imagefare', whereby one set of images is used to overturn or upstage another.

Whilst this state of 'imagefare' can undoubtedly be very effective, the problem is that it would appear always to have to remain an *incomplete* (or one-sided) form of critical engagement. John Berger (1997), in his writings on photography, makes this point well. Here, for 'photography', we can read equally 'image-events' (or simply 'images'):

You can use photography in all kinds of agitprop ways, you can make propaganda with photographs – you can make anti-capitalist propaganda, anti-imperialist propaganda. I wouldn't deny the usefulness of this, but at the same time I think the answer is incomplete. It's like taking a canon and turning it round and firing it in the opposite direction. You haven't actually changed the practice, you've simply changed the aim.

(Berger 1997: 45)

Berger himself is, of course, known to use images in his work for specific critique of social, political and economic circumstances.[10] However, in wanting to do more than simply change the 'aim', he describes an alternative practice. He argues, if we seek to put the photograph back into the context of its 'original' experience – a social experience or memory – we have to respect its original laws of memory, which run not in a unilinear fashion, but radially. That is to say, 'with an enormous number of associations all leading to the same event' (Berger 1997: 46). Understood this way, Berger's use of images for critical purpose is certainly different to that of their use in the forceful exchanges of imagefare. Berger similarly seeks to use images to contribute to and affect political, public debates,[11] but his approach is to create a space/writing – to fashion a new, complex context – in which a number of relevant associations and tensions are brought together all at once, so allowing us not only to see the image afresh, but also to see how it comes to be before us.

A key point for Berger in re-contextualizing images is this idea that we construct around them (or with them) a radial system of associations as a means to greater reflexivity, 'in terms which are simultaneously personal, political, economic, dramatic, everyday and historic' (Berger 1997: 47). The polyperspectival viewing that Berger alludes to means the spectator not only sees the image for what it is, but also for how it relates to the world around. Thus, the point (to use Berger's own analogy again) is certainly not anything so simple as to turn the canon around and fire in the opposite direction. Instead, it is has as much to do with bringing into view the canon's directionality, its very axis of turning. The critical image Berger describes (which I take to intersect with my definition of an image critique) is one that allows us to see – all at once – more than one view (along with the gaps or binding that lie between these views).

Arguably, the two films Helden wie wir and Goodbye Lenin! bring together multiple contexts of images of the fall of the Wall as a means to reawaken the event for critical re-examination. There is certainly more to these sets of images than simply an attempt to shatter all else that went before and to only replace one interpretation with another. In both cases, these films re-figure the site/sight of the fall of the Wall to allow for various layers of meaning and relationships to be contested and tested at the same time. This is not about imagefare, but rather a process that lets multiple images (or perspectives) of the fall of the Wall co-exist; appealing more to the radial nature of our (visual) social experiences and memories. The principle is one of building up complex, dense images, yet, equally in maintaining these images as images, there is also that sense of immediacy of the visual, letting us see things in rapidity, or even all at once.

So, for example, the effect of the films displaying their own narrative construction is that we know we are not watching a definitive account of the Wall. In fact, we are frequently alerted to the unreliable nature of their storytelling. In Helden wie wir and, in particular, the scenes relating to Christa Wolf, some commentators have come to question the status of the narrator's voice. Brad Prager (2004: 994) suggests that it is 'troublesome' that during these passages it appears we hear the author's voice, not that of Klaus'; or, at least, that 'Klaus sounds like an author taking a position in GDR culture debates'. In defence of the novel, however, Fröhlich (1998: 28) argues 'it is precisely the estrangement created through the foolish fictional protagonist that serves as a mask behind which Brussig can comfortably slip in his own views while simultaneously disavowing responsibility for the stance he attributes to his protagonist'. Interestingly, if we take either point of view, they both assert that Brussig is indeed imparting his view on the reader. Yet, in both cases, such an interpretation would seem incomplete. With the stakes raised as they are in broaching the thorny topic of the German literary controversy, it is surely inconceivable that an up-and-coming East German author would choose to either clumsily state his case (by temporarily appropriating the narrator's voice) or put his sole faith in a mask as flimsy as Klaus. Instead, I would argue, Brussig purposely engineers this confusion in order to enliven at least three different possibilities: that it *is* his authorial voice, that it is Klaus's voice or, in fact, that it is precisely a confusion of both his own and Klaus's voice we hear. The *drama* of these open possibilities helps bring out various tensions *all at once*.

To elaborate, it is useful to turn to the example of Spike Lee's *Do the Right Thing* and, in particular, the pivotal scene when the main protagonist, Mookie, smashes the window of the pizzeria at the centre of the story. Not unlike the scenes of protest in Seattle, this episode shows a public act of violence against private property, which again is not simply about a physical act of violence but a symbolic one too, for in this case the smashing of the window marks the occasion when Mookie is able to 'break out' of his passive and uncommitted stance. Nevertheless, unlike the smashing of the windows during the Seattle riot (ending up as images in a forceful exchange through the media), the image in the film sets up a more analytical experience.[12] Mitchell's (1994: 390–393) argument is that Mookie's 'choice' in this scene 'breaks the film loose from the narrative justification of violence' and, instead, 'displays it as a pure effect of this work of art in this moment and place'. It is an act/art, he argues, that makes 'perfect sense as a piece of Brechtean theatre, giving the audience what it wants with one hand and taking it back with the other'. It can properly be described as a piece of 'violent public art', since it allows for the multiple effects of being a representation, an act and a weapon of violence all in one. It is a work, Mitchell (1994: 392–393) argues, 'of intelligent violence...It does not repudiate the alternative of non-violence...it resituates both violence and non-violence as strategies within a struggle that is simply an ineradicable fact of American public life'. Crucially, what the film refuses to be is a 'prefabricated propaganda image of political or ethical correctness', instead it is 'a monument of resistance...a ready-made assemblage of images that reconfigures a local space – literally, the space of the black ghetto, figuratively, the space of public images of race in the American public sphere'.

In a similar vein, both *Helden wie wir* and *Goodbye Lenin!* can be considered (public) 'monuments of resistance' in that they do not assert a single, determined point of view, but instead re-situate both the sense of victory and loss associated with the fall of the Wall (i.e. victory/loss over political ideologies and of East German cultural identity) as concurrent differences; as ineradicable facts of the event of the fall of the Wall. Their alternative visions of the fall of the Wall take up a position vis-à-vis the 'prefabricated' euphoric image of the fall of the Wall that leads sequaciously to the celebration of an apparent end of ideological history. Through their ready-made assemblage of images, both films attempt to reconfigure, literally, the site/sight of the fall of the Wall and, figuratively, the space of public images of East German politics and culture both before and after the fall of the Wall.

Metapictures

If we accept the premise of the public screen – yet wish to go beyond mere 'imagefare' – there is need of a critical form that can service (and survive) the medium; to work from within 'publicity', yet maintain a critical function. Images of the fall of the Wall would appear to present both their antidote and problem at the same time, at least in that they seemingly make the event of the fall of the Wall the event that it *is*, that we witnessed and now remember. Yet, equally, the images present a certain critical dilemma, being images that arguably mask, or upstage, other important (political/historical) considerations. With the two East German films there is illustrated the potential to engage on the level of these images, with a view to re-figure, or re-stage, the event for new critical purpose. This, I want to suggest, is to create a 'metapicture' of the fall of the Wall; a picture that examines the picturing of the event. As Mitchell (1994: 57) explains, '[t]he principle use of the metapicture is...to explain what pictures are – to stage, as it were, the "self-knowledge" of pictures'. And with regard to the problem I have outlined of the public sphere, where debate and critique are most readily considered the domain of verbal reasoning, Mitchell's (1994: 82) point is similarly to get beyond the tendency to 'think of "theory" as something that is primarily conducted in linear discourse, in language and logic'. As he suggests, 'if there is such a thing as a metalanguage, it should hardly surprise us that there is such a thing as a metapicture', one result of which is that the picture, as a metapicture, is afforded a more assertive role, away from being merely a passive object of description and explanation. Thus, Mitchell's (1994: 35–82) discussion of the metapicture provides some further theoretical understanding of the use of images as an *embodiment* of critical thought, to demarcate not simply a critique *of* pictures, but rather a means to picture pictures, to critique pictures with pictures (as argued here with the examples of the films).

Mitchell describes various kinds of metapicture, though the one that we might take to underpin all of them is the dialectical, or 'multistable', image. Mitchell *illustrates* the concept of this image type with some well-known drawings of optical illusions. These images include, for example, the 'double' images 'My Wife or my Mother-in-Law', and the classic 'Duck-Rabbit', as well as the Necker cube, the perspective of which alters depending on our way of perceiving the drawing. The primary function of such pictures is 'to illustrate the co-existence of contrary or simply different readings in the single image' (Mitchell 1994: 45). Of course, given that these puzzle pictures are really only made up of simple lines and shadings on a flat surface, we may be tempted to think what Mitchell terms as the 'self-knowledge' of pictures really only amounts to a metaphor. Evidently, these illusions do not refer to themselves in any specific sense (i.e. as a form of reflexive meta-analysis), nor, in fact, do they reference any specific class of pictures. Yet, as a result of the fact that they 'employ a single gestalt to shift from one reference to another' (48), they at least illustrate the idea of a complex site/sight of images; indeed, they *show* us the effect of a multiple perspective. In the Duck-Rabbit drawing, for example, the very ambiguity of its referentiality 'produces a kind of secondary effect of auto-reference to the drawing as drawing, an invitation to the spectator to return with fascination to the mysterious object whose identity seems so mutable and yet so absolutely singular and definite' (48). The critical, revealing value of these kinds of multistable images perhaps helps best explain the way to understand (or 'see') Benjamin's concept of the dialectical image; and significantly how this differs from that of DeLuca and Peeples' account of a crucial, forceful image. Benjamin (1999) frequently refers to a 'dialectics at a standstill', a phrase that can be misleading. In itself 'dialectic' suggests a transition (a progression even) from one term to another, yet, as Sigrid Weigel (1996: 58) explains, Benjamin's dialectic 'does not culminate in a synthesis, but in a constellation of non-synchronicity'. Furthermore, its 'standstill' does not refer to a moment of stasis, or fixity (nor a collapse in the dialectic), but rather an oscillation, which like an irritant is at once object and subject. Or, to refer again to the Duck-Rabbit illustration, is akin to the instance in which we see both the duck and the rabbit – 'it's a duck-rabbit', we exclaim!

It is important to keep in mind that whilst the dialectical, multistable image can achieve a degree of self-reference and/or meta-analysis of pictures, this has 'as much to do with the self of the observer as with the metapicture itself' (Mitchell 1994: 48). It is a point that is relatively obvious when thinking about drawings of optical illusions, since it can be something as simple as the position of the observer's body that provides a specific reading. So, for example, the multiple views of the Necker cube 'are best activated by imagining oneself alternatively looking up and looking down at the image' (48). This kind of (physical) engagement in the image lets us reflect upon how

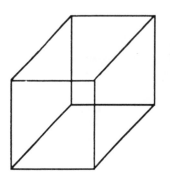

meaning is made, how it is achieved differently in different ways. In thinking about more complex images, such as we might describe with the images of the fall of the Wall in both *Helden wie wir* and *Goodbye Lenin!*, the observer's identity and cultural context is clearly going to have a bearing on how the various aspects of image constellation may or may not come to override or augment each other. Thus, we might come to think of the dialectical, or multistable, image 'as a device for educing self-knowledge, a kind of mirror for the beholder, or a screen for self-projection' (48). Indeed, it is precisely this idea of the metapicture as offering *itself* as a 'screen' for critical engagement that marks it out, against the 'imagefare' described by DeLuca and Peeples.

The dialectical image, as understood with respect to Mitchell's concept of the metapicture, can be seen to describe a critical, thought-image that incorporates the scene of its own making into what it pictures. It describes a *process* of scrutiny, which, if we extrapolate to the level of public forum and public debate, might more usefully prompt us to describe a public *screening*, rather than simply a public screen. In other words, it presents us with the idea of a complex engagement on the level of images which enables a process of 'screening' or working through various elements all at once (as a single gestalt site/sight or screen). These critical metapictures may still, of course, work their way through the public screen (i.e. through the media networks), but, nonetheless, they are distinctive in that they do not *finally* offer a crucial, forceful image, but instead hold within themselves an array of different (and even opposing) forces.

It is true that in both accounts of the dialectical image given here – Mitchell's oscillating site/sight of contesting forces/perspectives and DeLuca and Peeples' account of a visual-philosophical mind bomb – a lot rides on the principle of what we perceive to be the *immediacy* of the image. Yet, what separates these views is the degree to which their respective image critiques can offer contemplative, reflexive perspectives. Metapictures do not necessarily circulate the public screen to get a 'message' heard (indeed it does not have a single message) but, instead, in being its own 'screen', prompts us to keep looking, to keep probing, to ask questions not only of what is shown or how/why it was shown, but also what 'we', as spectators, bring to its spectacle. Keeping this in mind, a few brief observations can be made on the specific effects of the two East German films as presenting us with metapictures of the fall of the Wall. These accounts draw upon Mitchell's (1994: 38–45) further delineations of the metapicture. In the first case it is a metapicture of 'the picture itself', which provides one way of understanding *Helden wie wir* and, in particular, the closing sequence in which Klaus stands before the awaiting media as he crosses through to the West after toppling the Wall. In the second case, a metapicture of '*other* pictures', which provides some insight into how we might understand the fabricated news broadcasts in *Goodbye Lenin!*

Inside and Out: A Metapicture of the Event of the Fall of the Wall

To translate the idea of a picture picturing itself across to *Helden wie wir*, we need to remember that throughout the film its protagonist, Klaus, self-consciously narrates his own story (in the novel this is even more explicit since he is constantly recording his voice for a *New York Times* journalist). This narrative device establishes a frame for the narrative as a whole, within which Klaus is then further framed by the various scenes that we know of from real events of the fall of the Wall. There are also numerous references to real-life personalities, events and locations, all of which add to the frames or levels of this metapicture of the fall of the Wall, which all come to a head at the very end of the story.

As Klaus himself points out, however sardonic his account of the fall of the Wall, he cannot deny the occasion paved the way for one of the most joyous and momentous moments in German history. Thus, regardless of his scorn for the passivity of his fellow citizens, Klaus acknowledges he, too, found himself rejoicing during the night of the fall of the Wall. Crucially, it is in the state of reverie that Klaus suddenly gets his chance to speak out. It is a moment that can be viewed in at least two different ways. On the one hand the scene elevates Klaus' own sense of heroism, yet, on the other, we see it unravelling as he speaks:

> I was half demented with happiness, and it was at one of these moments of exultation that a camera crew stationed itself in front of me and held a microphone under my nose. Every revolutionary movement emancipates language as well, so listen carefully to what I, the veteran composer of aphorisms and quotable pronouncements, burbled to the international media. I was incapable of speech, having lost control of my ar-tic-u-lat-ory apparatus, but no matter, my utterance sufficed to become "the word of 1989": Cra-a-a-zy! Yes indeed, I was the person that uttered it on the Bornholmer Bridge on the night of 9 November 1989, and its status was officially confirmed, three months later, by the German Language Association.
>
> (Brussig 1997: 248)

What happens here is that Klaus – as a metaphor of 'the people' – comes to embody the joyous atmosphere of the event of the fall of the Wall. Thus, despite wanting to tell the reporters before him what 'truly' happened, he ends up repeating (indeed, he is swept along with) the scenes as we already know of them. So, the question arises as to which 'direction' we might read Klaus' exploits. On the one hand, if we take Klaus' own point of view we are drawn inwards, realizing that it is only as a result of his 'heroic' deed that we then get to see these celebratory scenes at all. In effect, Klaus is the maker of his own picture. He even manages to stoke up the euphoria giving the international media the kind of sound bite it hankers after when he utters spiritedly the single word 'Crazy!' Thus, Klaus shields his fellow citizens from their own passivity, he remains the unsung hero, the draughtsman of the whole event.

But read another way, outwards as it were and placing Klaus in a broader context (of journalistic media), we begin to realize that Klaus, as much as his fellow citizens, was not actually in control of what he was doing, nor even in command of the telling of his own story. Instead it is the media that has been guiding his actions – indeed his whole life story is one long media interview. The moment he blurts out the catchword of the year – 'Crazy!' – we realize all along that Klaus has been caught up in the media apparatus. It is this apparatus that prompts him to reduce the whole event of the fall of the Wall (and his 'fantastic' role in it) to a single, meaningless, though suitably dramatic word. This pivotal moment might be thought of as a highly condensed version of a broader process of the fall of the Wall as a media event, packaged uncritically by a pervading theme of celebration.

Importantly, however, neither one of these views of the event (i.e. as read inward or outward) can be said to dominate the other. Instead, we keep looking between the two, rather like a duck-rabbit gestalt. The closing scene of *Helden wie wir* presents a self-referential image that shows itself making its image. We are never entirely sure of the picture's beginning and end points, where it refers to production and where it is about reception. And, whilst this is an image about itself, that shows its own making, it does not prevent it from being about other things too, 'from calling into question the basic issues of reference that determine what a picture is about and constitute the "selves" referred to in its structure of self-reference' (Mitchell 1994: 41–42). Crucially, it calls into question the more complex significance of 'the people' (the ordinary citizens, those 'heroes like us') of East Germany. Yet, the story does not give us any definitive answers (Klaus himself is quite emphatic in his views, yet we are never able to take his word unconditionally). Instead, in being given *simultaneously* at least two sides of the story (one spiralling inward, the other unravelling outwards) there is always a prompt for further attention and (self-) questioning.

Another Re-Scaling of the Images of the Fall of the Wall

A similar oscillating thought-image occurs when watching *Goodbye Lenin!* Although, here, the metapicture is one that refers not so much to its own making, but to a collection, or genre, of images of the news media and to the potential for alternative, *other* versions of these images. The effect is achieved through the protagonist's fabricated news broadcasts, which function by one reading giving life to the other. So, for example, Alex manages to fashion a wholly humane vision of the GDR, a vision that he thinks will meet with his mother's untiring belief in the communist system. But, he can only do this by replicating the same kind of vision that was *really* reported during the event. In other words, the only way to make an alternative history of the fall of the Wall is to make a direct East German *equivalent* of the western media's theme of celebration. Anything else would not constitute the event of the fall of the Wall, it would be something else (and for Alex that would be of little use, since eventually he needs his mother to be able to relate to the *reality* of the dramatic changes that have taken place).

There is a further level to this picturing of other pictures, which makes the film that much more poignant. Running parallel to Alex's exploits in retaining a communist lifeworld, his mother, Hanna, begins privately to regret her allegiance to the state. Alex's father, punished under the

GDR regime for not being a party member, fled to the West many years prior to the fall of the Wall. Subsequently, having failed to follow him with the children as planned, Hanna now (in what she knows is the end of her life) makes a final request to see her husband. In addition to which, and just prior to watching Alex's final news report, we witness a scene in which we suspect Hanna is told the *truth* about the recent events of the fall of the Wall. Thus, when the final news report is screened, with the family all gathered around the television set, we watch not just for how Alex has finally managed to complete the reversal of history, but also for how Hanna looks at her son, moved by the care and attention she now knows he has taken over her. In this moment we are presented with multiple views, both public and private. And so by the close of the film we have become torn as to which memory of Hanna we might hold to. Her character is wholly fashioned by her life as a faithful citizen of her country. Yet, equally we know now that this life was predicated on a failure to follow her heart. We see the potential for *other* ways of picturing, in this case other, alternative public and private representations of the event of the fall of the Wall and the GDR more generally. In addition, as we try to decide about Hanna's true identity we question our own set of expectations. What if the images of the fall of the Berlin Wall really had looked something like Alex's home-made videos? Since we know these fabricated news broadcasts actually replicate the codes and conventions of the media apparatus we are so used to consuming, we realize we are not only watching 'new' pictures of the fall of the Wall (as made by Alex), but equally we are watching the *form* of their specific genre. So, like the camera shot which slowly pulls back to reveal the wider view, our realization parallels the scene in which Hanna watches Alex's final news report, which she does not so much for what it tells her about world affairs, but for what it tells her about her own view of her son's love for her.

It is perhaps worth pointing out the 'application' here of the metapicture for critical analysis of the two films remains perhaps only a heuristic endeavour; not least because as a theoretical idea the metapicture is still very much in its infancy. Moreover, the fact that the metapicture by default can not be explained or carried by words, means there must come a point when it is only by watching these films (and by extension other such visual culture phenomena) for *oneself* that the critical effects described here can be observed (or not). Nonetheless, it is hopefully the case that consideration of the metapicture vis-à-vis notions of the public sphere/screen enables some novel theoretical understanding of how the films manage and maintain various configurations of the images of the fall of the Berlin Wall. By extension, the metapicture may come to shed further light on the possible design and purpose of an image-based critique more generally. At root, the 'image' is not to be used as a prop for commentary or interpretation, but rather an enactment of theory and critique. An image critique, then, is to be itself a dynamic site/sight from which we can constantly be conferring (or screening) between different perspectives and discovering new critical possibilities.

Image Critique as Public *Screening*

Running through Daniel Boorstin's (1992) *The Image*, a classic and damning study of media culture, is a specific suggestion that somehow the expectations we have in wanting to understand the world around us are far too great. 'When we pick up our newspaper at breakfast', he writes, 'we expect – we even demand – that it brings us momentous events since the night before. We turn on the car radio as we drive to work and expect "news" to have occurred since the morning newspaper went to press' (3), and so it goes on. With the growth of 24-hour news broadcasting (bringing us events such as the fall of the Wall) and with the ever increasing demand on journalists and news production to be 'embedded' in the action, Boorstin's diagnosis is perhaps no less prescient. We are ruled, he suggests, by high expectations not only of what the world holds for us, but also over our power to shape that world, 'to invent our standards and then to respect them as if they had been revealed or discovered' (5). Of course, this chapter, having relied substantially upon the critical insights of DeLuca and Peeples (2002), who advocate use of the media apparatus for contemporary forums of political debate, takes a quite different view of the role and nature of the media.

By way of offering alternative viewpoints, both *Helden wie wir* and *Goodbye Lenin!* demonstrate the potential for new critical pictures of the fall of the Berlin Wall (and by extension perhaps other such media events). In particular, by foregrounding their own narrative constructions – in *Helden wie wir*, with the half-crazed monologue of its protagonist and in *Goodbye Lenin!*, its own diegetic requirement to make alternative news reports – these films enable an analytical kind of entertainment that provide *opportunity* for interpretations as opposed to promulgating any one single interpretation. In other words, these films keep open a mode of thinking or picturing; they afford a space or pause within which it is still possible to continue to experience and reflect on the complexity of the event in its own terms. Thus, we may in fact be more inclined to suggest an image-based critique actually helps *lower* our expectations (to afford greater humility) in understanding events, if only since we begin to look upon matters in greater complexity. And, by extension, these new critical pictures offer the potential for a renewal of the purported openness of the public sphere, a chance, then, to think in the light of all things (and images) that surround us in our daily and shared lives.

Of course, the two films discussed here are not without their problems. By the nature of being comedies the potential is there to undermine attempts at new critical reflections. So, whilst comedy is certainly an important part of the way in which both films combine various layers of meaning, the risk is always that the subtlety of these different levels to the narrative will be missed, overshadowed, by the immediacy of the slapstick sequences, the caricatures and outright absurdities. In short, that these films may simply be taken as a 'bit of harmless fun'. As Brussig himself somewhat wryly suggests in interview: 'The GDR was always harmless enough that today its icons can be used to celebrate a party with relative innocence' (Brussig 1999: 257). Moreover, the explicit play of *ostalgia* central to both films can soon lose its significance as a subtle marker of East German identity, becoming simply a one-sided, stereotypical sign of such purported cultural authenticity. As something of a caveat then, but which I have stressed throughout, neither of these films should be taken as exemplars of an image critique as such, only useful illustrations of aspects of what might be made possible in terms of the kind of polyperspectival complexity I suggest is particular of an image critique. It is a complexity that should also be the consequence of a public *screening*, conceived not simply as the dissemination of various images to adjust or change perceptions and political agendas, but as an opportunity for a public to work through debates, to screen or filter through various aspects of a political or ethical situation.

With such principles in mind, I will end here with a brief, final illustration or thought-image: the image of the Reichstag, the old parliament building which during German division was situated – in its then estranged, dilapidated state – just metres away from the Berlin Wall. Since the removal of the Wall the building has returned once again centre-stage in German

democratic life. The *image* of the Reichstag has undoubtedly attained iconic status, cutting across ideologies and histories, as seen, for example, with those horrendous pictures of devastation following the pogrom of *Kristallnacht*, or the much cited image of a Soviet flag raised on the roof of the building by Russian soldiers following the conquest of Berlin at the close of World War II. Today, following extensive renovation under the direction of Sir Norman Foster & Partners, the building houses the new seat of the federal government of a (re)united Germany, so offering once more a renewed political image. In addition, with its eco-friendly innovations and the suturing of old and new, it has become a key marker of the 'new architecture' of post-Wall Berlin. Each of these image associations (and many more besides) that have accumulated throughout Berlin's tempestuous history, were given an unusual public screening. A dramatic art event took place over two weeks in the summer of 1995, drawing to the site a reported five million visitors. The event was Christo and Jeanne-Claude's 'wrapping' of the Reichstag, which cloaked the building in a million square feet of fabric.

For many, this grand veiling of the building actually meant the 'screening out' of the darker pictures from the past. Needless to say, it was an 'ideal rite of passage marking the Reichstag's initiation into a new era' (Ladd 1997: 92). Any more formal or orchestrated a ceremony would most likely have stirred up controversy and unrest. The wrapping of the Reichstag was undoubtedly 'a huge public-relations coup for Berlin' (Large 2001: 612), not only because it brought together many different people, but also because in it Berliners finally found a successful way to celebrate the past. Notably, however, one of the reasons suggested for the success of this event has been its absence of any single or determined message. The artists certainly refrained from offering one, and 'neither their supporters nor their opponents had been able to agree on what it all meant'. The result was that this temporary re-figuring of the Reichstag 'could be a celebration for some and a commemoration for others, one person's work of art and another's spectacle, a political event and a giant party' (Ladd 1997: 95). In other words, what was maintained was a lowering of expectations, whilst simultaneously the enriching of the complexity of this slice of history. The event not only offered a new start, a blank canvas so to speak, but it also helped to underwrite the re-issuing of various aspects of the city's past, projecting them as images for the future. It is perhaps all but impossible to 'contain' an event of this kind on the dry pages of a book such as this. The wrapping of the Reichstag surely had simply to be visited for its effect to be felt. And whilst in this case the event might be said to lack an explicit kind of radial patterning (that Berger argues is necessary to respect social memories), the event, nonetheless, like the metapicture, which gives 'theory a body' (Mitchell 1994: 418), was something to be experienced, not explained. It is this kind of theoretical/philosophical embodiment that I suggest is the order of the image critique: it is not a form of imagefare, but rather a certain critical 'blankness' or openness allowing – as an incident of polyperspectival complexity – a combination of images and issues to be re-staged, not only in order to be experienced as a kind of thought-image, but to be *collectively* experienced; their responsibility shared.

Notes

1. With respect to the rather limited range of critical responses to the fall of the Wall, the two films I discuss here are among only a few examples that exhibit anything like the kind of creative, 'visual' critique I describe with an image critique. One possibility might have been Peter Schneider's *The*

German Comedy (1991), a follow-up to his highly popular book of fantastical tales of the Wall when it was still standing (*The Wall Jumper*, 1983). However, given the scope of this book, Schneider's book is concerned more specifically with reunification than with the actual fall of the Wall and does not work upon the images as such of the fall of the Wall. As a result, the kinds of complex and critical 'spaces' that I suggest make for an image critique are not particularly evident (if anything, his earlier book of fantastical tales of Wall jumpers is more in-keeping with an image critique, but obviously this book is not about the *fall* of the Wall). Another possible example is a BBC radio play, *Mars Flight* (2004). The story centres on Michael Hoffman, a 20-year-old East German mechanic, who signs up for a medical trial that will simulate the journey to Mars. This simulated 'mission' is used to represent the overblown dreams of the socialist project, both on a macro scale in terms of the workings of the state and the micro level with the narrative told through an exchange of letters between Michael and his doting family. The imagery is certainly dramatic and in numerous places intricately bound to media accounts of the events leading up to the fall of the Wall. Ultimately, however, in being a radio play it is not nearly as illustrative as the two film examples I have chosen. Also, generally, this play is only derivative of these films, echoing many aspects, but not necessarily developing them further.

2. The American film distributing company Icestorm, established only in 1997, have released on the domestic market over 400 East German classic films from the DEFA archives, as well as numerous cartoons and TV programmes. In addition various East German-made films formerly suppressed by the GDR regime are now available and many of which attracting the interests of film critics and scholars.

3. Brussig's novel *Helden wie wir* has been translated into English as *Heroes Like Us* (1997). Throughout this chapter, where I cite from the text, it is from the English version. However, since I tend to discuss the film and novel interchangeably, I have chosen to keep to the original German title.

4. It should be noted, however, there are a number of crucial scenes omitted from the film version of *Helden wie wir* (including those on Christa Wolf), which certainly lessens the political resonance of the story. In general, the film lacks the pace of the novel. Crucially, what is missing is the ongoing sense of a build-up to the finale in which we see Klaus 'open' the wall. Significantly, there is no reporter to which Klaus is telling his story, which means that the film does not present that double narrative of Klaus offering the media his story about the media event of the fall of the Wall. One result of this absence is that his heroic act at the Wall comes across as a somewhat isolated incident. In fact, the whole narrative trajectory, which in the novel always leads to the fall of the Wall, is replaced in the film by a love story (with a 'Hollywood ending' in which the boy gets the girl!). On one level (certainly for the fans of the novel) this is rather disappointing. However, with respect to my interests here in image critique this need not cause significant problems. As I have already noted, I do not look to *Helden wie wir* (nor *Goodbye Lenin!*) as an exemplar of an image critique. Nevertheless, in combination – as *both* novel and film – *Helden wie wir* undoubtedly offers interesting possibilities in respect of a consideration of what an image critique of the fall of the Wall might look like.

5. I am grateful to Martin Jan Stepanek for this careful translation.

6. Emphasis upon the authority and clarity of verbal reasoning is certainly not restricted to Habermas' notion of the public sphere. In fact, it underpins much of the liberal tradition that puts emphasis upon the need for 'reasoned dialogue' to negotiate power relations. For a useful overview see Benhabib (1999: 73–98).

7. Stuart Hall's (1980) encoding/decoding model of the media undoubtedly allows for more specific evaluations of the media message and to understand the ways in which messages can be negotiated at each and every stage of their articulation. Arguably, however, there is a tendency for this framework to be used to 'celebrate moments of "resistance"'; frequently borne out by the implicit desire not to integrate subordinate groups into a dominant ideology (Morley 1999: 140). In response to this criticism, and in revising his own study of news consumption, David Morley suggests a further need to 'differentiate the moment of comprehension more clearly from the moment of interpretation/evaluation of 'messages'. This is a point that I pick up in the following section, where I discuss the concept of the public screen, which relates specifically to *distraction* as being central to our contemporary mode of perception.

8. For a useful overview of the main themes and trends in contemporary interpretations of the two Germanies and reunification, see Fulbrook (2000).

9. This controversy was sparked off by Christa Wolf's publication of a short story, *Was Bleibt* (1990 [English trans. 1993]), in which an East Berlin writer (generally identifiable as Wolf herself) suffers from an identity crisis as she becomes a target of *Stasi* surveillance and harassment. The fact that Wolf writes about the *Stasi* in this way marks a contrast with the more personal, interior subject matter of her other works and can be taken as a direct attack on the system. However, the fact that the manuscript was dated as both 1979 and 1989 immediately prompted the question of why she had not sought to make it public *during* the time of the GDR regime. The allegation, particularly by West German critics, was that Wolf had sought, retroactively, to label herself a victim of the system she herself had supported. The controversy quickly extended to question the significance of East German literature as a whole. For more on this subject, see Vazsonyi (1996); Huyssen (1991); von Oppen (2000); Witte (1997); and Anz (1991).

10. Arguably, the critical importance of images (and in particular the photograph) develops more strongly in Berger's later work; notable, for example, with his collaboration with Jean Mohr on *Another Way of Telling* (1995). As Clive Scott (1999: 251) points out, in Berger's early work, he 'seems to be of the conviction that language alone can open out the constricted, presentative (rather inhabitable) space of the photograph, largely by the resource of metaphor', yet in his later work with Mohr, 'the photograph has become the adequate instrument of its own exploration'.

11. Berger's political commitments are central to his work. Indeed, some of his most well-known books, *Ways of Seeing* (1972) and, with Jean Mohr, *A Fortunate Man* (1967) and *The Seventh Man* (1975), are each concerned with very real, pressing issues relating to what he generally takes to be the brutalizing effects of modernization. Respectively, these concerns include issues such as the representation of women; the culturally deprived; and the difficulties faced by migrant workers.

12. Despite arguing here that *Do the Right Thing* offers an analytical approach to issues of race, it has certainly not stopped the director, Spike Lee, having been highly criticized for inciting 'real' violence. Paralleling my remarks, perhaps, regarding Thomas Brussig's role/intervention in his own narrative of *Helden wie wir*, Mitchell (1994: 391–392) notes the criticisms levelled at Spike Lee highlight a certain lack of transparency: 'Spike Lee's motives as writer and director – whether to make a political statement, give the audience the spectacle it wants, or fulfil a narrative design – are far from clear'). Thus, Mookie's 'ethical intervention' that diverts the violence away from people to property is not necessarily only to be interpreted as Mookie 'doing the right thing', but equally, perhaps, that 'Spike Lee himself "does the right thing" in this moment by breaking the illusion of cinematic realism and intervening as the director of his own work of public art'.

AFTERWORD: ECOLOGIES OF IMAGES, TOPOLOGIES OF CRITIQUE

Above all, the ideas drawn together in this book are situated within the context of an espoused pictorial turn. In explaining this notion, Mitchell (1994: 16) writes:

> ...it should be clear that it is not a return to naïve mimesis, copy or correspondence theories of representation, or a renewed metaphysics of pictorial "presence: " it is rather a postlinguistics, postsemiotic rediscovery of the picture as a complex interplay between visuality, apparatus, institutions, discourse, bodies, and figurality.

What is evident from these remarks is that a 'rediscovery of the picture' involves a wide range of concerns and interests. Yet, as Mitchell (1994: 417–418) himself notes, the concepts he raises in respect of these debates have been 'largely negative', forming part of a 'de-disciplinary effort whose ultimate outcome cannot yet be pictured'. In lieu of a single picture of his 'whole argument' Mitchell explains how his book, *Picture Theory*, was 'compiled in something like the manner of a photograph album'. It is a 'collection of snapshots', he suggests, 'of specific problems indigenous to representation, addressed on particular occasions, at a definite historical moment that [he calls] the end of postmodernism'. This would seem to raise not only an interesting point about what it means at this moment in time to 'do' theory, but also how this activity might be 'written' up. I share a similar concern in trying to negotiate an 'explanation' and illustration of an image critique.

There are two main concerns that arise from Mitchell's account of the pictorial turn that have been of significant influence. The first is the observation 'that visual experience or "visual literacy" might not be fully explicable on the model of textuality' (Mitchell 1994: 16). This has been a guiding principle in considering how and, more importantly, *why* an image critique can most effectively come to deal with televisual events such as the fall of the Wall. Events such as these have become a constituent feature of contemporary global politics, a fact that relates directly to Mitchell's second observation, that 'while the problem of pictorial representation has always been with us, it presses inescapably now, and with unprecedented force.' Significantly, this leads him to make the suggestion that '[t]raditional strategies of containment no longer seem adequate, and the need for a global critique of visual culture seems inescapable'.

It is, then, in light of these concerns (and possibilities) that I have sought to explain what an image critique looks like. I may well have described it as if it were something original, though more reasonably it is only my *analyses* of the use of images for critical purposes that are perhaps new – as well as the specific critique of images of the fall of the Berlin Wall. However, I have also tried to take a step on from Mitchell's account of a 'picture theory', at least in that I explicitly advocate the *use* of images for a creative, critical engagement in contemporary visual culture. Throughout, I have tended to make sense of an image critique by using spatial and architectural metaphors, having included references to all number of things, from the theatre stage and the Great Wall of China, to the zoetrope and the Angel of History. These latter two are not simply spatial, but also temporal designs. Frequently, in characterizing image critique as a 'situation of writing', I have inferred both a space and a time, or *pause* in which we can gain critical reflection. My habit of moving from one descriptive model to another is perhaps something of a 'fault' in my style of thinking, yet equally, I would argue it is the need to illustrate the unsystematic motion of image critique that has led me to think in this way. Here, I want to offer some closing (though surely not final!) remarks on the possible shape and design of an image critique, which relates above all to an extended, complex 'environment' in which various images are in play.

Nonetheless, in working towards these supposedly 'defining' remarks, I do still heed caution against seeking to explicate a theory of pictures. As Mitchell (1994: 18–20) suggests, were he to give some shape to a new disciplinary formation that might emerge from the theory of pictures/picturing of theory, 'it would have a thoroughly dialogical and dialectical structure, not in the Hegelian sense of achieving a stable synthesis, but in Blake's and Adorno's sense of working through contradiction interminably'. And (as discussed in the preceding chapter) it is in this respect that the metapicture might make visible to us the difficulty in separating out theory from practice, so 'to give theory a body and visible shape that it often wants to deny, to reveal theory as representation'. Importantly, Mitchell asks us to understand representation not as a particular object, but rather 'as relationship, as process, as the relay mechanism in exchanges of power, value, and publicity' (420). This is precisely how I suggest an image critique be envisaged – it is more about being the messenger than the message. Significantly, 'nothing in this model guarantees the directionality of the structure. On the contrary, it suggests an inherently unstable, reversible, and dialectical structure' (420). In following this logic, there can be no 'roadmap' for an image critique, no generic formula, either of its design or its use. Moreover, (whether we accept any pronouncement of an end of postmodernism or not) there is seemingly little use in seeking to overcome our present media/image contexts via some kind of mapping; the kind, for example, epitomized by Fredric Jameson's (1991) notion of 'cognitive mapping'.

Jameson suggests two different image strategies as a means to undermine what he considers the depthlessness of postmodernism and the 'cultural logic of late capitalism' (a 'cultural logic' that interconnects with what I identified as the neo-liberal celebration of economic 'freedom' and its associated end of ideological history). The first strategy is to adhere to the very 'postmodern political aesthetic' that one wishes to confront. Such a counter-aesthetic 'would confront the structure of image society as such head-on and undermine it from within'. It is,

Jameson suggests, what might be termed a 'homeopathic strategy...undermining the image by way of the image itself, and planning the implosion of the logic of the simulacrum by dint of ever greater doses of simulacra' (1991: 409). Andy Warhol is taken to be the exemplar of such an approach, yet, interestingly, the strategy would seem rather neatly to describe DeLuca and Peeples' (2002) concept of the image-event as it faces up to the 'logic' of the public screen. In either case, the problem is that the remedy can soon become its own malady. Thus – as relates to my argument in the preceding chapter – Jameson's suggestion of the process of undermining the image 'by way of the image itself' can all too easily lead to 'imagefare' where one image seeks to override another without bringing to light the actual framework in which the process of exchange takes place. By contrast, I suggest films such as Helden wie wir and Goodbye Lenin! offer examples of an image critique in which various images come together in new configurations and as a way of examining not only their various relations, but also the grounds of their own fabrication and spectatorship. This, then, relates better to Jameson's second and supposedly 'more modernist strategy' of cognitive mapping. Essentially, this is a strategy that, as Simons (2000: 95) describes, 'foregrounds the pedagogic and didactic functions of art as a means to foster a new as yet undreamed form of class consciousness.' Jameson conceives of the notion by extrapolating from Lynch's (1998) famous study The Image of the City, to transpose a spatial analysis to a social, cultural analysis of an unbounded postmodern global capitalism. The point of cognitive mapping is to find a means to navigate the unsystematic conditions of postmodern, multinational capitalism, not by removing oneself from it (which would not be possible anyway), but by staying within its 'logic', yet, concurrently, seeking to achieve a 'breakthrough to some as yet unimaginable new mode of representing...in which we may again begin to grasp our positioning as individual and collective subjects' (Jameson 1991: 54, emphasis added).

There are certainly a number of problems with this proposal, not least the bid to work towards a certain totality within the relativity of postmodernism, along with the fact that we are never actually given a working example. This 'new political art', as Jameson (1991: 54) calls it, always comes with the disclaimer 'if it is possible at all'. More significantly still, the very 'image' of a map, or mapping, presents a key dilemma for Jameson in properly explaining what is meant by cognitive mapping. Indeed, the very strength of its formulation is also its weakness. As he explains, the phrase 'cognitive mapping' is meant to have had a kind of oxymoronic value, 'to transcend the limits of mapping altogether', but in the end, the concept is seemingly 'drawn back by the force of gravity of the black hole of the map itself' (416). Oddly, then, the idea is that once we know what cognitive mapping is 'driving at', we are then meant to 'dismiss all figures of maps and mapping from [the] mind and try to imagine something else' (409). In the terms Mitchell describes of 'picturing theory' we might suggest the image of this critical concept not only ends up undermining its purpose, but equally it would appear to demonstrate the impossibility inherent in trying to map an image-based strategy in the first place. My penchant for deploying a variety of specific but, nonetheless, unfixed metaphors for picturing an image critique would seem either symptomatic or more hopefully a pragmatic means to overcome the 'force of gravity' of any single way of describing its method and form.

These problems aside, however, it is worth noting that my appeal to an image critique, in paralleling certain aspects of Jameson's idea for cognitive mapping, can come up against similar problems – particularly when it comes to defining and giving examples of its practice.

In common with the notion of cognitive mapping, I too advocate something like its pedagogical aesthetics. For Jameson this relates to a delight in cognition in revealing the actual structures underlying the resolute unsystemacity of multinational capitalism. Similarly, as I outlined in chapter two, I suggest an image critique can be likened to Susan Buck-Morss's methodology (as inspired by Walter Benjamin) in which images are used as philosophy or critical thought, providing the reader with 'a cognitive experience that surprises present understandings, and subverts them' (Buck-Morss 2000: xv). In addition, where Jameson argues we engage the actual *terrain* of the postmodern itself, I too suggest – as I have in the preceding chapter with respect to the image/media-event – a need to engage the 'terrain' of the image itself. Should this seem too suggestive of some metaphysical interior to the image, it is perhaps more accurate for me to say we need to find ways of critiquing *with* what we have available to us.

I have described how an image critique is intended as a *construction* 'for its own sake'. In other words, not a window or interpretation which seeks to frame an external object, but rather a kind of thought-piece which triggers and sustains critical reflection, as a means to embody theory. Thus, as an incident of writing/picturing an image critique should allow for 'theory' or critique to be *experienced*, rather than applied. There is a need to adjust our expectations (especially with respects to events in the world), in order not to seek critical *resolutions* (nor repeatable modes of analysis), but rather more critical spaces (or pauses) in which a greater complexity and polyphony of thoughts and voices can be heard. Cognitive *mapping* suggests (if unwillingly) a totalizing process or aim; to *map out* all possible directions and to provide a key or route to critical awareness. An image critique is seemingly less ambitious and goal-orientated. In this respect, whilst both conceptions might equally be said to embrace a certain instability and principle of open architecture, the 'image' of an image critique is hopefully rather less assertive, though no less critical and reflective in purview.

In formulating what might be described as a polymeric (image-based) critique, the intention is not so much to 'find our way', as we might with a map, but more – as in a refracting and reflecting crystalline space (whether textual or imagistic) – to find a time and place in which to keep thoughts open, to keep in circulation various image-elements, which allow for many different points of view. My description of a crystalline state is, in part, influenced by Deleuze's (1989: 68–97) puzzling 'crystal-image', which he expounds in his analysis of film. In particular, he refers to the 'time-image', an image (or engagement with images) which is described as breaking the movement or action image of conventional narrative film (as structured by a common-sense understanding of space-time). By contrast, Deleuze's interest in the time-image is its enabling of a more analytical, thought-provoking instance. It is an image which can be treated 'like something that is also readable' (24). It is an image that asks us to *reflect* on a situation; crucially, in breaking with the causality of the movement image, it poses a primary question of precisely what *does* connect one moment to the next.

To simplify, we might say the 'crystal-image' enables us to watch ourselves watching. In film, for example, flashback and dream sequences are an (all too) obvious example of time-images (which make up a crystal-image) since they break with the common-sense narrative flow. These images in themselves, whilst unhinging narrative time, are relatively conventional and easily subsumed within a structure of movement images. The significance of the crystal-image is its composite design of many such time-images, thus allowing different instances of the image to be maintained simultaneously. If we were to separate out each image that cuts the structure of its movement, they would appear as 'the shattered splinters of the crystal-image' (69). In its simplest form, the crystal-image can be thought of as a mirror reflection, as in a scene, for example, in which we can observe simultaneously an actor, a mirror and their reflection in it. This scene, akin to the duck-rabbit illusion (cited in the previous chapter), provides us with three concurrent moments of the image, its actual (the actor), virtual (reflection) and combined (actor-reflection) image. And, of course, if this mirroring effect is then multiplied further with respect to a crystalline structure, with each of its faces able not only to reflect images, but also to refract them, we perhaps begin to understand the complexity of such a composition.

Putting aside Deleuze's deeper preoccupation with time, which is perhaps not altogether relevant here, the point I want to make is simply that the crystal structure (making 'cuts' through what we otherwise take for granted) is a useful descriptive model for a complex space or situation in which we stage new opportunities of critical reflection. And by 'reflection' here I mean both the occasion of 'serious' thinking or consideration, as well as the reflection of the image itself which looks back as a means to awakening us to its present value. The crystal, then, provides yet another architectonic image to explain the workings of an image critique – an image that attempts to describe both what it looks like (how it is experienced), as well as how it is formulated (or at least how we might like to imagine it is formulated). In contrast to a map or plan (the tool of an architect and traveller alike), the crystal describes a complex, 'living' occasioning of the image. Its bounded, yet translucent, construction is a site/sight in which to witness and create (in a writerly sense) a whole series of interconnections, tensions and relations. Significantly, there is no original location (or starting point), nor is there any final destination. Thus, it is not something we can use to point with as such, as we might with a compass or map. Instead it continually and radially interacts with (and reflects) the wider 'ecology' of the world around us.

It is this radial patterning that – if only in a small way – I hope to have demonstrated through an exploration of images of the fall of the Berlin Wall. In chapter one, I characterized images of the fall of the Wall as moving images, which, beyond the temporal medium in which they are captured, refers to a philosophical understanding of a singular repetition or 'secret vibration'. This, I explained, was to be thought of as the profound idea repeated in its every iteration, which in the case of the Wall relates specifically to the celebration of an 'end of history'. I likened such 'repetition' (or continuum) to the writing through a stick of rock, which – with the force of a sharp edge – can be interrupted (and realized) at any point. It is in this sense, then, that as light traverses the many faces of a crystal its singular repetition is both free to travel, yet equally cut through at each angle of incidence. This is the 'art' of the image critique, for each slither of the crystal is like the Angel of History who 'looks back' to inflect the dialectic of the flow of time; to witness, as an awakening, 'what passes away in the becoming' (Weigel 1996: 59). In the case of the fall of the Wall, an image critique entails seeing how the image of celebration comes to fruition and what effects this has in framing our thoughts towards it, now and in the future. The aim is not to 'understand' such an image in a hermeneutically detached manner, but instead to be critically engaged with the image itself. As we find with the idea of the metapicture, which can 'make visible the impossibility of separating theory from practice, to give theory a body' (Mitchell 1994: 418), an image critique seeks the kind of praxis of thought that Sigrid Weigel explains underpins Benjamin's concept of the dialectical image;

where 'memory and action find articulation in images, [...] ideas are structured as images, and what is at stake is therefore a praxis that can operate with images' (Wiegel 1996: 9–10). This, then, is the crystalline state in which we find ourselves and in which we can make our thoughts (and those of others) come to light.

*   *   *

To work my way a little further through this 'terrain' of the image it is perhaps useful to re-cycle an image-theory from the past – and here I refer to Susan Sontag's (1979: 180) somewhat enigmatic idea of an 'ecology of images'. Sontag conceives this idea in her closing remarks on the nature of the photograph within the context of what she labels our 'image-world' – a world in which we have come to live according to a 'de-Platonised' understanding of reality, whereby it is 'less and less plausible to reflect upon our experience according to the distinction between images and things, between copies and originals' (179). In such an *environment*, she tells us, '[i]mages are more real than anyone could have supposed...[and if] there can be a better way for the real world to include the one of images, it will require an ecology not only of real things but of images as well' (180). The overriding point for this 'conservationist remedy' is to find a means to secure our capacity to respond to experiences (whether taken from 'reality' or its pictures) with 'emotional freshness and ethical pertinence', which is otherwise 'being sapped by the relentless diffusion' of all sort of images ('good' and 'bad') (Sontag 2003: 108–9). In the case of the fall of the Wall there are, of course, a bewildering array of images and associations. According to Darnton (1991: 74), even as quickly as the morning after the night of the fall of the Wall, its 'jagged wound in the middle of a great city' had become popularized as 'a dance floor, a picture gallery, a bulletin board, a movie screen, a videocassette, a museum...'. Indeed, overnight, the Wall in pieces became available to all. An ecology of images would imply perhaps that we sift through all of these images and things in order to make sense of their 'value' and to determine our responsibility (if any) towards them.

What I take most significantly from this allusion to an 'ecology of images' is its suggestion of an environment (or lived situation) that is constituted by images, an operational 'system' or flux that makes images a living, dynamic concern. An image critique needs to enter into this system, to work with it and to demonstrate it at work. In the preceding chapter, I analysed how the films *Helden wie wir* and *Goodbye Lenin!* overtly represent certain public images as images. These films not only (re)create an 'image-world' in order to re-circulate these specific images for new critical attention, but they also do so in such a way as to be reflexive about their own narrative construction. So, for example, in *Helden wie wir*, the 'real' scenes of the Alexanderplatz rally and the final fall of the Wall are shown from the new and strange perspective of the main character, Klaus. In *Goodbye Lenin!* the norms of television news formatting are applied in order to rewrite the news of the events leading up to the fall of the Wall, again to frame a new, alternative reading of the event. In both cases, they acknowledge the currency of certain images in contemporary society and allow them in all their specificity to *replay* (as much as re-figure) their meaning for new critical possibilities.

Admittedly, Sontag is ambivalent about any so-called 'ecology of images'. Her reference to 'ecology' as a remedy for our de-Platonic 'image-world' is arguably iconoclastic. Thus, in finding myself drawn to the idea, I equally find myself perhaps needing to work against the grain of Sontag's argument, against a certain melancholy that pervades her analysis. In her subsequent reflections on photography, Sontag (2003: 108) actively denounces the idea of an ecology of images, or at least declares it a non-starter. In discussing the growing tide of images of war, atrocity and terror, she remarks cuttingly '[t]here isn't going to be an ecology of images. No Committee of Guardians is going to ration horror, to keep fresh its ability to shock. And the horrors themselves are not going to abate'. Yet, in Sontag's typically circuitous argumentation, we actually find that there may not necessarily be a 'committee' of guardians of the images, but at least a number of committed artists, journalists and critics. Indeed, an ecology of images might most readily be achieved by those themselves involved directly in image-making. This, of course, echoes what I have said of the makers of *Helden wie wir* and *Goodbye Lenin!*

Sontag (2003: 123) provides an example with the artist Jeff Wall and in particular a huge anti-war image by him, which she suggests is 'exemplary in its thoughtfulness and power'. The picture, which depicts thirteen Russian soldiers who lie dead in a blasted hillside landscape of Afghanistan, is provocative not only with respect to war, but about our spectatorship of war. In this respect, particularly, it contributes well to an 'ecology' of war imagery, for it works to re-invest our sense of shock and awe. Sontag explains the point:

> The figures in [Jeff] Wall's visionary photo-work are "realistic" but, of course, the image is not. Dead soldiers don't talk. Here they do. [...] Engulfed by the image, which is so accusatory, one could fantasize that the soldiers might turn and talk to us. But no, no one is looking out of the picture. There's no threat of protest [...] These dead are supremely uninterested in the living: in those who took their lives; in witnesses – and in us. Why should they seek our gaze? What would they have to say to us? "We" – this "we" is everyone who has never experienced anything like what they went through – don't understand. We don't get it. We truly can't imagine what it was like.
>
> (2003: 125)

As Sontag declares in earlier reflections on photography, the camera is both 'the antidote and the disease, a means of appropriating reality and a means of making it obsolete' (Sontag 1979: 179). The real force of the photographic image she suggests is its *material* reality; the fact that, as Barthes (1981: 75–77) says, the photograph places tangibly in our hand something 'that-has-been'. These deposits of the past, or *creations* of the 'past' as we see here with Jeff Wall's work, provide 'potent means for turning the tables on reality', which in keeping with Sontag's reference to Plato's simile of the cave, means turning reality itself 'into a shadow' (Sontag 1979: 180); into images which dance upon the wall (or the various screens) of our lives. Crucially, the argument that underpins Sontag's idea of an ecology of images is always unequivocally 'a defense of reality and the imperilled standards for responding more fully to it' (Sontag 2003: 109). I must stress, for all my 'bluster' here about images and an image critique (with all its accoutrements of crystals, zoetropes, angels and even the Great Wall of China), there is always a reality at stake. In the case of fall of the Berlin Wall, this reality most readily refers to the concerns of individual East Germans, as well as those who find themselves sitting at home far from events, yet strangely wrapped up in them, indelibly altered because of them. The point is that images (as 'things' in the world) can play an important part in our responding – hopefully in responsible ways – to our everyday reality and social interactions. As a consequence it can be just as important not to over-analyse images or seek to 'understand' and interpret them as such, but rather to consider whom they surround, why they do so and what they actually do for us.

At the very start of this book, I perhaps reified Mitchell's idea of the image as 'go-between' when I suggested that images can be better thought of as the *messengers* than the message; and more specifically, when I compared images to that of angels, such as those which frequent Wim Wender's filmic depictions of Berlin. This marked the first of a number of references I have made to angels, with the most notable being Benjamin's Angel of History (which I take to offer a useful emblem of image critique). Of course, I referred to the figure of the angel for its liminal quality – a quality which in Wender's Berlin, for example, allows them to move in and out of the human world. My point for an image critique, then, has been to keep in view a similar kind of uncertainty or transitional quality. With images there is always a potentially blank expression – the kind of expression you see in someone's face when they refuse to answer, when you *just don't know* what it is they are thinking. However, rather than see this as an end to dialogue, I would rather consider it a precious resource – for it is at this time that images have the capacity to tell us things we otherwise did not know. I have tried to demonstrate this with the sites/sights of the fall of the Wall in the films *Helden wie wir* and *Goodbye Lenin!* In both cases we are confronted with new critical versions of the images of the fall of the Wall that leave us with all sorts of thoughts about the event – thoughts and connections that are not necessarily easy to put into words. As we pick our way through the 'image-world', these pregnant pauses or silences of images are easily lost to our words and actions. But rather than our words needlessly colonizing the image, an image critique is intended to establish different sets of configurations, with different critical purposes.

Image critique is ineluctably fragile. There can be no guarantees for its success, which, in turn, might seem quite frustrating. Yet, equally this can be its strength. Where it is wrongly prescribed there are seemingly no adverse effects. Yet, where it is aptly applied the effects can be both pronounced and challenging. Ultimately, what I have described as 'image critique' defines an approach that is experimental and undeniably heuristic in nature. In other words it seeks to provide a situation for someone to discover and learn something for themselves. It is a situation that must be experienced (an experience that perhaps may well be shared), but presumably it can never adequately be explained or catalogued in the confines of a monograph such as this, with its overly analytical 'long roll of thunder' of the text.

With these thoughts in mind, it is perhaps pertinent to return to one last rather obscure(d) image of the Berlin Wall. A particular stretch of the Wall remains today enmeshed in a host of different histories, some of which are concrete, some organic and others weightless memories that nonetheless hang heavy in the air. I refer, in particular, to an open-air exhibition known as 'The Topography of Terror', which lies in the heart of Berlin, on Prinz-Albrecht-Strasse. Here, only metres below some obsolete and battered sections of the Wall, lies the site of the former headquarters of the Nazi secret police agency, the Gestapo. For many years after the war – during the time the Wall served as a brutal East/West dividing line – this area remained a wasteland and dumping ground. However, in 1986, following ongoing pressure from the public for a confrontation with the Nazi past, the West Berlin city government sponsored an archaeological excavation of the site. As a result, the foundation walls of the former

headquarters and the ruins of the Gestapo cells were uncovered. Since this discovery, the site has remained an 'open wound', 'an intentional irritant and lasting reminder of [Berlin's] troubled past' (Ladd 1997: 165). Numerous attempts to galvanize the site as a more traditional memorial have failed, and, instead, the temporary cabin that serves as the 'Museum' office and the exhibition panels which detail the Nazi past have become, if only by default, a permanent fixture amidst the earth and weeds of this overgrown plot. Even after the dramatic end to the Berlin Wall and the sudden revival of the city's lost centre which surrounds this spot, it has still managed to remain in this fashion an ad hoc, open-air exhibition site.

It is by dint of its shifting topography that the exhibit exposes a rich seam of Berlin's recent and painful past and which continues to draw many thousands of visitors throughout the year. It can be argued that the presence of the defunct Berlin Wall is unnecessarily confusing to those who make a trip to this site. It is almost certain that some visitors go away thinking that the Nazi exhibit details the GDR regime that once lay behind it, or vice versa. While the organizers naturally have their own views on the correct interpretations, they have remained committed to the need for visitors to find the 'answers' for themselves – thus, the site remains one of documentation, not interpretation. In this way, then, 'The Topography of Terror' stimulates thought but does not direct it; in the ruins there is room for an appetite and openness for critical and public engagement. Here, quite literally, lies an 'ecology of images', a topology of critique, which allows its various pictures and memories to be perpetually pieced together and then taken apart again. The viewer is not only able to become aware of the past but also of their own present context in which they bring the various elements together. I would like to imagine that this is the *shape* (of 'things' to come) of an image critique, for like this complex street scene exposed above and below ground, an image critique does not aim to secure only one point of view, nor, indeed, any one critic's voice. Instead it is a space in which *many* can visit. If we consider an image critique always in pieces and made up of only fragments – with all number of images mixed up in its 'landscape' – it need not necessarily be taken as a sign of an unravelling, but rather of a healthy and edifying circulation. The task set by an image critique must be to engage such flux and complexity when writing and thinking about the world we see around us. In accepting the conditions of what has been referred to as a pictorial turn and more specifically when beginning to consider just what future research and/or writing on visual culture might actually come to *look* like, surely we need set ourselves the task beyond that of simply securing knowledge based upon a single point of view. An image critique is to afford us an opportunity to bring the visual (if not the multi-modal) world into our very words and theories. It is, to paraphrase Barthes, to suggest a hermenuetics that paints rather than digs. For unless it is possible to afford ourselves such 'situations of writing', we will no doubt ever be playing *fort-da* as we take up our pens in the face of a burgeoning visual culture.

BIBLIOGRAPHY

Alpers, Svetlana (1983), *The Art of Describing: Dutch Art in the Seventeenth Century*. Chicago: University of Chicago Press.

Amann, Jessica (2003), *The Fantastic in the Post-Wende German Novel*. Ph.D. Thesis, University of Nottingham, Nottingham.

Anderson, Perry (1992), *A Zone of Engagement*. London: Verso.

Anz, Thomas (ed.) (1991), *Es geht nicht um Christa Wolf*. Munich: Spangenberg.

Appadurai, Arjun (ed.) (1986), *The Social Life of Things*. Cambridge: Cambridge University Press.

Armstrong, Carol (1996), 'Reponse to Visual Culture Questionnaire', October, 77 (Summer), pp. 27–28.

Ash, Timothy Garton (1994), *In Europe's Name: Germany and the Divided Continent*. London: Vintage.

Ash, Timothy Garton (1999), *We the People: The Revolution of '89 Witnesses in Warsaw, Budapest, Berlin and Prague*. London: Penguin.

August, Oliver (1999), *Along the Wall and Watchtowers: A Journey Down Germany's Divide*. London: HarperCollins.

Bakhtin, Mikhail M. (1984), *Rabelais and his World*, trans. by Helene Iswolsky. Bloomington: Indiana University Press.

Bal, Mieke (2003), 'Visual Essentialism and the Object of Visual Culture', *Journal of Visual Culture*, 2 (1), pp. 5–32.

Bal, Mieke (2005), 'The Commitment to Look', *Journal of Visual Culture*, 4 (2), pp. 145–162.

Balfour, Alan (1990), *Berlin: The Politics of Order, 1737–1989*. New York: Rizzoli International Publications.

Balfour, Alan (ed.) (1995), *Berlin*. London: Academy Editions.

Barber, Stephen (1995), *Fragments of the European City*. London: Reaktion Books.

Barnard, Malcolm (1998), *Art, Design, and Visual Culture: An Introduction*. New York: St Martin's.

Barnard, Peter (1999), *We Interrupt This Programme...20 News Stories That Marked The Century*. London: BBC.

Barthes, Roland (1977), *Image Music Text*, trans. by Stephen Heath. London: Fontana.

Barthes, Roland (1981), *Camera Lucida: Reflections on Photography*, trans. by Richard Howard. New York: Hill & Wang.

Barthes, Roland (1982), *Empire of Signs*, trans. by Richard Howard. London: Jonathan Cape.

Barthes, Roland (1985), *The Grain of the Voice: Interviews 1962–1980*, trans. by Linda Coverdale. London: Jonathan Cape.

Barthes, Roland (1987), *Writer Sollers*, trans. By Philip Thody. Minneapolis: University of Minnesota Press.

Barthes, Roland (1989), *The Rustle of Language*, trans. by Richard Howard. Berkeley: University of California Press.

Barthes, Roland (1990), *A Lover's Discourse: Fragments*, trans. by Richard Howard. London: Penguin Books.

Barthes, Roland (1994), *Roland Barthes*, trans. by Richard Howard. Berkeley and Los Angeles: University of California Press.

Barthes, Roland (1999), *The Pleasure of the Text*, trans. by Richard Miller. New York: Hill and Wang.

Barthes, Roland (2000), 'Inaugural Lecture, Collège de France' in Susan Sontag (ed.) *A Barthes Reader*. London: Vintage, pp. 457–478.

Baudrillard, Jean (1994) *The Illusion of the End*, trans. by Chris Turner. Cambridge: Polity Press.

Baudrillard, Jean (1995), *The Gulf War Did Not Take Place*. Indiana University Press.

Bauman, Zygmunt (1992), *Intimations of Postmodernity*. London: Routledge.

Benhabib, Seyla (1999), 'Models of Public Space: Hannah Arendt, the Liberal Tradition, and Jürgen Habermas' in Craig Calhoun (ed.) *Habermas and the Public Sphere*. Cambridge, Mass.: MIT Press, pp. 73–98.

Benjamin, Walter (1987), *Berliner Kindheit um Neunzehnhundert*. Frankfurt am Main: Suhrkamp.

Benjamin, Walter (1992), *Illuminations*, trans. by Harry Zohn. London: Fontana Press.

Benjamin, Walter (1997), *One-Way Street and Other Writings*, trans. by Edmund Jephcott and Kingsley Shorter. London: Verso.

Benjamin, Walter (1999) *The Arcades Project*, trans. by Howard Eiland and Kevin McLaughlin. Cambridge, Mass.: Harvard University Press.

Benjamin, Walter (2002), 'Berlin Childhood Around 1900' in *Selected Writings: Volume 3, 1935–1938*. Cambridge, Mass. and London: Harvard University Press, pp. 344–415.

Bennett, W. Lance and Lawrence, Regina G. (1995), 'News Icons and the Mainstreaming of Social Change', *Journal of Communication*, 45 (3), pp. 20–39.

Berger, John (1972), *Ways of Seeing*. London: Penguin Books.

Berger, John (1997), 'Ways of Remembering' in Jessica Evans (ed.) *The Camerawork Essays: Context and Meaning In Photography*. London: Rivers Oram Press, pp. 38–51.

Berger, John and Mohr, Jean (1967), *A Fortunate Man*. London: Allen Lane.

Berger, John and Mohr, Jean (1975), *A Seventh Man*. Harmondsworth: Penguin.

Berger, John and Mohr, Jean (1995), *Another Way of Telling*. New York: Vintage International.

Bertsch, Georg C., Hedler, Ernst and Dietz, Matthias (eds.) (1994), *SED – Schönes Einheits Design*. Köln: Taschen.

Bialas, Wolfgang (1996), *Vom unfreien Schweben zum freien Fall: Ostdeutsche Intellektuelle im gesellschaftlichen Umbruch*. Frankfurt: Fischer.

Boorstin, Daniel J. (1992), *The Image: A Guide to Pseudo-Events in America*. New York: Vintage Books.

Bordo, Susan (1997), *Twilight Zones: The Hidden Life of Cultural Images from Plato to O.J.* California: University of California Press.

Borneman, John (1991) *After the Wall: East meets West in the New Berlin*. New York: Basic Books.

Borneman, John (1992), *Belonging in the Two Berlins: Kin, State, Nation*. Cambridge: Cambridge University Press.

Borneman, John (1998), 'Grenzregime (border regime): the Wall and its Aftermath' in Thomas M. Wilson and Hastings Donnan (eds.) *Border Identities: Nation and State at International Frontiers*. Cambridge: Cambridge University Press, pp. 162–190.

Bourdieu, Pierre (1998), *On Television and Journalism*, trans. by Priscilla Parkhurst Ferguson. London: Pluto Press.

Boyer, Dominic (2001) 'Media Markets, Mediating Labors, and the Branding of East German Culture at *Super Ill'*, *Social Text*, 19 (3), pp. 9–33.

Brockmann, Stephen (1991), 'Introduction: The Reunification Debate', *New German Critique*, 52 (Winter), pp. 3–30.

Bruner, Michael S. (1989), 'Symbolic Uses of the Berlin Wall, 1961–1989', *Communication Quarterly*, 37 (4), pp. 319–328.

Brussig, Thomas (1995), *Helden wie wir*. Frankfurt: Fischer.

Brussig, Thomas (1997), *Heroes Like Us*, trans. by John Brownjohn. London: Harvill.

Brussig, Thomas (1999), 'Jubelfeiern wird's geben' in *Der Spiegel*, nr. 36, 6.9.99, pp. 255–257 [Interview with Thomas Brussig].

Bryson, Norman, Holly, Michael Ann and Moxey, Keith (eds.) (1994), *Visual Culture: Images and Interpretations*. Hannover: Wesleyan University Press.

Buck-Morss, Susan (1989), *The Dialectics of Seeing: Walter Benjamin and the Arcades Project*. Cambridge, Mass.: MIT Press.

Buck-Morss, Susan (1994), 'Fashion in Ruins: History after the Cold War', *Radical Philosophy*, 68 (Autumn), pp. 10–17.

Buck-Morss, Susan (1996), 'Response to Visual Culture Questionnaire', *October*, 77 (Summer), pp. 29–31.

Buck-Morss, Susan (2000) *Dreamworld and Catastrophe: The Passing of Mass Utopia in East and West*. Cambridge, Mass.: MIT Press.

Buck-Morss, Susan (2002), 'Globalisation, Cosmopolitanism, politics, and the citizen (in conversation with Laura Mulvey and Marquard Smith)', *Journal of Visual Culture*, 1 (3), pp. 325–340.

Buhl, Dieter (1990), *Window To The West: How Television from the Federal Republic Influenced Events in East Germany*. The Joan Shorenstein Barone Center, Discussion Paper D-5, pp. 1–9.

Burgin, Victor (1986), *The End of Art Theory: Criticism and Postmodernity*. London: Macmillan.

Burgin, Victor (1996a), *In/Different Spaces: Place and Memory In Visual Culture*. Berkeley: University of California Press.

Burgin, Victor (1996b), *Some Cities*. London: Reaktion Books.

Cavell, Stanley (1984), 'The Fact of Television' in *Themes out of School*. San Francisco: North Point Press, pp. 235–268.

Chamberlain, Lesley (1990), *In the Communist Mirror: Journeys in Eastern Europe*. London: Faber.

Chaney, David C. (2000), 'Contemporary Socioscapes: Books on Visual Culture' *Theory, Culture & Society*, 17 (6), pp. 111–124.

Cheng, Meiling (2003), 'The Unbearable Lightness of Sight' in Amelia Jones (ed.) *The Feminism and Visual Culture Reader*. London: Routledge, pp. 29–31.

Childs, David (2001), *The Fall of the GDR: Germany's Road to Unity*. London: Longman.

Childs, David and Popplewell, Richard (1996), *The Stasi: The East German Intelligence and Security System*. Basingstoke: Macmillan.

Chomsky, Noam (1997), *World Orders, Old and New*. London: Pluto Press.

Connell, Matt F. (2002), 'Georg Wilhelm Friedrich Hegel' in Jon Simons (ed.) *From Kant to Levi-Strauss: The Background to Contemporary Critical Theory*. Edinburgh: Edinburgh University Press, pp. 33–49.

Connor, Steven (2000), 'Making an Issue of Cultural Phenomenology', *Critical Quarterly*, 42 (1), pp. 2–6.

Cooper, Marther and Chalfant, Henry (1984), *Subway Art*. London: Thames and Hudson.

Cormack, Michael (1992), 'Opening the Wall' in *Ideology*, London: B.T. Batsford Ltd., pp. 45–55.

Crary, Jonathan (1988), 'Modernising Vision' in Hal Foster (ed.) *Vision and Visuality*. Seattle: Bay Press, pp. 29–44.

Critchley, Simon (2001), *Continental Philosophy: A Very Short Introduction*. Oxford: Oxford University Press.

Darnton, Robert (1991), *Berlin Journal: 1989–1990*. New York: Norton.

Dayan, Daniel and Katz, Elihu (1992), *Media Events: The Live Broadcasting of History*. Cambridge, Mass.: Harvard University Press.

Debray, Régis (1996), *Media Manifestos: On the Technological Transmission of Cultural Forms*, trans. by Eric Rauth. London: Verso.

Deleuze, Gilles (1989), *Cinema 2: The Time-Image*. London: Athlone Press.

Deleuze, Gilles (1994), *Difference and Repetition*, trans. by Paul Patton. London: Athlone Press.

Deleuze, Gilles (2001), *Pure Immanence: Essays on a Life*, trans. by Anne Boyman. New York: Zone Books.

Deluca, Kevin (1999), *Image Politics*. New York: Guildford Press.

Deluca, Kevin and Peeples, Jennifer (2002), 'From Public Sphere to Public Screen: Democracy, Activism, and the "Violence" of Seattle', *Critical Studies in Media Communication*, 19 (2), pp. 125–151.

Dennis, Mike (2003), *The Stasi: Myth and Reality*. London: Longman.

Derrida, Jacques (1976), *Of Grammatology*, trans. by Gayatri Chakravorty Spivak. Baltimore: Johns Hopkins University Press.

Derrida, Jacques (1987), *The Post Card: From Socrates to Freud and Beyond*, trans. by Alan Bass. Chicago: University of Chicago.

Derrida, Jacques (1993), 'Back From Moscow, in the USSR' in Mark Poster (ed.) *Politics, Theory, and Contemporary Culture*. New York: Columbia University Press, pp. 197–235.

Derrida, Jacques (1994), *Specters of Marx: The State of the Debt, the Work of Mourning, and the New International*, trans. by Peggy Kamuf. New York: Routledge.

Descartes, René (2000), *Meditations and Other Metaphysical Writings*. London: Penguin.

Dikovitskaya, Margarita (2001), *From Art History to Visual Culture: The Study of the Visual after the Cultural Turn*. Ph.D. Thesis, Columbia University, New York.

Doctorow, E. L. (1982), *The Book of Daniel*. London: Picador.

Do The Right Thing (1989), [Film], directed by Spike Lee; screenplay by Spike Lee (Universal City Studios).

Elkins, James (2003), *Visual Studies: A Skeptical Introduction*. New York: Routledge.

Ellis, John (1999), 'Television as Working-Through' in Jostein Gripsrud (ed.) *Television and Common Knowledge*. London and New York: Routledge, pp. 55–70.

Evans, Jessica and Hall, Stuart (eds.) (1999), *Visual Culture: The Reader*. London: Sage.

Evans, Madeline (2000), *Meditative Provings: Notes on the Meditative Provings of New Remedies*. York: The Rose Press.

Faraway So Close! (1993), [Film], directed by Wim Wenders; screenplay by Wim Wenders, Ulrich Zieger and Richard Reitinger (Connoisseur Video/Argos Films/British Film Institute).

Feversham, Polly and Schmidt, Leo (1999), *Die Berliner Mauer Heute: Denkmalwert und Umgang/The Berlin Wall Today: Cultural Significance and Conservation Issues*. Berlin: Bauwesen.

Fieschi, Catherine, Shield, James and Woods, Roger (1996), 'Extreme Right-Wing Parties and the European Union' in J. Gaffney (ed.) *Political Parties and the European Union*. London: Routledge, pp. 235–53.

Fiske, John (1989), *Reading the Popular*. London: Unwin Hyman.

Forrest Gump (1994), [Film], directed by Robert Zemeckis; screenplay by Eric Roth (Paramount Pictures).

Foster, Hal (ed.) (1988), *Vision and Visuality*. Seattle: Bay Press.

Franz, Karen Annette (1996), '"Orientalism" at the End of the Cold War? Local Television Coverage of "The Fall of the Berlin Wall" in the United States. Visual Analysis of Three News Excerpts' in Ernst Schürer, Manfred Keune and Philip Jenkins (eds.) *The Berlin Wall: Representations and Perspectives*. New York: Peter Lang, pp. 255–280.

Fröhlich, Margrit (1998), 'Thomas Brussig's Satire of Contemporary History', GDR Bulletin, 25, pp. 21–30.

Fuery, Patrick and Fuery, Kelli (2003), Visual Cultures and Critical Theory. London: Arnold.

Fukuyama, Francis (1989), 'The End of History?' The National Interest, 16 (Summer), pp. 3–18.

Fukuyama, Francis (1992), The End of History and the Last Man. London: Penguin.

Fukuyama, Francis (2002), 'Has History Started Again?' Policy, 18 (2), pp. 3–7.

Fulbrook, Mary (1995), Anatomy of a Dictatorship: Inside the GDR, 1949–1989. Oxford: Oxford University Press.

Fulbrook, Mary (2000), Interpretations of the Two Germanies, 1945–1990. London: Macmillan.

Funder, Anna (2003), Stasiland. London: Granta.

Gerber, Margy and Woods, Roger (eds.) (1993), Studies in GDR Culture and Society 11/12: The End of the GDR and the Problems of Integration. Lanham: University Press of America.

Gerber, Margy and Woods, Roger (eds.) (1994), Studies in GDR Culture and Society 13: Understanding the Past – Managing the Future: The Integration of the Five New Länder into the Federal Republic of Germany. Lanham: University Press of America.

Gerber, Margy and Woods, Roger (eds.) (1996), Studies in GDR Culture and Society 14/15: Changing Identities in East Germany. Lanham: University Press of America.

Gilbert, Mathew and Ryan, Suzanne C. (2003), 'Snap Judgements: Did iconic images from Baghdad reveal more about the media than Iraq?' Boston Globe, 10.04.03, pp. D1.

Glees, Anthony (2004), The Stasi Files: East Germany's Secret Operations Against Britain. London: Free Press.

Glendinning, Simon (ed.) (1999), The Edinburgh Encyclopedia of Continental Philosophy. Edinburgh: Edinburgh University Press.

Gleye, Paul (1991), Behind The Wall: An American in East Germany, 1988–89. Carbondale: Southern Illinois University Press.

Gombrich, Ernst H. (2000), Art and Illusion: A Study in Psychology of Pictorial Representation. Princeton and Oxford: Princeton University Press.

Goodbye Lenin! (2002), [Film], directed by Wolfgang Becker; screenplay by Bernd Lichtenberg and Wolfgang Becker (X Filme/Twentieth Century Fox).

Grant, R. G. (1998), The Berlin Wall. Hove: Wayland.

Grass, Günter (1998), The Tin Drum, trans. by Ralph Manheim. London: Vintage.

Grimmelshausen, Hans Jakob Christoffel von (1999), Simplicissimus, trans. by Mike Mitchell. Sawtry: Dedalus.

Grix, Jonathan (2000), The Role of the Masses in the Collapse of the GDR. London: Macmillan Press.

Habermas, Jürgen (1989), Structural Transformation of the Public Sphere, trans. by Thomas Burger and Frederick Lawrence. Cambridge, Mass.: MIT Press.

Habermas, Jürgen (1994), The Past as Future, trans. by Max Pensky. Cambridge: Polity Press.

Habermas, Jürgen (1998), A Berlin Republic: Writings on Germany, trans. by Steven Rendall. Cambridge: Polity Press.

Habermas, Jürgen (1999), 'Further Reflections on the Structural Transformations of the Public Sphere' in Craig Calhoun (ed.) Habermas and the Public Sphere. Cambridge, Mass.: MIT Press, pp. 421–461.

Hall, Stuart (1980), 'Encoding/decoding' in Stuart Hall (ed.) Culture, Media, Language. London: Hutchinson & Co., pp. 128–138.

Hall, Stuart (1983), 'The Great Moving Right Show' in Stuart Hall and Martin Jaques (eds.) The Politics of Thatcherism. London: Lawrence & Wishart.

Hariman, Robert and Lucaites, John Louis (2003), 'Public Identity and Collective Memory in U.S. Iconic Photography: The Image of "Accidental Napalm"', Critical Studies in Media Communication, 20 (1), pp. 35–66.

Hartley, John (1992), *The Politics of Pictures*. New York: Routledge.

Hebdige, Dick (1993), 'Training Some Thoughts on the Future' in Jon Bird, Barry Curtis, Tim Putnam, George Robertson and Lisa Tickner (eds.) *Mapping the Futures: Local Cultures, Global Change*. Routledge, pp. 270–279.

Hegel, George Wilhelm Friedrich (1956), *Lectures on the Philosophy of History*, trans. by J. Silbree. New York: Dover.

Hegel, George Wilhelm Friedrich (1977), *Hegel's Phenomenology of Spirit*, trans. by J. B. Baillie. Oxford: Oxford University Press.

Heidegger, Martin (1977), 'The Age of the World Picture' *The Question Concerning Technology and Other Essays*. New York and London: Garland.

Heins, Cornelia (1994), *The Wall Falls: An Oral History of the Reunification of the Two Germanies*. London: Grey Seal.

Helden wie wir (1999), [Film], directed by Sebastian Peterson; screenplay by Thomas Brussig, Sebastian Peterson, and Markus Dittrich (Senator Film/BMG).

Heneghan, Tom (2000), *Unchained Eagle: Germany After the Wall*. London: Reuters/Pearson Education.

Hesse, Kurt R. (1988), *Westmedien in die DDR: Nutzung, Image und Auswirkungen bundesrepublikanischen Hörfunks und Fernsehens*. Köln: Verlag Wissenschaft und Politik.

Hilton, Christopher (2001), *The Wall: The People's Story*. Stroud: Sutton Publishing.

Hohendahl, Peter Uwe (1995), 'Recasting the Public Sphere', October, 73 (Summer), pp. 27–54.

Holly, Michael Ann (2003), 'Now and Then', *Journal of Visual Culture*, 2 (2), pp. 238–242.

Howells, Richard (2003), *Visual Culture: An Introduction*. Cambridge: Polity.

Huyssen, Andreas (1991), 'After the Wall: The Failure of German Intellectuals', *New German Critique*, 52 (Winter), pp. 109–143.

Huyssen, Andreas (1997), 'The Voids of Berlin' in *Critical Inquiry*, 24 (1), pp. 57–81.

Isaacs, Jeremy and Downing, Taylor (1998), *Cold War*. London: Transworld Publishers.

Ittenbach, Max (1968), *Berlin: Bilder aus der Hauptstadt der DDR*. Leipzig: Brockhaus.

James, Harold and Stone, Marla (eds.) (1992), *When the Wall Came Down: Reactions to German Unification*. New York: Routledge.

Jameson, Fredric (1991), *Postmodernism, Or, The Cultural Logic of Late Capitalism*. London: Verso.

Jay, Martin (1993), *Downcast Eyes: The Denigration of Vision in Twentieth-Century French Thought*. Berkeley: California University Press.

Jay, Martin (2002), 'Cultural Relativism and the Visual Turn', *Journal of Visual Culture*, 1 (3), pp. 267–278.

Jennings, Michael (1987) *Dialectical Images: Walter Benjamin's Theory of Literary Criticism*. Ithaca: Cornell University Press.

JFK (1991), [Film], directed by Oliver Stone; screenplay by Oliver Stone and Zachary Sklar (Warner Bros.).

Jones, Amelia (2003), *The Feminism and Visual Culture Reader*. London: Routledge.

Kafka, Franz (1961), 'The Great Wall of China' in *Metamorphosis and Other Stories*, London: Penguin, pp. 65–81.

Koehler, John O. (2000), *Stasi: The Untold Story of the East German Secret Police*. London: Westview.

Kojève, Alexandre (1969), *Introduction to the Reading of Hegel: Lectures on the Phenomenology of Spirit*, trans. by James H. Nichols. New York: Basic Books.

Kracauer, Siegfried (1995), *The Mass Ornament: Weimar Essays*, trans. by Thomas Y. Levin. Cambridge, Mass.: Harvard University Press.

Kramer, Julian (2003), 'Goodbye Lenin: The Uses of Nostalgia', *OpenDemocracy*, available at: < http://www.opendemocracy.net/debates/article-1-67-1433.jsp >.

Krauss, Rosalind (1988), 'The Im/pulse to See' in Hal Foster (ed.) *Vision and Visuality*, Seattle: Bay Press, pp. 50–78.

Krauss, Rosalind (1993), *The Optical Unconscious*. Cambridge, Mass.: MIT Press.

Kristeva, Julia (1984), *Revolution in Poetic Language*. New York: Columbia University Press.

Lacan, Jacques (1977), *Écrits: A Selection*, trans. by Alan Sheridan. New York and London: W.W. Norton Company.

Ladd, Brian (1997), *The Ghosts of Berlin: Confronting German History in the Urban Landscape*. Chicago: University of Chicago Press.

Large, David Clay (2001), *Berlin: A Modern History*. London: Penguin.

Lash, Scott (1990), 'Learning from Leipzig – Or Politics in the Semiotic Society', *Theory, Culture & Society*, 7 (4), pp. 145–158.

Leach, Neil (ed.) (1999), *Architecture and Revolution: Contemporary Perspectives on Central and Eastern Europe*. London: Routledge.

Leslie, Esther (2000), *Walter Benjamin: Overpowering Conformism*. London: Pluto.

Lewis, Justin (1991), *The Ideological Octopus: An Exploration of Television and its Audience*. New York: Routledge.

Life Magazine (2003), *100 Photographs That Changed the World*. New York: Life Books/Time Inc. Home Entertainment.

Lomax, Yve (2000), *Writing the Image: An Adventure with Art and Theory*. London and New York: I.B. Tauris.

London (1993), [Film], directed by Patrick Keiller; screenplay by Patrick Keiller (Connoisseur/Academy Video).

Ludes, Peter (ed.) (1994), *Visualizing the Public Spheres*. München: Wilhelm Frink Verlag.

Lynch, Kevin (1998 [1960]), *The Image of the City*. Cambridge, Mass.: MIT Press.

Lyotard, Jean-François (1988), *The Differend: Phrases in Dispute*, trans. by Georges Van Den Abeele. Manchester: Manchester University Press.

Lyotard, Jean-François (1989a), 'The Sign of History' in Andrew Benjamin (ed.) *The Lyotard Reader*. Oxford: Blackwell, pp. 393–411.

Lyotard, Jean-François (1989b), 'Universal History and Cultural Differences' in Andrew Benjamin (ed.) *The Lyotard Reader*. Oxford: Blackwell, pp. 314–323.

Lyotard, Jean-François (1992), *The Postmodern Explained to Children: Correspondence 1982–1985*. London: Turnaround.

Lyotard, Jean-François (1993), 'The Wall, the Gulf, and the Sun: A Fable' in Mark Poster (ed.) *Politics, Theory, and Contemporary Culture*. New York: Columbia University Press, pp. 261–275.

McAdams, A. James (2001), *Judging the Past in Unified Germany*. Cambridge: Cambridge University Press.

Magnus, Bernd and Cullenberg, Stephen (eds.) (1995), *Whither Marxism? Global Crises in International Perspective*. New York: Routledge.

Maier, Charles S. (1997), *Dissolution: The Crisis of Communism and the End of East Germany*. Princeton: Princeton University Press.

Manghani, Sunil (2003a), 'Adventures in Subsemiotics: Towards a New "Object" and Writing of Visual Culture', *Culture, Theory and Critique*, 44 (1), pp. 23–36.

Manghani, Sunil (2003b), 'Experimental Text-image Travel Literature', *Theory, Culture & Society*, 20 (3), pp. 127–138.

Manghani, Sunil (2003c), 'Picturing Berlin, Piecing Together a Public Sphere', *Invisible Culture*, issue 6, available at: < http: //www.rochester.edu/in_visible_culture/Issue_6/manghani/manghani.html >.

Manghani, Sunil, Piper, Arthur and Simons, Jon. (eds.) (2006), *Images: A Reader*. London: Sage.

Mannheim, Karl (1968), 'Utopia in the Contemporary Situation' in Chaim I. Waxman (ed.) *The End of Ideology Debate*. New York: Funk & Wagnalls, pp. 10–26.

Mars Flight (2004), [Radio Broadcast], directed by David Hunter; screenplay by Max Mueller and Alasdair Mangham (BBC Radio Four).

Marx, Karl (1990), *Capital: A Critique of Political Economy, Volume One*. London: Penguin.

Mayer, Sigrid (1996), 'The Graffiti of the Berlin Wall: A Semiotic Approach' in Ernst Schürer, Manfred Keune and Philip Jenkins (eds.) *The Berlin Wall: Representations and Perspectives*. New York: Peter Lang, pp. 214–228.

Merleau-Ponty, Maurice (1962), *Phenomenology of Perception*, trans. by Colin Smith. London: Routledge.

Miller, Barbara (2004), *The Stasi Files Unveiled: Guilt and Compliance in a Unified Germany*. London: Transaction Publishers.

Mirzoeff, Nicholas (ed.) (1998), *Visual Culture Reader*. London: Routledge.

Mirzoeff, Nicholas (1999), *An Introduction to Visual Culture*. London: Routledge.

Mirzoeff, Nicholas (2005), *Watching Babylon: The War in Iraq and Global Visual Culture*. New York and London: Routledge.

Mirzoeff, Nicholas (2006), 'On Visuality', *Journal of Visual Culture*, 5 (1), pp. 53–79.

Mitchell, W. J. T. (1986), *Iconology: Image, Text, Ideology*. Chicago: University of Chicago Press.

Mitchell, W. J. T. (1994), *Picture Theory: Essays on Verbal and Visual Representation*. Chicago: University of Chicago.

Mitchell, W. J. T. (1995), 'Interdisciplinarity and Visual Culture', *Art Bulletin*, LXXVII (4), pp. 540–543.

Mitchell, W. J. T. (1996), 'What do Pictures *Really* Want?', *October*, 77 (Summer), pp. 71–82.

Mitchell, W. J. T. (2002), 'Showing Seeing: A Critique of Visual Culture', *Journal of Visual Culture*, 1(2), pp. 165–181.

Mitchell, W. J. T. (2005), *What Do Pictures Want? The Live and Loves of Images*. Chicago: University of Chicago Press.

Mohr, Jean and Berger, John (1999), *At the Edge of the World*. London: Reaktion Books.

Morley, David (1999), 'Finding out about the World from Television News: Some difficulties' in Jostein Gripsrud (ed.) *Television and Common Knowledge*. London: Routledge, pp. 135–158.

Müller, Jan-Werner (2000), *Another Country: German Intellectuals, Unification and National Identity*. New Haven: Yale University Press.

Niethammer, Lutz (1992), *Posthistoire: Has History Come to an End?* trans. by Patrick Camiller. London and New York: Verso.

Nietzsche, Friedrich (1969), *Thus Spoke Zarathustra*, trans. by R. J. Hollingdale. London: Penguin.

Nietzsche, Friedrich (1974), *The Gay Science*, trans. by Walter Kaufmann. New York: Random House.

Nietzsche, Friedrich (2003), *Beyond Good and Evil*, trans. by R. J. Hollingdale. London: Penguin.

Omaar, Rageh (2004), *Revolution Day: The Human Story of the Battle of Iraq*. London: Penguin.

Opp, Karl-Dieter, Voss, Peter and Gern, Christiane (1995), *Origins of a Spontaneous Revolution: East Germany, 1989*. Ann Arbour: University of Michigan Press.

Peirce, Charles Sanders (1932), *Collected Papers of Charles Sanders Peirce, Vol II: Elements of Logic*. Cambridge, MA: Harvard University Press.

Pejič, Bojana and Elliott, David (eds.) (1999), *After The Wall: Art and Culture in Post-Communist Europe*. Stockholm: Moderna Museet.

Philipsen, Dirk (1993), *We Were the People: Voices from East Germany's Revolutionary Autumn of 1989*. Durham: Duke University Press.

Plato (1929), *Timaeus and Critias*, trans. by A. E. Taylor. London: Methuen.

Prager, Brad (2004), 'The Erection of the Berlin Wall: Thomas Brussig's *Helden Wie Wir* and the End of East Germany', *Modern Language Review*, 99 (4), pp. 983–998.

Richie, Alexandra (1998), *Faust's Metropolis: A History of Berlin*. London: HarperCollins.

Robins, Kevin (1996), *Into the Image: Culture and Politics in the Field of Vision*. London: Routledge.

Rogoff, Irit (1998), 'Studying Visual Culture' in Nicholas Mirzoeff (ed.) *Visual Culture Reader*. London: Routledge, pp. 14–26.

Rorty, Richard (1979), *Philosophy and the Mirror of Nature*. Princeton: Princeton University Press.

Rose, Gillian (2001), *Visual Methodologies: An Introduction to the Interpretation of Visual Materials*. London: Sage.

Rugg, Linda Haverty (1997), *Picturing Ourselves: Photography & Autobiography*. Chicago: University of Chicago Press.

Said, Edward (1978), *Orientalism*. London: Routledge & Kegan Paul Ltd.

Sardar, Ziauddin (1999), *Orientalism*. Buckingham: Open University Press.

Schneider, Peter (1983), *The Wall Jumper*, trans. by Leigh Hafrey. Toronto: Random House.

Schneider, Peter (1991), *The German Comedy: Scenes of Life After the Wall*. New York: Farrar, Straus and Giroux.

Schürer, Ernst, Keune, Manfred and Jenkins, Philip (eds.) (1996), *The Berlin Wall: Representations and Perspectives*. New York: Peter Lang.

Scott, Clive (1999), *The Spoken Image: Photography and Language*. London: Reaktion Books.

Sebald, W. G. (1996), *The Emigrants*. London: Harvill Press.

Sebald, W. G. (1998), *The Rings of Saturn*. London: Harvill Press.

Sebald, W. G. (2001), *Austerlitz*. London: Hamish Hamilton.

Sedlmayr, Hans (2000), 'Toward a Rigorous Study of Art' in Christopher S. Wood (ed.) *The Vienna School Reader: Politics and Art Historical Method in the 1930s*. New York: Zone Books, pp. 133–179.

Sennett, Richard (1990), *The Conscience of the Eye: The Design and Social Life of Cities*. New York: Alfred A. Knopf.

Sharp, Ingrid and Flinspach, Dagmar (1995), 'Women in Germany from Division to Unification' in Derek Lewis and John R. p. McKenzie (eds.) *The New Germany: Social, Political and Cultural Challenges of Unification*. Exeter: University of Exeter Press, pp. 173–195.

Sieg, Katrin (1993), 'The Revolution Has Been Televised', *Theatre Journal*, 46, pp. 35–47.

Simons, Jon (2000), 'Ideology, Imagology, and Critical Thought: the Impoverishment of Politics', *Journal of Political Ideologies*, 5 (1), pp. 81–103.

Sinclair, Iain (2003), *Lights Out for the Territory*. London: Penguin.

Sontag, Susan (1979), *On Photography*. London: Penguin.

Sontag, Susan (1994), *Against Interpretation*. London: Vintage.

Sontag, Susan (2003), *Regarding the Pain of Others*. New York: Farrar, Straus and Giroux.

Stafford, Barbara (1996), *Good Looking: Essays on the Virtue of Images*. Cambridge, Mass.: MIT Press.

Stein, Mary Beth (1993), *Berlin/Berlin: The Wall in the Expressive Culture of a Divided City*. Ph.D. Dissertation: Indiana University.

Stein, Mary Beth (1996), 'The Banana and the Trabant: Representations of the "Other" in a United Germany' in Ernst Schürer, Manfred Keune and Philip Jenkins (eds.) *The Berlin Wall: Representations and Perspectives*. New York: Peter Lang, pp. 333–346.

Stepan, Peter (ed.) (2000), *Photos That Changed the World*. Munich: Prestel.

Stoekl, Allan (1997), 'The Future of the End of History', *Parallax*, 3 (4), pp. 29–40.

Stokes, Gale (1993), *The Walls Came Tumbling Down: The Collapse of Communism in Eastern Europe*. New York: Oxford University Press.

Stone, Nick (2001), 'Hail to the Revolutionary Critique!' *Radical Philosophy*, 1007 (May/June), pp. 48–50.

Sturken, Marita and Cartwright, Lisa (2001), *Practices of Looking: An Introduction to Visual Culture*. Oxford: Oxford University Press.

Vazsonyi, Nicholas (1996), 'A Wall of Silence? The Case of Christa Wolf' in Ernst Schürer, Manfred Keune and Philip Jenkins (eds.) The Berlin Wall: Representations and Perspectives. New York: Peter Lang, pp. 181–190.

Veenis, Milena (1997) 'Fantastic Things' in Susan M. Pearce (ed.) Experiencing Material Culture in the Western World. London: Leicester University Press, pp. 154–174.

Veenis, Milena (1999), 'Consumption in East Germany: The Seduction and Betrayal of Things', Journal of Material Culture, 4 (1), pp. 79–112.

Verheyen, Dirk (1999), The German Question: A Cultural, Historical, and Geopolitical Exploration. Colorado: Westview Press.

Viehoff, von Reinhold and Segers, Rien T. (eds.) (1999), Kultur Identität Europa: Über die Schwierigkeiten und Möglichkeiten einer Konstruktion. Frankfurt am Main: Surkamp.

'Visual Culture Questionnaire' (1996), October, 77 (Summer), pp. 25–70.

von Oppen, Karoline (2000), The Role of the Writer and the Press in the Unification of Germany, 1989–1990. New York: Peter Lang.

Waldenburg, Hermann (1990), The Berlin Wall Book. London: Thames and Hudson.

Ward, Janet (2004), 'Berlin, the Virtual Global City', Journal of Visual Culture, 3 (2), pp. 239–256.

Ward, James J. (1996), 'Remember When It Was the "Antifascist Defense Wall"? The Uses of History in the Battle for Public Memory and Public Space' in Ernst Schürer, Manfred Keune and Philip Jenkins (eds.) The Berlin Wall. New York: Peter Lang, pp. 11–24.

Waxman, Chaim I. (ed.) (1968), The End of Ideology Debate. New York: Funk & Wagnalls.

Weigel, Sigrid (1996), Body- and Image-Space: Re-Reading Walter Benjamin, trans. by Georgina Paul, Rachel McNicholl and Jeremy Gaines. London: Routledge.

Whybrow, Nicolas (2001), 'Leaving Berlin: On the Performance of Monumental Change', Performance Research, 6 (1), pp. 37–45.

Wicke, Peter (1996), 'Pop Music in the GDR between Conformity and Resistance' in Margy Gerber and Roger Woods (eds.) Studies in GDR Culture and Society 14/15: Changing Identities in East Germany. Maryland: University of America, pp. 25–35.

Wings of Desire (1987), [Film], directed by Wim Wenders; screenplay by Wim Wenders (Road Movies/Argos Films).

Witte, Bernd (1997), Der Literaturstreit im sich vereinigenden Deutschland: Eine Analyse des Streits um Christa Wolf und die deutsch-deutsche Gegenwartsliteratur in Zeitungen und Zeitschriften. Marburg: Tectum.

Wolf, Christa (1990), Was bleibt. Berlin: Aufbau.

Wolf, Christa (1992), [No Title – Protest Demonstration at Berlin-Alexanderplatz, text of recorded speech] in Harold James and Marla Stone (eds.) When the Wall Came Down: Reactions to German Unification. New York: Routledge, pp. 127–129.

Wolf, Christa (1993), What Remains and Other Stories, trans. by Heike Schwarzbauer and Rick Takvorian. New York: Farrar, Straus and Giroux.

Young, James E. (1992), 'The Counter-Monument: Memory against Itself in Germany Today' in W. J. T. Mitchell (ed.) Art and the Public Sphere. Chicago: University of Chicago Press, pp. 49–78.

Young, John W. (1996), Cold War Europe 1945 – 1991. London: Arnold.

Zelizer, Barbie (1992), 'CNN, the Gulf War, and Journalistic Practice', Journal of Communication, 42 (1), pp. 65–81.

Zelizer, Barbie (ed.) (2001), Visual Culture and the Holocaust. New Brunswick: Rutgers University Press.

Žižek, Slavoj (1990), 'Eastern Europe's Republics of Gilead', New Left Review, 183, pp. 50–62.

Žižek, Slavoj (2002), Did Somebody Say Totalitarianism? Five Interventions in the (Mis)use of a Notion. London: Verso.

INDEX

Page references to illustrations are shown in italic. Where a reference ranges over an illustration page the numbers have been conflated, e.g. 61–2, 63, 65 appears as 61–4.